# HOW TO ANALYZE PEOPLE, DARK PSYCHOLOGY & MANIPULATION PROTECTION + BODY LANGUAGE MASTERY 4 IN 1

## THE GUIDE TO SPEED READING PEOPLE & TECHNIQUES AGAINST DARK PERSUASION & MIND CONTROL

### WESTLEY ARMSTRONG

DEVON HOUSE
PRESS

# CONTENTS

## HOW TO ANALYZE PEOPLE & BODY LANGUAGE MASTERY 2 IN 1

# DARK PSYCHOLOGY AND MANIPULATION PROTECTION 2 IN 1

# HOW TO ANALYZE PEOPLE & BODY LANGUAGE MASTERY 2 IN 1

## A PRACTICAL GUIDE TO SPEED READING PEOPLE, INCREASING EMOTIONAL INTELLIGENCE (EQ) & PROTECTING AGAINST MANIPULATION BY DARK PSYCHOLOGY

# INTRODUCTION

How many times has someone told you something but meant a different thing altogether? Words are easy to say, I can tell you anything I want. But how do you know if I'm being honest? How do you know if I have an ulterior motive, maybe even a bad one? How can you tell when a politician is trying to deceive you? How can you tell a conman from an honest merchant?

You can just read it! "Hold on," you may say, "we read words, and you just told me that words can be manipulated..." Yes, words can – actually very often *are* – manipulated! But we don't just read words! We also read smiles, lips, hands, even feet... I don't mean like palm reading though... What I mean is analyzing body language and that huge set of nonverbal signals we produce all the time!

Did you know that most of what we "say" is nonverbal? Technically we should say "communicate", but the point is that 60% of what we communicate on average is nonverbal. Only 40% of communication is made up of words (written, spoken, sung...)

So, don't you think it's strange that in all our communication studies (from learning to speak to learning English to studying journalism and reading Shakespeare) basically all we learn is how to read words?

No wonder there are so many misunderstandings. *We only learn to make sense of 40% of all we communicate!* Now, imagine if you could understand 60, 70 or even 80% of what people are actually telling you!

And before we go further, let's pause a second... You may be thinking, "Yes, but reading body language and nonverbal signals is a lot of work..." I fully understand you. Verbal language can already be tricky with some people. Just imagine politicians or insurance agents... They twist words, they use strange terms, they play with ambiguity... Fine but...

...Reading nonverbal communication does not need to be a hassle nor a hard task. You will not be taking out a notebook and jotting down all signs all the time... Like all things you learn, if you "digest it" well, it will become second nature to you. It will become spontaneous, effortless, automatic... Like driving a car in fact...

It is mainly a matter of becoming conscious of what's "beyond words and encoded in gesturers" and equipping yourself with a good set of "reading tools". Then it's all downhill!

And in fact, people who are good at reading body language do it all the time and naturally, almost unconsciously. Statistically, women are better than men at this. But there is more... Everybody does it to some extent, but we are not always very conscious of it...

Think about it... Do you remember any time when someone told you something, but you just didn't believe it, because "something wasn't just right?" Maybe that saved you a few bucks or even from worse, like a bad relationship? But you still can't put your finger on "that thing that did not click..." That's because it wasn't a word, nor a sentence... It was a nonverbal sign that you read without being aware of it!

And I will let you in on a secret... I too was very bad at reading nonverbal language. And in fact, as a child I was frustrated. People took advantage of me regularly and, well, I faced big disappointments. But then, when I studied psychology at university, I realized that most of what happens in our mind is not conscious, let alone verbal! I realized that if something is irrational, it cannot be verbal. Words express rational thoughts... But how about all creative, emotional and simply non rational thinking?

Then I studied pedagogy, and I learned that a good teacher is not one who says the right words... But someone who conveys concepts through many means of communication. And that only a minority of students have a primarily verbal way of learning. Some have visual learning natures, other kinesthetic (based on movement) etc.

Funny, isn't it? Verbal communication isn't even the most common natural learning method, but I trust your experience of school is one of – how to describe it – lots of words and verbosity?

So, I changed my course of study after my degree. I was a very rational person, I realized. But I wanted to learn all about "the other side of human intelligence and behavior". And I spent years researching it...

The consequences? Well, to start with, when I was all rational, I was easy prey to deceit and grifters... *After learning to analyze nonverbal communication, it became much harder to deceive me.* Now, think about it, I am not! So, if you are like I was, the one dishonest people can "smell at a distance" or even if you just get conned every now and then... You too will avoid a lot of problems.

And don't take my words as read (sorry about the pun)! It's not just me saying that analyzing nonverbal communication has massive positive effects on your life. It's science! There are loads of studies I could refer you to, but a recent one on how, for example, this can change your family relations is 'The Nonverbal Communication of Positive Emotions: An Emotion Family Approach' by psychologist Disa A. Sauter from Amsterdam University, which appeared in the peer reviewed psychology journal *Emotion Review* in July 2017. It concludes that most positive emotions are communicated only nonverbally! Think about how much happiness we are missing out on...

But *the benefits will heap up for you as they did for me* if you learn to analyze nonverbal communication... There are so many that I would not know where to start...

*Your social relationships will improve a lot!* This includes your relationships with significant others (friends, family, partner etc.) but also with people you are "just acquainted with" or you make casual encounters with.

And yes, *also with your colleagues at school or at work...* And this can make *a huge difference in your quality of life...* Think about it, what do you do as soon as you get home? Most people complain about this or that colleague, school friend, teacher, or, most frequently – boss! They can make our life a misery. And if you can bypass their verbal communication, you will be the one in charge now.

Do you want some more? *Your professional life will improve a lot!* You will actually see it change before your eyes. Again, if you only understand verbal signals at work, you miss out on a whole sphere of communication and information you could use for your actual work and tasks, for your colleagues and (why not?) for your career.

*You will grow in people's esteem.* Yes, because every time we miss a clue, every time we misunderstand a point (even hidden ones), we actually make fools of ourselves. Yes, our friends and family are understanding... but it's the cumulative effect that matters... And don't forget – people remember these small events subconsciously.

*You'll become more intelligent.* Especially, you'll become *more emotionally intelligent.* You may've heard of this, because it is a very important topic in psychology and self-development these days. Emotional intelligence is very much based on nonverbal communication. *People with good emotional intelligence are on average happier and more successful than those who are lacking.*

As a consequence, *your quality of life will skyrocket. You'll be happier, more confident, you'll waste much less time solving problems you didn't foresee,* and you'll have better relationships.

Last, but by no means least, *you'll not be manipulated easily*. Let's call a spade a spade... When you watch an ad, you're exposed to a picture or short clip made by an expert in manipulation and with a lot of means at his or her disposal... We're being manipulated all the time.

Every time you buy something and after a while you say, "Why in the world did I buy it?" the answer is always the same: you have been manipulated into doing it! *Politicians are professional manipulators.* This is nothing new. They have been so since the times of Classical Greece! Their speeches were masterpieces of crowd manipulation... Now they just got better and have bigger means.

But hold on – do you know that politicians (like actors and actresses) are literally trained to use body language and nonverbal communication? It's one of the most important parts of their training and success! "He looks presidential," we say, because he (one day she) learnt to stand, look, move, use his hands etc. in a way that projects confidence and calm.

You're right! Politicians and professional con-people are a step ahead. But let me tell you a secret: even for them it's very hard, actually impossible to hide their real thoughts. A little twist in Bill Clinton's lip cast deep doubts about his "straight face" and defense in the Monica Lewinsky case...

And you must have seen psychologists analyze people's nonverbal communication on TV. You can do it too now. And if politicians and grifters have an advantage now, it is one more reason to start soon!

Taking about that... Do you know when the next manipulator, conman or dishonest colleague will metaphorically knock on your life's door? No, but it may well be tomorrow!

Do you realize how every day you spend without being capable of analyzing people's body language and other signs is a day you miss out on a lot of happiness and confidence?

How long are you ready to wait before you do something to improve those relationships that frustrate you so much? And even good relationships have frustrating moments, we all know!

Now, honestly think about it: *you could be on the way to solving all these problems in minutes...* Or you could put it off, and waste valuable time.

And *this book is really based on actual research; it is scientific in everything it says.*

But *this book is also a nice read!* True, there is hard science behind all the *strategies, skills and even exercises* in this book. But you may have guessed that we want to make this experience pleasurable, even bubbly. I told you I studied pedagogy at postgrad level (the science of teaching and learning). And you know rule number one of learning? Statistically *people learn better when they are having fun!* There goes another stuffy urban myth out of the window... lessons didn't need to be boring at school...

And *this book is also practical.* In the end, you need to learn *to analyze people's nonverbal language – not about it!* There are activities and exercises you can carry out without disturbing your daily life.

They are short, but also "noninvasive". Let me explain... They are designed so that you can do them while you go about your daily life... When you are shopping, when you are on the bus etc. I don't want to take more of your time than is necessary.

*You will see real and visible changes in your life.* The promotion at work won't be immediate maybe, but you'll see improved relationships, confidence and in the overall quality of your life.

It's sad that analyzing nonverbal communication is not taught at school! *Think how many lives it would improve...* But hey, we should not cry over spilled milk, instead we should try to do something about our gaps...

And now you know what to do, and you know it is only a click away, I wish you a good read?

# FUNDAMENTALS OF BODY LANGUAGE

## WHY BODY LANGUAGE?

I f you still need convincing about the importance of body language, let me show you a quotation by writer, trainer and consultant Allen Ruddock:

---

*"Your body communicates as well as your mouth. Don't contradict yourself."*

— ALLEN RUDDOCK

---

There are two points we can get from this statement:

1. That if you understand body language, you also understand when people's words don't match their nonverbal communication.
2. That if you understand body language, you can improve your nonverbal communication and become more convincing, confident, trusted, and even respected.

It's a win-win situation. If you're aware of other people's body language you become more aware of your own as well. It's logical, isn't it?

But let me ask you a question. Do you think it is easier to be aware of:

1. Your own body language?

or

2. Other people's body language?

Decided? Now, here's the truth. It's far easier to be aware of other people's. And this is primarily what we are concerned about. But you will also see improvements in yours. It's not fully automatic. Meaning that you'll not automatically apply all you have learned about other people to yourself. We all know that the most difficult person to observe is oneself.

But you *will become more aware of your own body language,* which is necessary to then correct it.

Now, why understand body language? Do you know what they say about job interviews? That the panel decide if you get the job or not in the first 60 or even 30 seconds? "Nice waste of time," you may think... I agree. But let's say that not everything gets decided in the first minute or so...

It is more likely that they decide if you make the (final) cut in those few seconds... But what interests us is this: how many words do you actually say in the first 30 seconds?

The answer is very few, and none of them of any relevance at all to the job. It's usually like this:

Panel: "Good morning."
You: "Good morning."
Panel: "Did you find the place alright?"
You: "Oh yes!"
End of the 30 seconds...

So, their decision about your whole future cannot be based on these words, can it? In fact, it is based on the huge set of *nonverbal signals we give away when we meet someone.*

We will see that there are times when nonverbal communication goes into overdrive. And one of these moments is when you meet new people or start an interaction in any case. While they decide if the way you stand, walk, shake hands, even dress or look around the room give them the "right impression" for you to be a valid candidate... well, you can do the same to them!

You can see if they actually like you, if they trust you, if they are interested or they are thinking about the next candidate... *They will not tell you; but they will show you.*

We briefly talked about it in the introduction, but here are some key reasons why *body language shapes and even determines our quality of life!*

### Body language is key to social relationships

Think about that school mate no one ever cared about... That wallflower... Look at her or his body language? Do you want to bet that she or he had most of these in varying degrees?

- Slouching shoulders
- Often lowered his or her gaze
- Shabby or uninteresting clothes (accessories, shoes, hairstyle etc.)
- Hunching posture
- Often crossed his or her arms
- Feet pointing inward (ok, you may not have noticed it)

Basically your "missed friend's body language" told people to stay away. No wonder they did it... And this is not necessarily because that person (you now feel sorry for, I know!) actually wanted it. Our minds are more complex than that... Maybe that was all due to a lack of confidence... Maybe it simply meant, "Stay away unless you are the most trustworthy and non-judgmental person in the world"?

Yes, in most cases that body language means just that... But we don't know it. Especially as teenagers... How many people have met horrible teens because we couldn't read their actual signals to us? Here is a super reason to learn body language in my view...

And if you were one of those, then you really know what I mean...

### *Body language affects your success (at work but not just)*

There's more to life than work. There are family relations, friends, hobbies etc. And body language does affect how successful you are at all these. Here, both analyzing body language and using positive body language can make a huge difference to your life.

We know it implicitly, don't we, that "successful people *look success-ful.*" Now, remember the wallflower in your class? How many successful people slouch? And I am a sloucher by nature, so I say it out of personal experience.

Allow me a personal tip from my heart, in fact... If you do slouch, by all means correct it. Please, please, please do! Your life will change like you wouldn't even dream!

And this leads us to the next point...

### *Body language makes you "safe or vulnerable"*

Talking about slouching and the way you walk. Do you know that people who walk with their shoulders out are far less likely to be mugged or assaulted (in a dark alley?) So, *body language can even improve your very physical safety!*

You see how even criminals act upon body language... And I am sure you know about it. They look around for someone who "looks vulnerable" and that's how (consciously or unconsciously) they choose their victims.

Yet again – and vice versa! You too can spot someone with bad intentions from their body language. Follow me... We often "assess people's intentions" using the wrong tools. Very often they are prejudices the media and society force on us like:

- People with an unkempt look
- People who look "different" one way or another
- Young and tall males
- People with tattoos
- People with scars
- Unfortunately, even people with a darker skin than ours.

This leads only to the perpetuation of stereotypes and prejudice. How about if you knew how to tell if someone actually *does have negative and aggressive intentions* independently from these prejudices?

Let's look at nature for a lesson. Have you ever seen a lion walk bang in the middle of a herd of zebras and they just don't care? Of course, you have. So, zebras don't have a prejudice against lions. But as soon as the lion gets hungry, his attitude and body language change and the zebras start running!

You see, even nature uses body language as a tool of survival... And we still don't... Instead, *well trained officials (like FBI and CIA agents) are literally taught to spot body language signs that show a hidden threat.*

There's no reason why you should not know them too!

### Body language makes you less "gullible"

Let's play this game… Joe and Sarah go to the market to buy groceries… Joe is really careful, he has his eyes fixed on the apples, potatoes, zucchini and tomatoes he is buying… Sarah, on the other hand, when she is buying something, she does not look at it… No… she looks around and in particular, she looks up, at the merchant or seller.

Who will end up with the best deals? The chances are that while Joe is staring at his tomatoes, the dishonest merchant feels perfectly safe! Yes, that's the word. Safe. The best way to fend off someone's grift is to look at them straight in the eyes. So, Joe may be thinking that the apples look fine while the dishonest merchant is fixing the scales…

Try it even as a game. Call a friend and try to play a little trick on her or him… For example, offer them a glass of wine (or a coffee) and then try to take it away… But looking at her/him straight in the eyes… Can you feel how difficult it is? You will literally feel frozen, or as if there's a huge energy in your body that you need to overcome…

Now look away and you already feel you only need to say something along the lines of, "Hey there's a squirrel!" and the trick is done!

Looking at the body language of the person you are striking a deal with is the best way to get a good deal (or dropping the deal if you don't trust him/her).

### Body language is fun!

Allow me a personal touch as the last reason why learning nonverbal communication is good. It is actually fun to read how people move, stand, smile, their little strange gestures... It really fills your day with beautiful details. In my view, it makes you love the human psychology and behavior even more...

And it turns you into a good writer, if you have literary ambitions... Just think about what great writers have in common, an attention to detail about body language... *Body language is the best way to present a character...*

Aw, I was forgetting: Agatha Christie's Poirot! Of course, great detectives are also great body language readers!

## HISTORY OF BODY LANGUAGE

Let's play another game, shall we? Okay, I'll give you some well-known names and you need to tell me what these people have in common. Newton, Darwin, Einstein, Marie Curie, Freud, Galileo, Mendel... Of course, they all had a great role in the history of science...

Like all sciences, even body language has a history. Many people will argue that it started in the Seventeenth Century, but I am a maverick and I will argue that, in some ways, we can push it well before that. Maybe not as a *"conscious and rational study of how people communicate non-verbally"* but as the *"awareness and symbolic representation of how people communicate non-verbally".* In the end we do not start the history of physics with Newton (we go back to at least Zeno, an early Greek philosopher!)

Anyway, my point in telling you this is that civilizations have been culturally aware of body language, even if they looked at it from a less scientific perspective than today. So, how far can we go? Look at a hieroglyph, that far back, yes! Do you notice that the way the body is positioned has a symbolic and expressive meaning? I know, they don't tell you at school, but in Egyptian art, you give with the left hand and receive with the right hand. A habit still strong in many cultures around the world.

This was not just a "ritual" though. The left hand is connected with the right side of the brain, the less rational and more emotional side of the brain. Giving with the left means giving "with the heart". It's a sign of honesty.

Fact is, the Egyptians left us a large set of "standardized gestures", even ritualized ones, but no actual textbook of analysis. So, in their case, we cannot talk about a conscious analysis of body language (not that we know of).

But this keeps going through art till the modern times. You will see in most paintings the importance of people is represented by *proxemics.* This is where people stand in relation to one another, and it is one of the things we use to analyze nonverbal communication.

So, kings stand higher up than their subjects in almost every painting. Protagonists go in the middle, standing and sitting down are not casual etc. But again, this is not scientific analysis; it only shows that the awareness of body language has never wavered over the centuries – actually millennia.

It is true though that we started looking at body language in a rational, empirical and overall scientific way at the beginning of the Seventeenth Century. Of course, that was a time when science was starting to assert its method. In 1605, famous English philosopher (civil servant, secret agent etc.) Francis Bacon, published a book *The Advancement of Learning* (the whole title is *Of the Proficience and Advancement of Learning, Divine and Human*) and in it he is alleged to be the first who actually linked the meaning of words with that of gestures, with a famous statement:

---

*"As the tongue speaketh to the ear, so the gesture speaketh to the eye."*

— FRANCIS BACON

---

Like all scientific fields, body language analysis needs a *starting hypothesis* (like "the world is round") and this then needs to find evidence in real data. Those were the beginning of this new science, and that was the starting point.

For us, Bacon's statement may sound totally granted and commonsense. But every idea needs to be checked and then proved or disproved with facts and data in science, even the most obvious. And in fact, it took decades before someone actually took Sir Francis Bacon's statement seriously enough to check his theory with data.

It was the year 1644 and an English doctor (physician) and philosopher now forgotten actually looked at one single part of our body, our hand, and set out to describe all its gestures and their meaning. His name was John Bulwer and the book had the strange title, *Chrinologia, or the Naturall Language of the Hand* ("natural" with a double L; that was the "fancy spelling" of the time).

In science, we often start with a long list of correspondences and patterns. So, Carl Linnaeus is a founding father of biology, because he spent years categorizing plants and animals (he invented the double Latin name we still use nowadays).

In the title of Bulwer's book, however, there is more than just a list confirming that a certain gesture corresponds to a certain meaning, which proved Bacon's statement... There is the idea that all hand gestures are natural...

This is important for different reasons:

1. It states that hand gestures are not a social and cultural product, but they are fully spontaneous.
2. It states that hand gestures always have the same meaning.

Both statements, we will find out later, are not fully correct. We now know that *some gestures are cultural products* (and Italians prove it all the time!) But at the time, science was in the grip of a century (millennia) long debate: *nature vs nurture.* This debate continues nowadays (is intelligence genetic or cultural, how about the "cancer gene"? or is it only pollution and the environment that causes it?).

Nowadays science tends to take a middle position in this debate: there are some natural (genetic etc.) factors as well as environmental (culture, pollution etc.) factors.

This debate is so core to science and long that we still have two schools... And along the line, even towering figures of science took part in the debate, and one in particular Charles Darwin, used body language even as evidence for his famous Theory of Evolution.

It was the year 1872, 13 years after Darwin published his controversial *On the Origin of Species* (full title *On the Origin of Species by Means of Natural Selection, or Preservation of Favoured Races in the Struggle for Life...* you couldn't fit the average book title into a tweet back then!) Anyway... You must have seen those paintings of chimpanzee faces that express emotions like human beings. This picture became famous and even a worldwide scandal!

Why? Put simply, Darwin wrote a book, *The Expression of Emotions in Man and Animals* where he used facial expressions to show the similarities between humans and animals. The closer we were on his evolutionary tree, the more similar the facial expressions were. And this was used as evidence for his famous theory.

As a note, this is the book that makes us believe that Darwin said that "humans come from apes", while he actually never said that, and he refused to say it all his life. So, body language analysis finally got into the spotlight of science, with a book that shook the academic world the same way as 'Like a Virgin' shook popular culture in the 80s.

You see that Darwin took Bulwer's position? He followed his lead and said that "because humans and naturally related animals express themselves with similar facial expressions", it must mean that "facial expressions are produced naturally and not culturally". This is what he said for us, for psychologists and those who study body language.

In reality he said the opposite for biology: "because facial expressions are produced naturally" then the fact that they are similar between humans and other species means that "humans and other species are closely related". From a philosophy of science point of view this is a circular argument. You prove a theory with another unproven theory.

In fact, nowadays we know that not all gestures are congenital, or of natural origin. In Bulgaria, they nod sideways to say "yes" and up and down to say "no"... The rest of the world does the opposite... There is nothing in the DNA that makes it so, therefore it must be a cultural gesture.

But science is not fixed in time, and things improved from the point of view of body language... While Darwin was talking about apes and humans, another towering figure in the history of science, philosophy and above all psychology came along: Dr Sigmund Freud. His impact on psychology and psychoanalysis is colossal but he also gave us one concept that we sorely needed to understand body language:

---

*"The mind is like an iceberg; it floats with about one seventh of its bulk above water."*

— (SIGMUND FREUD, *THE UNCONSCIOUS*,

1915)

---

Nice metaphor, but what does it mean for us? It means that the main source of our behavior is not our conscious will and mind, but our unconscious! This is huge in terms of body language.

Freud allows us to move away from the rather academic debate of nature vs. nurture to new frontiers when it comes to body language analysis. You see, now that we know that most of our gestures, facial expressions etc. are not "meant", not "planned" and not even conscious, we can use these gestures and expressions to look behind the façade that people put on when talking.

*We can analyze body language to look beyond what people want us to believe and "read" what they actually mean.* Body language analysis becomes then the main tool people have to understand what people actually feel, think, want etc. Basically, now we can tell a fake smile from a real smile, at the simplest level...

Luck strikes again, and it's star studded! When Hollywood was enchanting millions with its popular movies, actors and actresses had to learn to speak, but without audio! The first films were silent in fact, and they had to improve their facial expressions and body language to communicate to their audience.

They borrowed heavily on the long tradition of the theatre, and you can see that the facial expressions and movements of early movie stars are somewhat exaggerated and stylized... But it gave drama teachers a huge chance to study actual face expressions and natural gestures, a databank of human behavior that still forms the bedrock of modern studies.

Those were the early years of the Twentieth Century, but then two horrifying wars came along and science was busy with the "war effort". But as the Second World War came to a close, the world found itself with an amazing new face...

It was the face of the 1950s, that decade we can describe with those pastel ads of washing machines and vacuum cleaners... And those adverts are full of body language analysis... The housewife who "smiles to the camera", the husband coming back from work and picking up his children for a hug – unrealistically smiling, of course!

And while companies employed professionals who told us with gestures and facial expressions why we would be happier with a washing machine rather than the new cake mix, a US anthropologist by the name of Ray Birdwhitshell was funding *kinesics,* the science of reading "facial expression, gestures, posture and gait, and visible arm and body language."

He's basically the father of body language analysis. By now, we had all we needed for a full-blown scientific field:

- A *sound theory* on which to build the field.
- A *large body of data* to study.

What really matters from now on is actually the growing body of evidence collected and the precision of analysis that professionals all over the world have been learning and displaying.

Body language can be used in court as well as for psychoanalysis. It has become a reliable way of understanding what goes on "behind the scenes" when politicians or other famous people are under scrutiny...

In the meantime, however, the long argument between nature and nurture has continued. So, zoologist Desmond Morris published *The Naked Ape* in 1967 where he stated that humans resort to animalistic behavior when under pressure. He looked at the behavior of people in cities to do so. This of course wanted to prove the fact that body language is fully natural.

Unfortunately, "animalistic" is a very personal definition, in itself a cultural one... But those were times when science leaned towards the "all is genetically motivated" theory, and even our field felt that shift.

And it was in the 1970s that US psychologists Paul Ekman and Wallace Friesen produced a long, articulated and consistent body of work that resulted in *FACS*, or *Facial Action Coding System.* This is very important because it gives us a sort of "dictionary of facial expressions", including clear ways of detecting deception. You can understand how useful this has been for investigators all over the world.

But it is also important that they looked at the cross-cultural patterns and similarities of these expressions. They are not the same in all people from all over the world. And the similarities are stronger where cultural identities are more similar. They came out with a synthesis of the nature vs. nurture debate. According to them, there are universal signs (a universal non-verbal code) but also cultural codes that "mask it", cover it or changes it.

So, coming to the present time, where are we now? We are in a very good place with body language analysis... *We have a large body of data to analyze all nonverbal communication*, from facial expressions to proxemics and much more.

We also know that *the analytical methods we use do work*. We are sure about it because it has been tested over and over again for decades, and the results are reliable.

And what's happened to the nature vs nurture leitmotif of the history of body language studies? Let's say that scholars are getting on "fairly well". They still argue, and that seems to be their nature (a pun, again...) but they argue less.

Basically, there are two *models* that scholars use to describe the different theories:

- *The cultural equivalence model,* which believes that the *main cause of body language is natural...*
- *The cultural advantage model,* which states that culturally similar people understand each other's nonverbal language better. So, *culture is key to body language.*

In 2008, Jessica Tracy and Richard Robins published an interesting study entitled 'The Nonverbal Expression of Pride: Evidence for cross cultural recognition' (*Journal of Personality and Psychology*). In it, they allege that pride and shame have the same overall body language all over the world. This is important because we may be starting to find archetypes of body language, and in science and especially psychology, discovering a set of archetypes is a huge step full of opportunities for future developments.

# BE WARNED!

You know now that body language analysis is a serious science, with a long history and some very, very famous contributors like Freud and Darwin. Like mathematics or physics, or psychology itself though, it is a double-edged sword! So... Be warned!

Be warned because *when you have a powerful tool at your disposal, like body language analysis, you have responsibilities.*

It's like when you are a journalist, a politician, or a social service agent... You have the power to change people's lives. Well, I would say that more than the "bare power" (what a disgusting concept) we should look at it like this: *you have the responsibility of using it in the respect of others if not for their own good.*

Imagine a doctor who uses her or his knowledge to hurt patients! They can, of course, but they literally swear an oath not to do it. Psychologists too have a professional code. It states that you will *never use your knowledge or skills to harm anyone.* And you are going to learn some of this knowledge and skills... So, *use them wisely but above all responsibly.*

Be warned because *you can make mistakes.* And I don't mean only at the first stages. Even great experts at their fields make mistakes. Napoleon lost at Waterloo, and yet he was the greatest general on Planet Earth. Einstein made famous mistakes as a scientist. But Einstein was an honest man and he admitted them.

But when your mistake has already caused some consequences, admitting it is useless. Imagine you misinterpret a friend's body language and you abandon that friendship. Years later you find out you were wrong. Fine, you can admit it as much as you want, but that's not going to give you back your friend! You could try to make up, and that would need some talking and convincing. But what are the chances of you two actually having as good a friendship as before? And even then, the lost years would be lost forever, you can't turn back time. How about if your friend passes away before you make up?

**Be warned,** *because you are dealing with people's lives, including your own.*

Let's play a "specular game". This is quite common in psychology. I'll show you. Imagine that your boss has not really favored you at work because s/he misunderstands your personality. This is actually very common and if it is not happening to you now, it may have happened in the past and will very likely happen in the future...

You very likely (did/will) miss out on opportunities because of this "personality reading" mistake. And that means giving up on that holiday of your dreams... It's not a little thing... Or seeing others make careers steps while you stay behind... frustration follows... in the long run, this is a major cause of depression...

Now, let's turn the mirror... You are that boss. And we all are "bosses" in some areas of our lives. I am the boss in the kitchen at home, for example. Do you realize the impact you could have on other people's lives, even those close to you? Your family, your friends?

Be warned, *because analyzing body language should not go to your head.* You should always keep a humble and modest approach to your knowledge. Knowing more than other people does not make you better than them nor does it give you any rights over them.

Be warned, *because there is always more you can learn.* You will get to an excellent level with this book, I promised it and it will happen. But remember that there are people who have more experience than you, even than me – actually. It's a bit like with everything, with history... You know a lot, but someone will know more than you... So, in case you are in doubt, consult more experienced people about it.

Psychologists, psychotherapists, psychoanalysts etc. are usually very good at reading body language. Don't be afraid to ask a friend from those professions if you are not sure about an analysis. There are other people too, of course who can help you. And this leads me to my next point.

Be warned, *a hurried analysis is never a good analysis. Always leave the door of doubt open.* An analysis may be good, convincing, even crushingly convincing, but there is always the chance that you missed something. A good professional always keeps the "I made a mistake" option open. Not the other way around. People who are sure about everything they do are not professionals, they are bullies and very likely with personal issues...

Be warned, *because there are cultural differences.* From our brief history of body language analysis, you know that the idea that we all have the same body language all over the world has been abandoned. In Arabic countries, for example, you do not point with your hands;

that is rude. Imagine one of them reading our body language and not taking the cultural "language" into account...

Be warned, *because you cannot see everything.* You will mainly see people from one point of view, at a particular moment and in a place. Sometimes there are parts of the body you cannot see, and that may change your analysis if you saw them.

But also, the time matters. Maybe someone looks fidgety and nervous and you interpret it as dishonesty? Fair guess from what you know. But how about if I told you that this person is waiting for an important health test result? Or a telephone call from his or her partner after a massive row? Or that s/he is about to simply miss the bus home and you are holding him or her behind?

We will look at how *the context is part and parcel of the analysis.* But keep in mind that you will never know "all the context", that is humanely impossible, so, think accordingly.

What does it mean in practice? *Does it mean you should avoid analyzing body language?*

I would not think so. You need to train; you need to learn. It means, however that:

- *You should not act on your analysis unless you have to, and you are sure about it.* If you suspect that someone is about to grift you and you wish to cut the conversation, by all means do! But before you take away an opportunity from someone (a job, for example) on the basis of your analysis, think twice.

- *You should be particularly careful when emotions and other people's lives are concerned.* If your analysis just tells you that you will not buy that particular phone because the merchant was not honest, you have all my sympathy. If you want to change a relationship based on your analysis, I must call for caution.

- *Distinguish between analyzing body language and acting upon it.* The beauty of school is that you get to learn about the world without the consequences... You learn about a war without acting upon it... The same should be with learning about body language, learn how to read it, practice it etc. But then do not act upon it especially when it involves relationships. Do it only when you are near 100% sure.

On a sad note, talking about school... the only area where we are not protected by simulation (we learn about history without actually starting one, about gravity without crashing a plane etc....) is in social relationships... We learn about friends and love by actually living real relationships... There is no simulation there!

But this last point remains as a final thought... From the point of view of a psychologist, knowing about the human mind, society, how to analyze people etc. is beautiful... But *nothing compares with the beauty and sacredness itself of human feelings, thoughts, experience and of course relationships.*

*Be professional and put these values first.*

# 2

# THE SCIENCE BEHIND BODY LANGUAGE

Who studies body language? I mean, which field does it belong to? By now, you should know that body language analysis is not a "random practice" with no scientific value. As we said, it is even used by investigators, intelligence agents, etc. Basically, *there is hard science behind body language analysis.*

In the previous chapter we looked briefly at the history of this science. But you may be a bit confused because there are psychologists, biologists (actually Darwin was a theologian!), anthropologists etc. So, where does body language analysis fall?

Like most scientific developments, *it draws on many fields and disciplines, but as a whole, it falls roughly within psychology.*

The main fields it is related to are:

- Psychology

- Sociology
- Anthropology
- Linguistics
- Semiotics
- Biology
- Neurology

But we should not forget the contributions of the arts, like drama, painting, and the cinema... And yes, psychology has often used the arts in its studies, just think about how Freud uses literature in *Interpretation of Dreams...* But not just psychology. The link between the arts and science are deeper than we think – and I am thinking physics and mathematics in particular...

But I am digressing... Let's see what the key scientific foundations of body language analysis are, one by one. This may sound a bit theoretical. I promise you that we will start getting "our hands dirty" with practical analysis. But you will need it. You will need it to develop your skills but also to study further if you wish to.

To start with, there is a *regular and steady correspondence between some nonverbal signs and their meaning,* for example:

- *Smiling* – happiness
- *Slouching* – insecurity or physical uneasiness
- *Eye contact* – trust and interest
- *Lack of eye contact* – distrust or lack of interest
- *Looking up* – thinking, taking a pause to think
- *Looking down* – avoiding confrontation and conflict (some

may read it as submission, and it may be at times; but the actual core meaning is "I don't want to fight").

- *Lateral eye movement* – often means that you "want to get out" of that conversation or situation.
- *Pupil size can tell us lots of things about internal feelings and states of mind* – a large pupil means you are liking what you're seeing or experiencing, if it squeezes, it means the opposite. Dilated pupils are often also the sign of drug use (both legal and illegal).
- *Stepping back* – taking emotional distance; this may mean disapproval or just the need to have "your space".

The list goes on... For example, there's a whole branch that deals with *handshakes*... Talking about which, it may be one of the most important things at interviews. As we are on the topic... Firm but not strong, tight but formal, not "I am with family" warm, like the Pope does and by all means no double hand! The double hand in handshakes shows familiarity, warmth and protection.

To recap, *body language analysis is part of psychology, but it is linked with other sciences and it has its own branches and fields.* Some as specialized as handshakes, or hand gestures, or eye movement!

We will see all these branches as we go along, but for now let's look at two with weird sounding names: *haptics and proxemics*

## HAPTICS

I bet few people have ever heard this word in the right context, and it means *"the branch of body language that studies how people touch and what it means"*. Of course, touch is a very important part of body language.

Haptics in particular has *strong cultural influences.* Look at the difference between a Japanese person who does not even shake hands and a French guy who kisses his friends (of any sex) every time they meet! The Brits do not like to touch each other, while Italians do it all the time... So, my piece of advice is to be very aware of the cultural baggage people carry with them when you analyze haptics.

Then there are people who are "touchy feely", who like to touch and to be touched, and others who don't. This is a very complex psychological and personal matter. It may depend on many things, including past experiences, upbringing, confidence with your own body etc.

A moment of reflection: you see now that you need anthropology, sociology and psychology (cultural, social and personal factors) to analyze haptics correctly?

And there is a key division here:

- *Touching yourself*
- *Touching others*

When we talk or communicate, *we often touch ourselves. Most of the time we do it involuntarily.* Here are some typical gestures, for example:

- Scratching your head
- Touching your nose
- Rubbing your hands
- Touching your chest
- Scratching your leg

There is a general misconception, and it is that every time you touch yourself when talking you show discomfort or even deceit. No. That's wrong! You may scratch your leg because it is actually itching. Otherwise, for example, it is far more likely to mean uncertainty than deceit.

Rubbing your hands has been taken by movies, drama, and popular culture to describe dishonest merchants who are about to grift you... But that is not the science! That's fantasy! *Rubbing your hands is a sign of excitement.* It usually means anticipation, but sometimes also "Oh good!" the discovery of some good news.

The meaning of *touching your nose* has become part of popular culture too. Ask around and they will tell you that it means "I am telling you a lie"! That is one of those silly simplifications that do not help the reputation of this science!

First and foremost, *never read a nose sign on its own.* With the nose, you *always need other sings to interpret it.*

Secondly, touching your nose is very often a *sign that you do not trust what you hear.* The exact opposite.

Finally, remember that the nose is a very sensitive part of our body and very often we touch it or scratch it just because it is slightly itchy or dry... Don't confuse a cold with a lie!

So far, we can see that there is a huge difference between the actual science of body language analysis and popular beliefs about it...

A very interesting use of haptics body language experts all over the world actually comes from Queen Elizabeth II. It is part of her posture, but have you noticed how she holds her own hands in front of her lap? That has been noted as an impressive sign...

In fact, it isolates her in her position of superiority to anybody else around. Holding hands shows equality, but she cannot be seen as "equal", so she only holds her own hands. Then she gives (shows) her knuckles to the audience. That means "stay off". And it finally resolves a problem for very powerful people: what to do with your hands? They far too often give away your insecurities, fears, subconscious thoughts... This way, no one can "read into the Queen's mind through her hands". It is in fact regarded as one of the most impressive signs of authority.

Compare that with George W. Bush, who often put his hands in his pockets and pushed out his elbows. That hid his hands, and he looked like a peacock trying to look bigger than he actually was... A display of power, for sure, but which to the expert eye showed a huge abyss of insecurity.

The way we touch ourselves gives away great signals about us. And we can develop our own ways to touch ourselves, to look more confident, calm, self-assured, positive etc. But learn from Bush Jr's mistake; it can backfire!

Let's talk about *touching others* now. This is very much influenced by culture and personality, as we said. But apart from this, *the way we touch others depends a lot on how at ease we are with each other.*

For example, body language analysts noticed that very often, at the very beginning of a romantic relationship between people who have not been friends before, there's *indirect touching.* What do we mean by that? We mean that people touch each other's objects, clothes, accessories etc., instead of actual bodies.

It is more often the male partner in a heterosexual pair who moves first and touches an object belonging to the woman. The first actual touch then can make all the difference... If it is the hand, it gives an idea of respect, equality, friendship etc. That would be ideal. And for people who are so inclined personally, it should come naturally.

If the first touch is on the leg, it will very strong sexual signals, and it may show that the person is mainly or only interested sexually. Shoulders are also common as "first place to touch", as touching them may give a sense of protection.

There are so many variables to consider when we look haptics when touching other people.

- Who touches who (first)
- How the other responds

- How long is the contact
- Which part of the body touches which
- How large is the contact surface
- When and why this happens
- Cultural and social factors.

The point is that *touching people is always a matter of social, emotional, interpersonal negotiation.* We all know it from experience. Just think about that most beautiful but often difficult of body contact acts, a hug!

Hugging is a sign of empathy and care basically like no other. You need to be very intimate and at ease with each other for "a good hug". Of course, there are societies where hugging is common, others where it is rare. In some countries, friends hug, in others, especially male friends do not (female friends may do more often, as visible in many social and cultural backgrounds in the USA or GB).

The "Mississippi" count for hugging may not be correct, but it gives the idea of *how much we invest in a hug.* And I am not talking about money, but confidence, intimacy, even "face" (self-confidence).

So, haptics help us understand two things mainly:

1. How people feel about themselves
2. How people feel about each other

And this is just one of the many branches we will see in this book! But let's see another now...

## PROXEMICS

Proximity is super important in reading body language. And "proxemics" means the *"study of where people are and how they move in relation to each other".* This includes:

- The distance between people
- The position in relation to one another (left, right, behind, in front etc.).
- The levels people are at (higher, lower, equal)
- The direction people face and turn (towards each other, away from each other)

Imagine two people back to back with their arms crossed... How would you interpret it? That they have had a massive disagreement or row and don't want to talk to each other? You'd be very likely correct.

Imagine two people facing each other. Now imagine if they lean forward, towards each other. Isn't that a sign of "agreement", of mutual interest etc.? And how about if they lean back? That may show "distance", "disagreement"...

This is why sitting back with your arms crossed at a job interview means losing it. It shows you take a distance from the panel, but also that you're closed to them (arms crossed) and if you also cross your legs then you just show that you are overconfident and "look down on them". And they will "keep in touch"... yeah trust it!

But proxemics also studies *how we react to each other's positions and movements.* Actors spend a long-time training to react to other actors; it's in fact a core part of learning acting. But on a stage, you will also exaggerate and sometimes ritualize these action-reaction gestures.

In fact, in reality *we tend to "downplay our reactions" in real life.* This becomes more so in formal situations. If you are at the pub or bar with friends, it is far more likely that your gestures and movements will be much bigger, much "grander" and much more dramatic than during a meeting with your boss! At least we hope so...

"What is more difficult," you may ask, "reading proxemics in formal or informal situations?" The honest answer is that in formal situations, proxemic signs (and other verbal signs) are smaller, "downsized", if I can use this word. On the other hand, fewer things happen; there isn't much "background noise" to pick up the signals.

The opposite is true, and it depends on how formal or informal situations are. From a simple informal meeting between acquaintances and a full-on stag party on one side, and from a simple fairly informal office meeting to being knighted by the Queen of England on the other...

The fact is that *the more informal the situation is, the more people feel dis-inhibited and free to move and gesticulate etc.* But if gestures and facial expressions become clearer, more definite and "bigger", so does the "background noise" caused by other people moving, talking loudly, gesticulating etc....

Both have their difficulties. *In formal situations, you will have to focus on details. In informal situations, you will have to exclude all that disturbs your focus.*

Having said this, let's see some *core principles of proxemic action-reaction*. Let's take 3 examples to illustrate them.

1. John and Sheila are sitting facing each other. John leans with his chest towards Sheila and she *mirrors it*; she leans with her chest towards him too.
2. John and Sheila are sitting facing each other. John leans with his chest towards Sheila and she leans back with her chest, still facing him.
3. John and Sheila are sitting facing each other. John leans with his chest towards Sheila and she turns sideways away from him, so that she is no longer facing him.

These are simple everyday situations that you must have witnessed many times in your life... But now I am asking you to look at them from the perspective of a body language analyst...

In case (a), we have the action known as *mirroring*. This always expresses *accord, empathy, agreement, appreciation, and even, in some cases, physical attraction or love.* In this case, whatever is going on between John and Sheila, we know that they are "on the same page".

Mirroring, be aware, is often used by charlatans and grifters to gain your trust, so now you know it...

In case (b), Sheila does not mirror what John does. Instead she *neutralizes it.* She basically does not allow him to close their distance. She keeps the same distance by moving back. This is a sign of *diffidence, discord, disagreement, mistrust or simple insecurity and uncertainty.*

Finally, in case (c), Sheila actually *breaks away*. She basically "gets out of the physical dynamics with John". She literally "exits" their proxemic relation... A bit like leaving a meeting halfway through, or a party if you prefer... In this case, *Sheila is subtracting herself from John's authority.* She is not showing simply disagreement: *she is rebelling, claiming her freedom.*

Like there is rarely a sudden switch between "love" and "hate" or "friends" and "enemies" in real life, so there is rarely a sudden change from mirroring to braking away in proxemics. When it happens, it all looks so visible and dramatic. Like in those old Hollywood movies when an old authoritarian aunt would suddenly turn her back on her niece's suitor and walk off with a grand gesture...

It does happen, but it is rare. People usually move from mirroring to mirroring less, then to neutralizing softly and with garb, then more, then intently, and only if that fails people start breaking away. And even here, first partially and only then fully.

Observe when people meet in the streets and one wants to leave... You will first see movements going back, claiming distance. Then a little step to the side. Then a bigger one, then the chest turns. This is actually often mirrored by the other person most of the times. Otherwise, the thing gets embarrassing as one is holding the other behind, being "insistent" or "sticky" ...

In many cases, using proxemics to signal these things is understood subconsciously by others and the whole process becomes consensual...

It almost looks like a parting ritual we all understand... But we actually do it without even being aware of it...

So, keep in mind there are three key action-reaction principles and in fact, yet again, observe them in the people you meet every day. At the office, you may find out things that had escaped you for months... Maybe that there are "feelings" between two colleagues (or that the "feelings" are long gone) or that your boss (or teacher) favors someone (mirroring gives it away very often).

And now we can move to a practical chapter... I want to show you some of the key rules and even "tricks of the trade" of body language analysis. And we are going to do it right now!

# 3

# THE BASICS OF BODY LANGUAGE ANALYSIS

Frowning, scowling, sighing, ogling, scratching, slouching... The list of words we have for body language is huge... Why? Put simply, there are loads of expressions in body language. But can we try and make some sense out of this huge language system we so often ignore? Yes, we can. And this is exactly what we are going to do.

Let's start with a little experiment... Think about your favorite teacher at school. Picture him or her in front of you, by the white-board (or blackboard if you are my generation!) Done? Keep the image in mind. Now, we all had teachers we couldn't stand the sight of (the voice of etc.). Pick your least favorite teacher ever.

Done? Great... Now, draw the contours of the two images you have in mind. Just pretend you have a big marker and draw their silhouettes. If your least favorite came out as one of those chalk shapes police people draw on the street in movies, then you really didn't like him! Jokes aside, overlap them...

I bet they had different postures... Am I right? Of course, because studies show that the thing students remember most about their schoolteachers is their "antics", like their weird posture, original body language, facial expressions, strange habits of tone of voice. Not the actual words, not the actual lessons...

But if you compare the two postures of the two teachers, one will give you a positive impression, the other a negative one. You see, you already "read" their body language. And you kept all this knowledge in your subconscious until now. And with a simple analysis, you now have a rational understanding of their body language (or part of it).

This exercise tells us a lot about body language. For example:

- We pick it up even if we are not aware of it.
- We react to it even if we don't know we are actually reacting to it.
- It influences our opinion of people.
- We remember it for a very long time. Longer than we remember words, in fact!
- People give off body language signs all the time.
- Some signs are positive, and others are negative.

Reading body language is like opening a book full of secrets. That book has been on the shelf for years, and we have not picked it up... It's time we did it now...

## POSITIVE AND NEGATIVE BODY LANGUAGE

Let's start from a basic distinction. *Positive and negative body language.* And we will do it with a little experiment... Tell me, of these two, which one is positive, and which one is negative?

a. Punching your fist on the table

b. Smiling

Of course, you will agree that (a), "punching your fist on the table" is negative while (b), "smiling is positive. But now let's add a few more...

c. Frowning

d. Touching your nose

e. Tapping your foot

f. Leaning backwards on a chair

Now things become a bit less straightforward, don't they? You may think that frowning is on the whole negative, but not as negative as punching your fist on the table. And I would agree. This tells us that there are *levels of negativity and positivity in body language.*

*Negativity and positivity are on a cline, on a gradient, from very negative to very positive.* In between, you have 'quite a lot negative/positive", "a little negative/positive" and all the grades in between you wish to use...

I can hear your question, don't worry, "Is there neutral body language?" Great question actually!

The idea of *neutral body language* is interesting for me... Let me tell you why. By neutral body language we mean "relaxed" and "at ease". So, in body language "neutral" is actually "positive"! I think it tells us a lot about the real meaning of life... But maybe this is something we will discuss in a philosophy book...

Now, back to positive and negative. What makes us measure negativity in body language? I mean, which attitude makes body language negative? There are a few:

- *Aggression*: of course, aggressive behavior makes body language negative.
- *Hostility*: it may be less overtly expressed than aggression. So, it will be more difficult to detect. But it really makes a huge difference if you can spot hostility on those you have in front of you...
- *Emotional distance:* this often translates into physical distance, as we will see.
- *Diffidence and lack of trust:* it is related to emotional distance and it can be its cause, but it's not the same. A friend may feel a lot for you but not trust you on some points. And yes, you can understand it from your friend's body language.
- *Disinterest:* this may not be as negative as outright hostility or aggression, but it is still negative and finding out about it will save you a lot of disappointments in life...

These are different "types" of negativity, or better different "sources" of negativity.

So, what you need to do when you spot general negativity in someone's body language, is to *work out which of these emotions or attitudes it expresses.* Understanding that your interviewer at a job interview is disinterested will tell you a lot about your prospects of getting a job. You know when you get home from a job interview and they ask you, "How did it go?" You usually give an impression, then waste days in anxiety... How about if you could actually tell rationally that it didn't go well because you read it in the panel's body language? Less anxiety, less disappointment, more time to move to your next interview...

You see, people nowadays often have a bad attitude about "knowing the negative" ... It's a sociological matter. Society has become so difficult and frustrating that as a defense mechanism many of us prefer "simply not to know." But if you know it rationally beforehand, you will not get the emotional blow when the news is broken to you.

Emotionally, being told something negative by someone in a position of power or knowing it beforehand is hugely different. The second immunizes you from disappointment, frustration, loss of face. And it gives you more time and energy to dedicate to your next move.

Let's pause for a little *reflection.* As a pedagogue, in fact, I have to tell you that a good learner is a reflective learner. So, every now and then we will pause and think back a bit... Have you noticed that *you have already started analyzing body language?* Analyzing means "breaking into parts" ...

So, what we can say about *analyzing body language is that we need to understand what the attitude is (emotion, thought etc.) behind nonverbal signs.*

And we can start with three steps:

1. *Divide between positive and negative.*
2. *Decide the level or degree of positivity and negativity.*
3. *Identify the core attitude behind the sign, gesture etc.*

It is a bit like mind reading, yes... Honest mind reading though...

"But how about the positive?" I can hear you! Talking about mind reading... Okay, I kept it last to end on a positive note.

Here again, of course there are *levels of positivity.* From "enthusiastic", "enamored" or "ecstatic" to "lukewarm" and "not fully hostile" ...

But *what causes a positive body language sign? What are the attitudes behind it?* Here they are:

- *Empathy:* this is by far the overriding attitude or feeling behind all positivity. When people understand what you feel, whether you are expressing a problem or expressing joy, they will open up both emotionally and physically (with body language).
- *Trust:* if people trust you, you will see it in the way they sit, move, smile, speak, look... And this is very important... Think grifters and what they may know about our body language! We'll come back to this... Trust me (I love puns!)

- *Interest:* if people are interested in what you say they will show an openness and positivity about your ideas, feelings etc. through their bodies.
- *Agreement:* it is not the same as interest. Understanding agreement through body language puts you a step ahead.
- *Relaxation:* you can't imagine how being relaxed changes your body language. Of all the attitudes (states of mind) that influence body language relaxation is "the big switch". You see, if you empathize, trust, agree etc.... you are relaxed! If you feel aggression etc. you are not! It's like "the bedrock of all positive attitudes". Or the consequence of them all? Let's say both.
- *Confidence:* we will have to look at this in detail, because there is a key difference between overconfidence (which is aggressive) and real confidence (which is protective). People who are positively confident have a warm, mother or father like body language. Overconfident people have an "army general" type of body language...

If you know which signs project positivity, you can do two things with it:

- You can *learn to read positive signs.* So, you will know when your teacher or boss *actually* agrees with you.
- You can *learn to project positive signs.* And this is as life changing as it gets. People who project positive signs have better lives: they have more respect and esteem, they are more trusted, they are happier, they receive more

information (yes, people talk openly to positive people), they have a better life experience and even better career prospects.

Now we have made lots of progress. But there is much more to say.

## BODY LANGUAGE IN CONTEXT

Let's take an example from verbal language and linguistics. Look at this statement in two contexts:

1. "What a nice day!" (The Sun is shining and it's hot).
2. "What a nice day!" (It's pouring down, it is cold and miserable).

The sentence is the same, but the *meaning is the exact opposite.* The second statement is ironic. And we cannot understand irony without some form of context. Yet irony changes the meaning of statements to their exact opposite!

As we do with verbal language, *we need the context to understand body language. We need contextual information.* But what is context exactly?

Context is everything that "comes with" a sign, which can be immediate (near and clear) or even very remote. It can actually be another nonverbal sign.

Imagine children coming back home all dirty and muddy. At the door the mother is waiting for them and you see:

- She has her fists on her hips, akimbo.
- She is tapping her foot.

What do you understand from this?

Your *first reading* would tell you that she is angry, that she has a scolding attitude and posture, very authoritative and even impatient.

But now I want to show you the mother's face: and she has a beaming smile!

*The smile is contextual to the other two signs.* And now you understand that she too is actually playing with the children. How often do we do it to "pretend scold"? It is actually an important social and educational activity. I won't get into the details, but for example it plays down the role of severe punisher-parents often have; it teaches children that even that is a role, not something parents like doing, showing self-irony etc.… Beautiful!

But for what we need to learn, there is a key point: *your analysis is only as accurate as the completeness of the sings and contextual signs you collect.*

It is a bit like "playing detective", like Columbo, for example… You need to collect a lot of data, in fact as much as you can and then piece the puzzle back together.

So, we can agree that *you should absolutely never interpret a body language sign in isolation. Read them all together, as different letters of the same word, or words in a sentence…* None alone can give you the full meaning.

If the smile is another nonverbal signal, and it is immediate context, now forget you ever saw it. But now I will give you another piece of information: *you know the mother's mindset and cultural values and you know that she does not care that her children get dirty. Actually, she values children's freedom and contact with nature above all.*

This is a very important piece of information which changes the whole perspective, once again. *We do not live in a cultural vacuum.* Personal, social, family, and culture and even traditions affect all we do and express.

Let's look at it this way. When you don't understand someone, very often you go to a friend of his/hers to get a "final interpretation". The "trust me s/he didn't mean it" from someone who knows him/her well... Why? That sentence is based on knowing the context, which includes the history of the person and his/her values...

"Hold on," you may be thinking, "I can't know everybody's past!" You are right, and you will not need it most of the time. If you are trying to find out if that shop assistant is trying to fleece you, then you won't need it.

But this is to show you how far we can go with the data we use, and how important the context may be. Still, with the shop assistant, you will want to take into consideration other contextual factors as well, for example:

- Is this a reputable shop?
- Have you shopped there before?

- Are you a regular customer?
- Is the shop assistant permanent or just filling in for one day?
- Do you know the shop assistant from outside this shop?

Like when you read a book you may need to know about the times it is set in, the culture it comes from etc.... the same will apply to analyzing body language.

## CONTEXT AND AMBIGUITY OF BODY LANGUAGE

At the beginning of this chapter we looked at a list of nonverbal signs, remember? We started with "punching your fist on the table" and "smiling" (assuming with a real smile!) These two are pretty *unambiguous.* A bit like the words "good" and "bad", "love" and "hatred", "happiness" and "pain".

But then we added "frowning", "tapping your foot", "touching your nose" and "leaning back on a chair". And these are not unambiguous, in fact, they can be *very ambiguous out of context and on their own.*

Tapping your foot with music means that you are feeling at ease and "getting into it". Tapping your foot without may be a sign of nerves (or maybe that you have a tune in your head?) Tapping your foot while standing may be a sign of disapproval, but sitting may be a sign of boredom.

So, if it is a formal meeting and you tap your foot under the chair... I'd bet you are bored... But if you are standing and staring at someone or at a particular place, I would think you are showing disapproval and impatience...

In this case, *you need the context to resolve the ambiguity of the nonverbal signal.*

Frowning can be a sign of perplexity but also of concern... If you are telling a friend that you had a bad experience and you see a frown on his or her head, you'd assume that s/he is expressing empathy, an honest concern about your happiness, health etc....

If you give in your homework and your teacher frowns – well, that can't be positive now!

Here again, it is the *context that tells us how to interpret a nonverbal sign.*

*Everything happens in context.* As a body language reader that makes all the difference. For example, in a *formal context* people will be stiffer, less expansive, less expressive. And this means that *body language becomes:*

- More controlled and less spontaneous
- More limited (smaller gestures, smaller movements, less expressive facial expressions)
- Slower and more predictable (there is like a "script" to follow in formal situations)

In short, our body language changes according to the situation:

- where we are
- why we are there
- who we are with

And this is all part of the context.

## BODY LANGUAGE AS A HOLISTIC PRACTICE

Let's go back to our foot tapping mother. We started from her foot and ended up to a conclusive reading only after seeing her face... That says a lot about how we read body language. You see, it is not "foot language" or "elbow language" for a reason. *We read the whole body, as a continuous and coherent expressive body.*

There are *specific branches of body language analysis for face, position and distance, hands etc.... even for eyes...* And we will see them very soon indeed! But the meaning comes only after looking at all the signs a person gives off and then putting them together. It's like reading a book... You don't just read verbs, or only adjectives or only nouns, do you?

"But is there a direction, an order? Where do I need to start from?" you ask quite correctly... No there isn't. But there is a professional trick I will teach you in a second.

Most times, *and most body language readers are caught by particular movements or gestures*, exactly like everybody else does. So, the foot tapping of the woman will very likely be the first thing a professional and an amateur body language reader would notice.

This is simply because *there are very visible gestures, expressions and movements that stand out.* It's a bit like shouting or raising your voice or laughing in verbal communication. You cannot fail to notice these signs.

The difference is that while everybody notices it, the expert body language reader "activates".

Let me explain this to you. What would you do, with your very eyes, if you saw someone punching the air? You would *zoom in on the strange, eye-catching and anomalous gesture, movement or facial expression,* right? That's the most natural thing to do. In fact, it's unconscious, spontaneous, it's a reflex, an instinctive reaction.

Now let me tell you what a professional body language reader would do... *She or he would zoom out from the strange, eye-catching and anomalous gesture, movement or facial expression.* The exact opposite, and that's what I mean by activate.

Why? How can you see signs from the rest of the body if you zoom in on a little detail? It's like people who play sports like basketball... They keep an eye on the ball but keep their peripheral vision on teammates and adversaries... They are trained to do it. Or while you focus on the ball, someone can steal it from you...

So, this is a bit of an insider secret, a trick of the trade, but I wanted you to know it. This way, you can start with the right tools, means, habits and attitude you need to become very proficient.

And the very first exercise I will ask you to do is just this. Go out (when you have to, don't rush out just because of this!) Go where there are people, maybe when you go shopping or you are going to school or work...

Okay? As you are out, look at people around you. If they move, some particular movement or gesture will catch your attention. Instead of zooming in though, "activate" and zoom out ready to catch any other signs his or her body gives off.

And after you have done this, we can meet again for the next Chapter, where we will learn about the very nature of body language, why we react the way we do...

# 4

# WHY DOES THE BODY REACT THE WAY IT DOES?

## BODY LANGUAGE

**B**ooooooo! Did I make you jump? Probably not because you're just reading this. But if I had shouted it from behind your back... The question is, why do we jump when someone scares us?

It is a reflex, and a very visible one. Like when the doctor tries your reflex with the little hammer (or gavel) on your knee. You cannot avoid it. In this case, the heart itself "skips a beat" (metaphorically, it beats faster actually). When the heart is affected, the whole body responds. You feel an adrenaline rush. Your mind suddenly resets and goes into defense mode. Your nerves and muscles stiffen. Sometimes even bladders have reactions...

This is a glaring example that *we are not fully in control of our physical actions and reactions.*

But how about if similar but much smaller, less visible episodes happened to you all the time? You don't consciously look away when someone irritates you most of the time, do you? You *can do it*, just to *show your disapproval*. But even if you don't want to show it, your body will.

In fact, *our body tends to respond to almost any experience and even any emotion we have.* And this is where *natural body language comes from.* If you're happy, you smile. If you're angry you scowl. If you're nervous your body stiffens etc.

"But how about actors and politicians," you're asking? We could spend hours talking about the long tradition of "looking at how the body communicates to then reproduce it as naturally as possible". In a way, the *ability to reproduce seemingly natural body language* is one of the things that makes an actor convincing. Centuries ago they had ritualized and exaggerated gestures no one would take as natural. At the times of Shakespeare, actors did not want to "look real". Then things changed and this art was perfected.

And of course charlatans, grifters and politicians jumped on the gravy train and learned how to use *recitation body language.* This is a form of *acquired body language* which is very conscious and intentional.

And in the middle? Is *recitation body language* the whole of *acquired body language*? No, not at all actually! We pick up body language unconsciously all the time. There is a theory in language studies called *Accommodation Theory.* It means that when we like someone, we imitate their language (tone, choice of words, even accent), but also their nonverbal communication (like body language)

... The opposite happens when we do not like someone we are talking with.

This happens all the time and for sure you have found yourself using "the words of a friend", meaning her or his typical language. We actually notice string relationships because people start "talking the same and moving the same" ...

So, in your own personal body language there is a *cultural inheritance* you carry with you. That facial expression from your beloved relative, that gesture from your old friendship group... all these signs you picked up along the way will surface every now and then subconsciously.

So, we have seen that there are at least three types of body language:

1. *Natural body language*
2. *Acquired body language*
3. *Recitation body language*

We go back to the nature vs. nurture debate... Well, in the end it turned out to be more practical and less academic than we thought!

## UNDERSTANDING WHAT THE BODY IS TELLING YOU

Now that you know that body language has different origins, you can start making a distinction. Let's take a practical example... Imagine you are a professional body language analyst. Imagine there's a famous politician on TV and she is making a big speech. Imagine they ask you to analyze the speech to find out "what she is hiding"...

Fine, now, you will need to find out:

- What she wants you to believe.
- What she actually feels about what she says.
- If there are any cultural interference that confuses the reading.

*Her body is telling you all these things at the same time.* And it's your task to tell them apart.

If you have seen professionals at work, maybe you noticed that often they say things like, "He used his hand this way but at the same time he frowned..." Finding *contradicting signs* is actually a door into deception. Not necessarily, don't take me wrong. There are *no ultimate absolutes with human sciences.* We are not machines.

But you see, *reading signs in conjunction can give us a clue whether the person feels consistently with what he is communicating or not.*

And how about the body language that is culturally acquired? Sometimes, it can give us the sympathy for or affiliation to a cultural group. Rappers are a clear example. Their hand gestures really tell us "I belong to the rapping cultural tradition", with all its links to urban, Black etc. communities.

The way people cross legs in the UK can tell you if they come from the upper class or the lower class... Allow me a cultural reference... Have you ever seen the TV series *The Jeffersons,* with a fantastic Sherman Hemsley as the unforgettable George Jefferson? Do you remember his iconic stride? What did it tell you? He told all the viewers that he was "deeply proud to be a member of the Black community".

When you read body language you then come home with three different sets of information about the person:

- *His or her cultural background.* This may be relevant according to what he or she is saying, or, in some cases, you may need to remove these signs as "noise" because they confuse your assessment. For example, if someone is selling you a vacuum cleaner you may want to focus on whether it is a con instead...

- *What he or she wants you to believe.* Finding out which gestures and nonverbal signs were "planted" there to convince you gives you a great advantage. Note though... It does not mean that if someone is "acting" they are also lying. The politician in question will of course use his or her body language training... The point is finding out if *his or her body is telling a different story from his or her lips.*
- *What the body involuntarily says.* Which, of course, will confirm or disprove what the person is saying.

This is very important when racing body language... In many cases, it is a bit like "cleaning out everything" till you can actually see the truth... And in many cases, it is a lot of cleaning! But it isn't always like that.

We looked at a big and important example. Actually, if people understood every time politicians lie to them, we would be much better off...

But at other times you may want to *read body language to help the person.* Psychologists do it all the time. If you are breaking a piece of bad news to someone, you can't expect the person to respond honestly all the time...

There may be many reasons for this:

- The person is in shock.
- You are not in a relationship of confidence.

- The person may not want to upset you with his or her pain...

If you have to break bad news to someone, always look at their body language. They may be in much more need of help than they actually admit. Any sign of *closure*, especially in front of their chest and stomach, is actually a sign of extreme pain in these moments. Your friend needs comforting.

Slouching or bending forward is a bad sign too... Your friend may be giving up, or literally "felling the weight of the situation"...

The worst sign, however, may just be the blank stare and expressionless face. That is a sign of emotional shock...

Yet again, the context is all important in these situations. You may even expect a fairly string and detached reaction when a doctor gives a patient bad news. This is why it should not be the doctor that gives it, but a psychologist... But if it happens in a friendly relationship, you should expect a request for help in the body language. Even a hug...

## HUMAN REFLEX, INEVITABLE OR NOT?

Some people are like marble statues though. They never seem to give off any unwanted signs. Maybe the most impressive of all in this is our old acquaintance the Queen of England. It may look like it is possible to *control human reflex and unconscious body language totally.*

In this case, of course it would be very hard to find out lying and cheating. But is it really possible? The answer is yes... and no!

*Yes, it is possible to control natural reflexes. No, it is not possible to control them completely.*

In fact, great part of the body language that politicians (and actors) go through involves not expressing nonverbal signals, but repressing them. "Getting into character" means "becoming a blank slate" and that involves calming down the body to a point where it does not have to express itself non-verbally.

Actors and actresses do it all the time. Luckily, most politicians and insurance agents are not that good at acting. But they still train to avoid spontaneous body language.

To do this, you need a trainer that checks on how you move, gesticulate etc. and then tells you to "stop this and stop that" till it becomes easy and then second nature for you to hide your body language.

But no one can do it perfectly and all the time. There are some obstacles to this:

- *Some areas of body language are harder to hide, some impossible. Eyes especially cannot be easily controlled and faces too.*
- *It requires an effort and energy to hide your natural body language. People can do it for a short time but not all the time.*
- *Sudden and unexpected events can suddenly bring out natural body language.*

In fact, political speeches are almost always, filmed at a distance, short and controlled, there is no sudden "boo!"

Look at the Queen again. She has been training for this all her life... But still you will rarely see close ups of her, and rarely when she is giving a speech. Her appearances are very short. Everything is under control all the time.

Having said this, I want to give you a tip... Imagine you are in the middle of a transaction with a guy who really hides his natural body language well... What can you do?

- You can tire him out if you have time. This way, his defenses and energy will drop, and natural body language will resurface.
- You can *surprise him.* No need to go "boo!" but a sudden and unexpected gesture, sentence, proposal etc. And be ready to read his body language immediately after you surprise him...

## THE HUMAN BODY

Reading body language also means focusing on different parts of the body at the same time. Think about it; it is not easy to read feet and eyes simultaneously. That's why, first of all, *you should keep at a decent distance when reading body language.* This is also because if you are very close to the person you are analyzing, you will literally be interfering into his or her body language. You don't read body language on elevators...

So, where can you stand?

- You should not be too far, because you need to see the person's eyes.
- You shouldn't be too near, because you need to see the whole body and let the person feel safe.
- You should not even be directly in front if in person. You may become the person's focus.
- About 10 feet away slightly to the left or right (about 30°) is fine.

Now you know where to position yourself, shall we have a look at some key areas of body language analysis? These all look like technical words, and they are. But we will explain them in simple terms, and you will learn the basics of these fields.

## KINESICS

*Kinesics is the study of movement within body language.* We don't just communicate when standing, with facial expressions and gestures. *We also communicate through movements.*

The way you walk, the way you run, when and where you go… Which way you turn… There are so many aspects of movement that the list could go on for days. We have also seen that kinetics is important in proxemics (how we stand and move in relation to each other). All the different fields of body language analysis are linked, of course.

But let's look at some core elements of kinesics…

- *The direction of movement.* Which way does the movement

go? Does it go towards someone or away from someone? Or maybe something?

- *The speed of movement.* Running away is not the same as walking away. And walking away slowly is not the same as walking away in a hurry.
- *The size of the movement.* Walking totally out of the room is a clear sign that you intend to finish an interaction, even peacefully... Instead, just stepping away may mean that you want to stop the interaction, but not just yet. How far you move does matter, of course.
- *The accentuation of the movement.* By this we mean how big, theatrical, exaggerated etc. the movement is. And this can show either intention (if the person wants to make a dramatic gesture) when intended, but total lack of control if it is natural.
- *The complexity of the movement.* Simply walking is not the same as walking and jumping, or walking and waving, or walking and shaking your head. We need to analyze movements in all their complexity.

To these, of course we need to add the different types of movements, like:

- Walking
- Sitting down, squatting etc.
- Standing up
- Moving hands (waving etc.)
- Moving arms

- Head movements

The list is long… An interesting one, for example, is crossing your legs. This can be a sign of ease, a cultural sign, or even a sign of discomfort according to how you do it.

It is a sign of ease because you lift a foot from the ground. You are less "grounded". Usually, when we feel unsafe, we want to feel in touch with the ground as much as possible.

It can be a cultural sign. Just think about the difference between resting your ankle on your knee, a sign of great confidence, often used by men and even frowned upon when women do it in some cultures. Now compare with aligning the knees one on top of the other. In Britain it is common but among middle- and upper-class men and all women. Working class men do not use it often…

It can be a sign of distress, especially if the lifted foot tends to drape back onto the other leg. This is quite a common sign by women especially, and it shows that the woman is "closing up completely", even that she feels sexually threatened, or at least that she wants to cut off the sexual sphere from the encounter.

Always keep an eye out for how people move, and you will find out much more than you may imagine…

## OCULESICS

Talking about keeping an eye out, *oculesics is that branch of body language analysis that studies eye movements.* It is actually a subfield of kinesics. You know that eyes move, but have you ever actually observed them? They move all the time!

Of course, their movement is limited in space (unless you count eye focus as well), but there are many other things to look out for in eye movement:

- The direction
- If it is repeated, constant
- Linearity (eyes can rotate, for example)
- The length of the movement
- The focus

Taking the last first, there are two key *directions of focus:*

- Inside focus
- Outside focus

Think about it carefully and you will notice that when people look "inside themselves" or outside, you can notice the difference. An outside focus is piercing, an inside focus is vanishing.

Then again, where someone focuses one's sight is of course very important. The famous looking at a watch during a (romantic) meeting says it all. But also, the frequency of *focus shift* is important. If you are out on a romantic date and you look at someone else once, your partner may not notice it, pay no attention to it or forgive you. Start doing it a bit more often and I am not sure your date will end up in a "happily ever after' scenario...

Everybody changes focus every now and then. But doing it constantly shows *interest in someone or something.*

While we are here, I will tell you an acting secret... Actors always look *above the heads of the audience.* So do good teachers... Why? They have to avoid *eye contact,* which is far too powerful to hold especially if you are, in a manner of speak, telling a story, a "lie" of sorts... You will find it hard to stay in character and loom at the audience in their eyes.

So, sometimes even in a very frank and honest conversation, people look away, they change focus. But that is just like "taking a break, a breath". Sustaining eye contact is very hard indeed.

On this topic, no... If you can stare at someone in the eyes for three second you are not necessarily in love with each other. Another urban myth about body language we have to dispel.

Let's see some typical eye movements.

- Looking up. This may mean many things. From desperation, to the fact that you are thinking, disbelief, confusion etc.
- Looking down. This usually shows disappointment and a will to avoid eye contact. It may also show shame and lack of self-confidence.
- Looking sideways briefly. That is usually a way to take a small break, maybe to think or reflect.
- Looking sideways intently. That is usually a sign that the person is actually very interesting in someone or something else.

- Repeated lateral movement. This is usually a sign that the person is trying to get away from this interaction.

And here is possibly the biggest urban myth we have to dispel. No... eyes up and left does not mean someone is telling the truth and eyes up and right does not mean the person is lying... It's been debunked and proved wrong by actual research... Sorry it is not that easy.

The *key to understanding if someone is lying is to find a contradiction between what someone says and what his or her body says.* There is no "one tell-tale sign" of lying... And we will see this in the next chapter.

The *sequence of shifts instead is important.* Let's go back to our romantic dinner which didn't start too well. Jack caught Rose look away at the other table, and not at the food... There's a very good-looking man over there...

Now, Jack gets worried and it does not happen anymore... Of course Jack may think it was a chance.

Next scenario, Rose looks that way once more... If before she did not know there was a good-looking man, now she shows that she liked the surprise... or at least this may be what Jack thinks.

But how about if Jack catches her eye as she is looking over at the man on the other table?

Imagine she moves her eyes and looks at Jack straight in his eyes...

Now imagine she shifts her eyes to the other side first, then down on the table and only later she looks into Jack's eyes?

You will agree that in the first case, we can be quite sure that Rose has "nothing to hide". But her behavior, actually the sequence of eye shifts in the second case leaves us bug doubts about it. Doubts which we will have to investigate, as body language analysts.

We have seen two important sub-fields of body language analysis which you can add to the two we have seen already: haptics and proxemics.

These four fields together will give you a good framework to work with.

Of course there are specific fields, for all the different parts of the body, and we will come across them soon enough.

Before we move onto the next chapter, where we will learn to interpret body language in the light of what people say and what their bodies tell us, let's recap and see how many areas (branches) of body language analysis you know so far.

- *Haptics* – which studies "how people touch" themselves and others.
- *Proxemics* – which studies "how people stand and move in relation to each other."
- *Kinesics* – which studies "how people move".
- *Oculesics* – which studies "eye movements".

Keep these in mind because you will need them next, when we actually get to the chapter you have been waiting for... the one on detecting lies!

# 5

# IS WHAT HE'S SAYING THE SAME AS WHAT HE'S ACTUALLY DOING?

Mayla gets home from her new job. She starts talking to her husband about her first day at work, but she gets the impression that he's not paying attention, so she says:

*"Are you listening Chris?"*

And he replies, "Yes, of course, Mayla, I'm all ears," looking out of the window...

You get the point. What Chris says does not match what his body language is saying. Beware, this is not a clue to jump to conclusions. But it is a *"gap between two realities we need to investigate"*. See yourself primarily as an investigator, not a judge. And in any case, the value of a judgement depends on the accuracy of the investigation.

In this chapter, we will focus on this gap (or lack of) ... We will look at different ways of communicating and what discrepancies can tell us about the real meaning behind the words (and behind gestures too).

## HOW HUMANS COMMUNICATE

Look at Michelangelo's *David*. Watch Leonardo's *Mona Lisa*. Listen to Beethoven's $9^{th}$ *Symphony*. Read a novel or watch a play by Shakespeare... These are all forms of communication. Written words, spoken words, even the weird noises we make are communication. But so are lines, colors, shade, perspective in paintings. And so are notes, beat, tempo in music... In cinematic language, zooming, cutting, close ups, photography, the soundtrack... they are all ways of communicating.

Communication is far more than a grammar book of any language! It is true, however, that we *humans heavily rely on verbal communication.* Much more than other animals. For example, fish communicate with colors and movements very often. Some birds communicate by singing, others by displaying their feathers or even doing ritual dances... Other animals are very verbal, on the other hand (cats, dolphins, elephants, whales etc.).

And dancing may be a very good example to use. Think about dancing. Think about how *you dance. Most of us, see, live and use dance as a way of expressing ourselves freely.* Most of us don't do the splits; most of us don't plié, sauté etc... We dance spontaneously and naturally.

But if you dance regularly, soon you will learn maybe to waltz, or to twist, or to rock 'n' roll (that's actually hard) or to tango (hard too!) Then if you progress you move to figurative tango etc.... Of course, to be a ballet dancer you need to start learning all those moves when you are a child

But what does this tell us? It tells us that we naturally communicate through dance. But the more we learn about it, the more we become experienced and then even professional, the more we learn "new signs", new "words" new "units of communication" as well as new styles etc.... We can express more because we have more tools.

And this is true of art, singing, acting... all forms of communication in fact! Think about it. You may not be a great singer, but we can all hum a tune (even off key, okay) when we are happy. No, you may not be as great a singer as Aretha Franklin or Natalie Dessay. But they had a massive natural talent and they studied and practiced!

Similarly, you will never paint as well as Leonardo or Caravaggio, but you can do simple drawings. And the more you practiced painting, the more you equipped yourself with "painting words", "painting phrases" etc....

You see, plants even communicate through smells. And some animals understand that language. We too understand if something is good to eat or not from its smell. So, that is another form of communication, but in our case it's only passive. Meaning we receive it, we "read" it. Well, some people may "speak it" too in what they think is a funny situation...

What matters is that *when we say "language" most of us mean "verbal language" but there are loads of languages we "read and speak" all the time, each with its structure, its "words".*

These languages, or ways of expression, can be divided into *visual and auditory*, mainly. We Humans have fairly good sight (and we depend on it more than all other senses), and below average hearing (it's good, but it does not match that of most mammals). Sharks also have the ability to detect electromagnetism, a sense we apparently do not have... Dogs have an incredible sense of smell...

What it tells us is that *our main means of communication depend on our best developed senses.* Cats for example have impressive hearing and they communicate even at frequencies we cannot hear (like dolphins). Dogs only communicate visually at close range, because their eyesight is poor, but wolves howl to speak to other wolves miles and miles away. We can't do that, and our sense of hearing is much weaker than theirs...

How many ways do humans use to communicate? The list is huge, but it is mainly divided into visual and auditory:

### Visual languages:

- Painting
- Sculpture
- Written words
- Visual symbolism
- Mathematic signs (they are a form of communication)

- Dancing
- Body language

*Auditory:*

- Spoken words
- Music
- Singing
- Whistling

Then, we also have *forms of communication that mix visual and auditory*, like:

- The theatre
- The cinema
- The opera
- Ballet
- Many concerts nowadays, since Madonna transformed concerts to a mainly auditory experience to a visual and auditory one.

Finally, *some forms of communication also have a kinesthetic nature*. This means that they use *body movements and gestures to express ideas, feelings etc.* For example:

- Drama
- Dance and ballet

- Opera
- Miming
- Juggling and similar arts
- Skateboarding, synchronized swimming
- Body language!

And we have come full circle.

All these have a mean of communication (hands, feet, movement, oil on canvas, sound etc.) and then a code, which is a series of meanings and then a "grammar" to put together these meanings.

## EXCHANGING INFORMATION WITH VERBAL COMMUNICATION

Is verbal language exceptional? Yes and no. No, it is not at all unique to humans, as we believed only a few years ago. We mentioned dolphins, but even closer to home, cats use a verbal language (they actually use 6 different verbal languages!) with clear meanings and quite expressive indeed.

Yes, it is because *we use verbal language as our main form of rational expression*. This does not mean that we cannot use verbal language for irrational communication... When you read or write a poem, a novel, or sing a song, you are actually expressing, in many cases, emotions, not ideas... But to express irrational concepts, in verbal language we need things like imagery, metaphors, similes etc.... We need "figurative" or metaphorical language.

What's more, *our society places a lot of importance on verbal language*. Peace treaties are written in words, not painted nor expressed through ballet. Similarly, laws are written on paper and signed. They are not presented as a statue nor as a symphony...

But there is more; *verbal language is at the core of education and it is taught extensively.* We mainly *learn through words* (books, discussions, presentations) and we *learn a lot about verbal communication.* Think about how long you spent learning English in your formal education and how long you spent learning music? Drama? Art (usually a tiny bit more)? Ballet? Body language? Never even heard of at school.

Now I will ask you to wind back a moment... What did we say about dancing? That the more you learn about it and the more you practice it, the more you become proficient. This means that:

- *You can express more concepts and with more precision.*
- *You have more control over what you express.*

This is the reason why most of us *prefer verbal language: we can control what we say very well.* We take it for granted but think about how a child speaks. They don't control what they say as well as we do. They start picking it up from family members, then they learn it at school etc....

This is a double-edged sword... On the one hand, it allows us to communicate with confidence and great precision. On the other hand, people who are very skilled at it may hide their true intentions...

This is why sales agents are all very good at speaking and verbal communication. They have the "gift of the glib". And if they don't have it by nature, they learned it!

This very point shows us *why learning nonverbal communication is very important:* we are not balanced. We need to look at "the other side of communication" which is often ignored, but which can also show things and intentions which are easily masked with verbal communication.

## PAYING ATTENTION TO NON-VERBAL COMMUNICATION

Of all the forms of non-verbal communication, the *most common is body language.* Not everybody paints, not everybody dances, not everybody sings. Everybody uses body language. Similarly, even painters, dancers and singers aren't always painting, dancing or singing. But *we (and they) use body language all the time, whether we (they) want it or not!*

But there is more.... When singers are singing, when dancers are dancing, when artists are painting, they know exactly what they are doing... *they are in control of their communication. With body language, in most cases, people are not in control of what they are saying.*

We often listen and look away (like Chris did in the example at the beginning of this Chapter). Mayla, on the other hand, was paying attention to Chris's body language. This is why she had "the impression that he was not listening". And this is why she is unlikely to believe that he is "all ears".

Did we say at the very beginning of this book that women, statistically, pay more attention to non-verbal communication? It is not a mistake that women, on average, have better EQs (emotional quotient, like the IQ but for emotional intelligence). *Just paying attention to body language and non-verbal communication stimulates your emotional intelligence.*

## NON-VERBAL COMMUNICATION AND LIE DETECTING

But I know what you are thinking... "How do we actually find out if someone is lying to us?"

Good. Let's debunk myths first. I said it but I will repeat it: *there is no one tell sign that tells you someone is lying.* Those are myths about body language analysis. However, do not despair, because...

*There is a method, a procedure to find out if someone is likely lying or telling the truth.*

To start with, notice the "likely". We said that body language is used by detectives. True, as evidence, to find clues etc. Not as definite proof. This is not because it is not scientific. It is because we simply cannot be inside people's minds. And there may always be a reason for gestures etc., that we cannot see...

So, what is this method? First of all, it uses *both rational and irrational thinking and communication. You should never draw a conclusion on an "impression". But you should let impressions come into your analysis.* You see the trick?

These are the core elements:

1. *Listen very carefully to what people are saying.*
2. *Watch carefully all the non-verbal signals they give off while saying it* (this usually happens at the same time, but with recordings we can change it).
3. *Match, overlap what they say with their body language.*
4. *Eliminate noise* (cultural signs etc.)
5. *Find inconsistencies between words and body language, between verbal and nonverbal language.*
6. *Analyze the probability that the person may be lying.*

These are the key steps. You have learned and are learning quite a few details and techniques about the first five steps. As to the 6$^{th}$, which is where you draw all the observations you have made together, we need to add some information.

Think about body language as someone bouncing on a mattress. The mattress is your subconscious. We react to it through non-verbal communication. However, the subconscious is never really steady. It's like a water mattress in continuous movement.

In a way, a bit of "waving, undulating, bouncing" is continuous and very normal. We are never on safe firm land psychologically speaking. At any "wave" we have a lack of balance in body language. That may result in a facial expression, movement, eye movement etc. These are usually small, because they come from small waves.

But they also have a certain regularity because these waves are sort of regular. A sudden wave, however, will cause a sudden non-verbal sign. And that is what you want to detect in particular.

The fact is that when we lie and we know we are, we "disturb the waves of our subconscious". It's like we drop a heavy weight on the water mattress... You see, the movement of the lie inside our person upsets the subconscious which reacts by pushing us off balance causing a dis-harmonic nonverbal sign.

Or, for another comparison, imagine you are reading a seismographer... You need to detect the odd peak in the line...

Once you detect the peak, the odd wave etc.... you need to go back to what the person has just said and analyse her or his body language in detail (easier with recordings).

Here, verbal language becomes again very important. *Can the actual sentence be a lie?* If the person said, "Good morning," it's far more likely that the sudden nonverbal signal is due to a stomach cramp than a lie...

Also *look at repeated patterns.* If a person behaves like there's been a bigger than usual bounce in the water mattress *(almost) every time s/he mentions a certain topic, then there is a clear emotional problem with that topic,* and you may well be on to something.

Yes, it is, on the whole, far easier to find out a lie if the person has to talk for longer... And this may come in handy, because very often, swindlers talk to us for a long time trying to convince us. And in this case, just show that you are not convinced and force them to keep talking, so you can find the telling pattern of unusual body language. That would be enough evidence to reasonably suspect a lie.

## AVOIDING MISCOMMUNICATION

But there are positive applications of verbal and nonverbal communication studies as well. We have already said that learning to control your body language, in an honest and moderate way, is actually very good for you.

Let's jump back onto the water mattress. You see, our subconscious can get into "patterns of waves" that produce repeated patterns of gestures we often are unaware of, and at times, we cannot control. To one extreme, we have nervous tics, on the other, we have less visible, small movements that, however, other people notice (more or less consciously) and sometimes they clash with what we intend to communicate.

Let's get practical. Imagine you have the tendency to rub your hands unconsciously. It's a very, very common habitual gesture. In fact, it may even come from a need for safety, solace, protection. However, also because magazines have made a huge disservice to our science, most people see it as a sign of dishonesty.

Trust me, no sales representative will ever be successful with this hand rubbing habit!

Let's take another common example. Feet pointing inward. It tends to project lack of confidence and a desire to protect oneself. But it can also be just habitual posture. Now imagine having to take on an authoritative role, like being a teacher, or a parent who has to give rules to children... Be sure that the children in both cases will need lots of convincing... Even with a good tone of voice etc. *that mismatch will stick in the children's minds and contradict what you say.*

These are all examples of *miscommunication. Being aware and correcting your body language can avoid miscommunication.* You should not, and you cannot, change all your body language. You should focus on one or two habitual signs that have caused you problems in the past. Slouching is a major example of this.

But being aware of body language also avoids other, maybe worse, miscommunication events. An example... This is something teachers in multicultural countries know or should know. Some communities, in particular the Black Caribbean community, you do not stare at someone you are not friends with. Eye contact has to be short and you need to move away, or you will be seen as aggressive.

Do you know how many times teachers have thought that students if this community "are rude", "don't care about what I say" or "never listen" simply because they associate eye contact with interest?

Similarly, when the teacher stares at the students in the eyes, do you know how many students from this community feel that the teacher is "being a pain", or "challenging me?"

Just knowing about body language allows you to get on well with many people and avoid sometimes really unpleasant misunderstandings. And changing this or that habit can make a huge difference to how well you can express your messages to others.

And now, get ready for a couple of very practical and straightforward chapters. The next for example, will look at all the different parts of body and how they speak.

# READING BODY MOVEMENTS

We couldn't possibly write a book on body language without looking at all *the different parts of the body and how they communicate.* It's a bit like reading different parts of a sentence. Each body part has its own characteristics, its own way of speaking. They also have different limitations. For example, you can't move your head as far as you move your legs and feet. And you can't move your feet as well as you move your hands... There are physiological differences.

But there is more... some body parts tend to communicate certain thought processes or feelings, while other body parts are better for another set of feelings and thoughts. At the same time, even cultural factors influence how we use body parts. We have seen it with hands and handshakes.

Last, but not at all least, *some body parts are easier to control than others.*

Let's compare these:

- Eyes
- Mouth
- Feet
- Arms

## Which ones are easier to control? Which ones are more difficult?

You may end up with a list of arms – feet – mouth – eyes from easier to most difficult and for the average person, you would be correct. But there are differences between people. Some people can even move their ears! I can move my scalp... And how about those who have prehensile feet?

Feet in fact show us that we can learn to use and control parts of our body that we would not expect to. People who paint with their feet (or their mouths) are a shiningly beautiful proof of it.

But we will talk about feet in a moment. For now, we shall start with the top... the head.

## HEAD AND FACE

We are very conscious of our head and face. Most of us imagine our "essence" to be placed somewhere in our head. That's where we "feel" we are thinking, watching, listening etc.… It's the center of our focus, basically.

Ironically though, *we hardly control our facial expressions at all.* Mind you, we can, and we try very often. We "pull faces"; we "wear smiles"; we "make faces" etc. But to the expert eye, eyes, ears, eyebrows, lips, nose and even facial muscles always give away much more than we think.

It is also true that we focus on people's faces when talking. So, this means that *people are aware that their faces are "under scrutiny".* And this means another thing for the skilled body language analysis… That if someone wants to hide a non-verbal expression, most likely that will be on his or her face.

Let's put it like this. If you know you are lying, and you know people are staring at your face, you will try to control your facial body language… It makes sense…

But every time a person tries to control and repress a natural nonverbal signal, expert body language analysis can notice it. It's like stopping twitch… You need energy to do it, you need to stiffen your muscles… It's never completely successful.

## *Head*

Your *head tilt* is important. Think about students daydreaming at school. They tilt their heads very often. This does not mean that they are not paying attention. It means that they are relaxed and creative.

In fact, *head tilt left or right* usually shows relaxation, comfort and even deep mental processing.

A *head leaning back*, instead, is a sign of disconnection, usually caused by deep frustration or total exhaustion. It often means something like "I can't bear this anymore." But beware, this does not need to be what we think. In a lesson "this" may be a personal thought, a family problem, an emotional disappointment. It does not have to be your lesson!

A *head leaning forward and down* can mean many things, from shame, to feeling guilt, to feeling tired. Sometimes it is a simple way of avoiding eye contact (often fixing the eyes on hands, feet etc.)

A *head leaning forward but straight ahead* is usually a sign of great interest, but it can also be used ironically, especially by young people, meaning "Okay, now, you see how much I listen?" but in a challenging, even mocking fashion. This last sign is usually accompanied by eyes open in an exaggerated way.

### Eyes

They say that "your eyes are the window of your soul" and there is far more than commonplace in this. For example, did you know that your eyes are in fact physically part of your brain? Yes, we look at each other's brains all the time. Sorry if I left you with a weird picture.

And our eyes are by far the most difficult parts of our body to control. Try not to blink! Impossible. Try staring at someone into his or her eyes for long; you will have to move away at some stage... Try keeping your focus fixed on a single point for long... It gets hard... But above all, try hiding your feelings... Eyes speak, and they do it independently from us.

So, let's see some of the most important signals our eyes give off...

- *Dilated pupils* express interest, pleasure, even sexual or emotional attraction.
- *Shrunk pupils* show dislike, even repulsion.
- *Eyes up* usually show thinking and doubt.
- *Eyes up right or left* usually indicate visualization. This does not mean "lying"; it means that you are using your visual brain, even to recall real facts in a visual way, like remembering your primary school friend's face.
- *Eyes sideways left or right* usually denotes attention to what you are hearing, attention to your auditory sense.
- *Eyes down right* usually show you are having an internal dialogue.
- *Eyes down left* usually show that you are checking facts.
- *Eyes down* shows you are focusing on your sense of smell.
- *Eyes shifting left and right* usually means "I want to get out of this"; the person feels embarrassed, not at ease, or wants to leave.
- *Eyes shifting in different directions* are rare, and they show great confusion most of the time, even panic.

Now, don't take these as "hard and fast rules". To start with, always keep in mind the option that someone is following a fly. This is a silly example, but with a serious message. There are external factors that catch our attention all the time. It may be a light, a flower etc.... People do not have any obligation to stare at you straight all the time...

But there is more to eyes than where they move... There is of course the expression. Sadness, joy, worry, concern, fear, care etc. all appear in the expression of our eyes.

This may be difficult to explain in few words, also because eyes, their shapes and their overall expressive qualities vary from person to person (actually from eye to eye as no two eyes are the same, even on the same face!) But all research shows that we all recognize the feelings and emotions expressed by eyes very easily.

In fact, this was used as evidence for the argument that body language is natural, because everybody can recognize eye expression "naturally". Okay, that was again a bit of the nature vs. nurture debate. But hey, I told you it went on, and on... and on again...

## Eyebrows

Did you know that we tend to look at eyebrows very carefully when talking to people? Those two hairy lines under our forehead are one of the main focal points we have... Thinking about it is funny because we don't think much of eyebrows...

Perhaps we subconsciously know that eyebrows are a very important area for body language... They tell us if a person is happy, angry, confused etc. To read them, divide each eyebrow into two parts:

1. *Inner eyebrow* (the part towards the center of the face)
2. *Outer eyebrow* (the part towards the temples)

On the whole, it is the inner eyebrow that leads the movement of the outer eyebrow. So, focus on this part and check out for:

- *Raised inner eyebrows*: that shows openness. It is often interpreted as a sign pf honesty and trustworthiness. But it can also mean interest and the fact that the person is trusting you or what you are saying.
- *Lowered outer eyebrows:* this usually shows sadness, pain, suffering.
- *Lowered inner eyebrows:* this usually shows anger, or at least frustration.
- *Whole eyebrow raised:* instead of being led by inner or outer eyebrow, this movement is led by the central part of the eyebrow. Here the eyebrows form arches with the center part being the highest. This shows surprise or astonishment.
- *Whole eyebrow straightens and lightly lifts.* In this case, when you see two eyebrows raising lightly but becoming straight, it means the person is excited.
- *Eyebrows pulled together:* this happens when we pull them both in the middle above our nose, and it usually shows confusion, or at least an attempt to understand what you are hearing, seeing etc.
- *Slightly raised eyebrows together with half open mouth (with flattened lips) and a stiff brow* usually means fear.

There are lots of things to read on eyebrows, as on people's mouths, and we'll see it next.

### Mouth

The mouth is a very expressive part of our body, not just because we use it to speak... It is also, note, an opening into our inside, and as such it has a very intimate function.

- *Flattened lips:* this is a very clear sign of tension, nervousness, or worry. Do note, however, that lips also flatten when we are tired. A good body language reader knows when her or his colleague has had a bad night.
- *Full, plump and relaxed lips:* this is of course a sign of relaxation and ease. Note that you need to adapt this concept to the actual natural shape of the person's lips. Some have naturally plumper lips. But they all change.
- *Pouting lips:* this is actually a very innocent sign. It does send us back to our childhood. However, many people know that this is a sign of physical attraction. The fact is that because you "drop your defenses", it may actually mean that you find the person attractive.
- *Lip biting* is one of the most noticeable signs. It shows that the person is in trouble, or perceives danger or conflict... This is one of those gestures politicians are told to avoid at all costs.
- *Partly open mouth showing top teeth (incisive teeth):* this is a sign of relaxation, attraction and interest.
- *Higher lip distorted with one side raised higher than the other:* this is a sign of disgust or great disapproval.
- *Broad smile showing teeth:* usually the upper teeth show more than the lower ones, but it may depend on the mouth's shape. This is outright joy and happiness. But it is also a sign

of approval. How many smiles by teachers have shown
students that they are on the right path?

But here we need to make an important point. *Always look at the sides, the tips of the lips.* People are quite aware of the function of mouth body language. This is because they are easy to read but also for the reason we said before: they are a very intimate part of our body and one often under scrutiny.

So... many people have learned to fake their mouth body language. But there is a problem... The "fakery" shows up at the very tips of the lips. It's a physiological thing. When you are lying your muscles tighten.

So...

- *Relaxed tips of the lips:* this goes with positive expressions and it shows that they are genuine.
- *Tense tips of the lips:* this goes with negative expressions. With a positive one, you may wish to question whether it was genuine or not.
- *Tips of the lips pointing up:* real smile.
- *Tips of the lips pointing down:* disgust or fake smile.

Go quite safe with the up and down tips... There's basically consensus on these two particular signs.

### Breathing

This action involves our head (nose and mouth), chest and even belly. Belly breathing is a little trick I would suggest you learn if you don't do it yet. It is much more relaxing than chest breathing. We use it when we sleep. Singers use it, actors use it... But does breathing tell us about a person's inner thoughts and emotions?

Breathing is such a vital function that it really goes deep as body language meaning. To start with, notice that breathing is both:

- Spontaneous
- Controlled, voluntary

When we stop controlling our breathing the natural "autopilot mode" steps in immediately. What an amazing gift we have! Or sometimes, the "autopilot" takes over without our consent because we receive a shock, a surprise, we worry, we lose energy etc.

And this is exactly what you have to do:

- *Check for sudden or even slow changes in breathing patterns.*
- *Check for unusual breathing.*

To be precise, use these two parameters:

- *Slow breathing means relaxation* (confidence, lack of worry etc.)
- *Fast breathing means excitement or worry, tension, fear etc.* Keep these two separate. Excitement can be positive.

Your breathing becomes fast also when your partner
proposes to you, or you to your partner!

However, in many formal situations (meeting at work, or dealing with an insurance agent, giving a speech...) the idea is that you will project confidence if you have a slow, well-paced and relaxed breathing pattern.

And going back to the beginning, you see why learning belly breathing can make a huge difference in your life? You can control your breathing so much better with belly breathing. Really, just try it!

### Shoulders

Shoulders do not move that much, but when they do, you can't miss them! The metaphorical meanings of shoulders (strength, support, confidence, stamina etc.) are basically the same as their overall body language message of this part of our body. Soldiers wear their rank on their shoulders, kings and queens wear ermine, managers in the 80s went crazy for shoulder pads because they made them look more "bossy".

Read shoulder movements in two main directions:

- *Shoulders out and back:* the person feels safe, confident, strong or/and calm, in control.
- *Shoulders in, forward and slouched:* these show lack of strength, tiredness, a sense of having lost, lack of confidence and of control.

- Careful though, *shoulders that look excessively and unnaturally raised can project arrogance.*

They are such a big and visible part of our body that we cannot hide them. So, do be careful about what your shoulders say about you.

## Arms

Arms are very mobile parts of our body. This means that they have a great expressive range or potential. But there are some very important characteristics of arms:

- They are one of *the parts of our body we are most in control of.* Very often arms say what we want them to say, rather than what we actually mean. But not always.
- Arms are often *used to "take possession of the space around us".* In this, they play an important role in power games, hierarchy etc.
- The *size of arm movements and gestures is very important.* This may change culturally (shall we mention Italy again?) but it is also a sign of *how confident, how in control and how much you think of yourself.* People who think they are bosses have often very broad arm movements.

Arms can even be threatening, as they are a primary fighting tool. Then again, which *type or arm movement we see* is also important. Thus...

- *Moving arms close to your sides especially turned inward, towards the center of your body:* this is a sign of discomfort, even fear. It is an attempt to defend yourself and at the same time to "make yourself small" and less visible.

- *Folding your arms* projects confidence but it also closes channels with the person you are talking to. You defend yourself and distance yourself. It's a "no" ...

- *Arms that open sideways* can have different meanings. Especially with palms forward or at times upward, they can be a protective sign, while with fists or downward palms they may be menacing or a way of taking control of space.

- *Arms upward* are a sign of freedom, joy and release.

- *Arms behind your back* is a rare occurrence nowadays. It was a favorite position of army, navy etc. officers. I have also seen dukes, bishops and prelates use this, even Popes... They actually project authority and self-confidence, especially when walking. Having said this, they hide your hands, so, many people may not like it. The position here is that where you have an arm stretched down behind you and you hold it with your hand at about elbow level.

- *Swinging arms when walking* is a sign of well-being, confidence and freedom. Excessive swinging though may look funny and clumsy and even indicate the opposite, lack of confidence. It really is a flexible sign and a lot will depend on the context.

- *Elbows out and hands in pockets or on hips,* as we have seen, is a way of making yourself look bigger. A sign that the person wants to take a controlling position but at the same time it shows weakness and insecurity.

- *Hands on hips or in pockets and hands forming V shapes backward,* basically when your elbows point backward is another disappearing gesture, but it shows openness and at the same time a "submissive" or at least very non-confrontational attitude. It's always been more common among young people, especially men, possibly as a "social marker", meaning they do not occupy a dominant role in society.

What matters most is that you look at the *quality of arm movements.*

- *Fast arm movements* often indicate confusion, stress and lack of control (not always though).
- *Powerful arm movements* can show aggression an engrossed person.
- *Calm and controlled arm movements* show, well, calm and control.
- *Exaggerated arm movements* are rare in most situations. That's because we know they would give away our lack of control and that is exactly what they tell us when they happen.
- *Sudden clumsiness in arm movements* shows that something has gone wrong in the person's perspective: doubt, uncertainty, maybe even fear or concern.

## Hands and Fingers

Hands are likely the most communicative part of our body outside our face. We use them to give rational signals, codes, indicate, explain, count, greet… But there are some key hand movements that can give the right or the wrong impression about ourselves…

- *Hiding hands* is a bad sign. It gives the impression we are hiding something. Sometimes this is true, but it may just be that the person is shy or embarrassed, or even worried for that matter. Never hide your hands at job interviews!
- *Front or back of hands.* This is a huge difference. Your *palms show openness.* When we want to mean "I swear", what do we do? We raise our hands and show our palms. On the contrary, *the back of your hands shows closure.* It means "keep away" and showing you knuckles in particular is a sign of aggression.

Here I need to tell you a story. A real one. Do you remember Tony Blair? He was noted by body language experts for always "waving his knuckles" at the audience during speeches. He also had very big hands, and the effect was even bigger. In any case, this was seen as both defensive (but accepted) and as a sign of strength. Even of dishonesty, maybe, but overall the audience read it as "confidence".

Not a pleasant gesture but wait till the next and short-lived UK Prime Minister came along… Gordon Brown too showed the back of his hands in speeches but in a lower position than Blair. Blair was actually "in your face" with his hands (surprise pun!) Brown seemed uncomfortable with his own hands… And people read it as? Weakness first of all, and a touch of dishonesty too.

This shows that really, *the way these movements happen, in a qualitative way, makes all the difference.*

- *Fists* are always an aggressive sign when shown to other people. The more towards the face they point and go, the more aggressive they are. But also waving them, pretend punching etc., matter, as well as facial expressions. But fists by the side of your body with arms stretched down show rebelliousness, or that the person is trying to control her or his anger or strong emotions.

- *Raising a fist in the air* is voluntary body language and it simply means solidarity with those you are with. From there, it was then taken by socialism and communism, with the left hand, as a greeting.

- *Raised open and hand in extended arm* is another voluntary sign and it means "obedience". The Nazi and fascist salute are all forms of submission... In fact, look at how Hitler used it... ever noticed that he never showed his palm to his subordinates as they did to him? That floppy hand of his ended up showing his palm upwards... to the sky... He owed loyalty to none of them... only to the "cause" is what his salute symbolized.

- *Palms of your hands attached to your body* mean that you are keeping calm, or even that you are protecting yourself.

- *Palms of your hands touching, joint* can have a lot of meanings. They don't necessarily mean "I beg you". The fact is that this position opens up an energy bridge inside your body. So, it may be a sign that someone is restoring his or her energy circulation, that the person is at peace with him or herself. Or it may just mean that the person is thinking in earnest about what you are saying.

- *Scratching your palms* is often (not always) a sign of confusion, discomfort or uncertainty. But remember, it could always be physical itching!
- *Palms up on the table, knees etc.* is an extreme sign of honesty and collaboration.
- *Palms down on the table, knees etc.* is instead a sign of control and it may denote that the person does not want you to know something.

Lots of things we can say with our hands, and still we have not seen them together with fingers!

With fingers, first of all, look if they are *relaxed, so bending slightly or tense, which means that they are either stretched out straight or in a fist.* A sudden tensing of the fingers of a person is a clear sign that something isn't quite right... Then of course, we have to look at how we move and position our fingers.

- *Pointing at people* can be a necessity but, in many cases, pointing at the person we are talking to is aggressive especially with a straight finger.
- *Pointing with a soft, arching finger* especially at things is often misunderstood. People may think it means "lack of character", "sloppiness" and "weakness". On the contrary it is often a sign of very strong and deeply rooted self-awareness and self-confidence. The fact is that pointing is always a way

of establishing a relationship. The soft finger is *protective and respectful* towards the pointed thing or person. It is a *sing of confident kindness*, which we often mistake for weakness.

- *Playing with the ring,* whether you are wearing it or not, is actually a sign of distress most times. It's a way of touching yourself to reassure yourself.
- *Little finger stretched out sideways* either means that the person is a piano player or... that s/he feels very at ease. That finger feels vulnerable, doesn't it? So, exposing it like that means that you feel perfectly safe.
- *Fingers touching forming a ring* too may have a lot of different meanings, mainly positive like connectivity, interest, deep thought or looking for a solution.
- *Nail touching and scratching* can be a sign of embarrassment, disagreement, doubt, discomfort or just boredom...
- *Checking your fingernails* is now rare in important situations. Why? It's so clear that you are not paying attention. And it does mean that, or, worse, that you are but you disagree or even that you think what you are hearing is total nonsense! Again, avoid it in a job interview...

Even fingers, you see, say lots of things about us.

## Legs and Feet

... and we need to add legs and feet to complete the list... On a general note, we are *less aware of our legs and feet than we are of hands and arms.* Because they are "down there", because they are often out of sight (under tables etc.) they tend to get forgotten quite easily.

At the same time, hands and feet body language is very much influenced by culture. The US "feet on the desk" may cost you your job in some countries, while they project authority and relaxation in the States... Arabs point with their feet and showing the sole of your foot is an insult. The same in some Asian countries.

In some countries, crossing your legs with the whole leg draped over the other is a "feminine" sign, and men avoid it. In others it is perfectly okay with their masculinity (or perceived masculinity). In many countries still nowadays women who open their legs when they are sitting are frowned upon. Still, let's get some general guidelines.

- *Legs open, apart* show confidence, self-control and at times relaxation.
- *Knees tight together* show lack of confidence even a perceived threat.
- *Crossed legs* too show a sense of informality, willingness to relax.
- *If the foot wraps on the calf* it may show a perceived threat, even sexual, or total closure, as we have said already.
- *Swinging leg while crossed* can be a sign of total ease, even happiness or, if nervous, it may show restlessness.
- *Legs lightly apart when standing, with feet forward* means self-assurance, self-control and calm. This is the singing position, the one professional singers use because it is relaxing.

- *Legs tight together, especially with feet together or point inward when standing* indicate a strong lack of confidence or sense of being unsafe.

- *One foot forward one pointing sideways when talking or standing* is quite common and it shows a certain level of arrogance, of determination, but not always. In any case it points to the idea that the person is interpreting the meeting, event, moment as a transactional situation... Basically it's business and not a social experience for him or her. In fact, you will often see it in speeches, conferences, lectures and presentations...

- *Feet up* is of course always a sign of relaxation and ease.

- *Feet backwards when sitting,* especially if "grabbing the leg of the chair" often show worrying or discomfort. This is very often accompanied by a leaning forward position of the upper body. This is not a dishonest person; this is a struggling person who needs help, but s/he is ready to collaborate fully and even go the extra mile.

- *Shaking foot* is always a sing of restlessness, but note that some people do it all the time and they are almost incapable of stopping it. In this case, they are more likely very nervous by nature.

- *Touching feet when talking,* usually when sitting and often with crossed legs. You must have seen people touching their feet in these situations. This is a sign of introversion... The person is internalizing what s/he is hearing or looking inward, not outward.

- *Crossed feet at the ankle* depend a bit on the situation. If at home and relaxed it's just a sign of relaxation. If it is during a discussion, meeting etc., it may show closure. Maybe the person is refusing to accept what s/he is hearing. Look at other signs in the body to make sure (folding arms, inner eyebrows lowered etc.).

Once more, always check if the movements look:

- Natural/unnatural or contrived
- Relaxed/tense
- Proportionate/exaggerated
- Controlled/out of control
- Friendly/aggressive
- "Going with the flow"/sudden and out of place.

Do this with legs and feet but also with all parts of the body and you will soon get a very good reference framework to analyze people quite deeply...

In fact, take a stroll in the park and look at how people move their bodies... Make a mental note... At first divide between positive and negative, then try to add the actual emotions and attitudes that their bodies are revealing to you.

You could do it before you move on to the next chapter. In fact, if in this chapter we have used cubism, by which I mean that we have broken down the human body into its components, in the next we will use an impressionist perspective. What do I mean? You are going to find out right now...

# 7

# SEEING BODY LANGUAGE AS A WHOLE

A cubist painting breaks the different parts of the body and places each on a flat plane for you to see. But it does make it hard to see the whole body, to give an overall reading of the general picture. We stressed very early on the importance to read the body in a holistic way, as a whole. And this is what I meant by "impressionist reading". Look at a Monet painting and you will get a general impression while the details are not well defined. But they do make sense as part of the whole.

So, without further ado, we shall now get out of our artistic metaphor and see what you need to look at a person's body as a whole. Now we will look at how posture is part of body language, different types of posture, we will go back to where you should stand in relation to the person and to a link between verbal and non-verbal language. Ready?

## EXPRESSING WITH BODY POSTURE

Posture in itself is hard to define, isn't it? It's "the way one stands" but also "the way one moves". It is broad and general, much more like an "impression" than a detailed and specific element. But you do know, for example, that many people decide just with posture if they are going to like someone? We also recognize people without seeing them well, in the shade etc. and we use posture to do this.

This tells us that we are very aware of posture, and we use it to make very big decisions, including the "like/not like", "trust/not trust" and "beautiful/ugly" ones. But we do it without being fully conscious of it. And this is why at the beginning of the book I begged you to correct your slouch if you have one. People see it, they do not rationalize it and yet act upon it very strongly.

General though it is, we can categorize body posture along *broad lines*. One such lines is the distinction between *dynamic posture* and *static posture*. Let's start with the latter.

### *Static posture*

Static is quite easy to understand. It means that it does not move or, more broadly, tends not to move. The Queen has a very static posture, to go back to the most analyzed person in body language all over the world. Very often, people in a position of power and in a formal setting (a speech etc.) have a very static posture.

It tends to project *authority*, *confidence* and even *reliability*. A person who does not move, or moves very little is fine when standing on a stage, behind a desk, in front of a camera... It's not a good posture to keep when you are mixing with friends, interacting with people etc.

And then there is the *degree of how static you are.* Very static postures end up looking "stiff". Not everybody can carry the super static posture of the Queen of England successfully. Even US Presidents tend to be more fluid, less "stuffy". They move slowly, but they do, even in formal speeches. The Queen does not even blink and even when she is walking, she makes it look like she is not moving at all...

## *Dynamic posture*

A dynamic posture is one where the person tends to move. This does not mean "walk" (it may), it means move legs, shoulders, head, arms etc. Here too, it all depends on the *context and the degree.* Moving too much may be good for some comedians just because it looks funny. Politicians will not move too much, nor will medical doctors, nor will sales agents...

You see, a *dynamic posture* projects a *lively personality,* a *likable* one, a *friendly* one, and even a *healthy one.* This is also why US Presidents tend to be more dynamic than monarchs like the Queen or the Emperor of Japan. They have to be liked, and they also need to prove they are healthy all the time.

At the same time, it all depends on the situation. If you are dancing... I don't need to finish the sentence. If you are playing with children, having fun with your friends etc. you want to be dynamic. If you are at a job interview, you want to be more static.

When the posture is *far too dynamic*, and especially if the movements do not look coordinated, you give the impression of being out of control, and sometimes this may well be the case. As usual, use other clues to confirm your suspicion (tone of voice, facial expression etc.).

### Dynamic and static postures

Here too, we talk about a gradient with many levels. From someone who is dancing around in an ecstatic and free fashion to someone who does not move at all. But I wanted to look at a special category here: teachers. Good teachers manage this very well. They have to move, you see, otherwise their students would fall asleep (or would not wake up!) On the other hand, they have to project authority, so they also have to offer some static postures to the class.

They change very well from one to the other... For example, they will be static when they need to talk to the whole class then become relaxed and dynamic when they walk around the desks to check on the students' progress.

## FORMS OF POSTURE

Another quality of posture is what "form" it takes. By this, we mean how *open, inviting, welcoming and non-confrontational* you are on the one hand (*open posture*) or on the contrary how *closed, defensive or even aggressive* you are (*closed posture*).

This too goes on a cline with many gradients. From a person holding arms out ready to embrace to the child clasping his knees while sitting on the ground with his head between his legs.

That last position, you see, closes the whole world off. There is no way to "enter" the child's space, and the child is only showing non vulnerable parts of his body: his shoulders, legs, back and feet. He is hiding his face, his belly, his palms and the inside of his legs. At the same time, the child is looking "within his own body shape".

In between, you can have the person with arms open but not yet ready to embrace, the person with arms folded and legs crossed... There is a potential infinity of positions we can take.

Again, context is very important. If the posture matches the context and situation, then fine. A manager facing a hostile board of directors, a politician who needs to criticize (attack) his adversaries etc. will *need a closed posture.*

Conversely, wishing your grandmother happy birthday with a closed posture will raise some important questions about your attitude, feelings, state of mind etc.

To analyze postures, I suggest you look at children and parents. There is a reason for this... They often quarrel. It's part of growing up. Parents have to be friends and at the same time severe educators, even punishers if necessary. This means that their relationship is in continuous swing between closed and open postures.

Go to the kid's corner of the local park. Look at all the parents and children on the slides and swings and in the sand pits... Look around and find those who are being "friends" and those who are being "naughty child and angry parent" by just looking at their postures.

## HOW FAR SHOULD WE BE?

We already said about 10 feet away and not in front, but at a slight angle (30 degrees or so), but is this a general rule? Yes and no. It is a general rule but with two provisos:

- That you can take that position.
- That you can observe properly and hear properly.

Let's see what this actually means... Imagine you are at a party... There is loud music and lots of people... Can you stand ten feet away? You can, but you won't hear anything, and you won't even see much with all the people walking by... or dancing... or spilling drinks...

Similarly, you go to a speech by a very famous politician. There she is, on the stage... then there is a barrier, and security and the first rows of course are all taken... Goodbye ten feet, welcome 100 feet if you are lucky!

Let's see another example. The person you are analyzing whispers. I don't mean that she or he whispers once... I mean that s/he does it all the time... What's the point in listening at that distance?

You are on a busy road... You are watching the person in a video... There are so many different situations.

So, we need to be very flexible but keep in mind these guidelines:

- Make sure you *see well, both the whole body and even small parts of it.*
- Make sure you *hear well.*
- Make sure *you are not top visible.* You should be a *discreet presence.*

So, the 10 feet 30° to one side rule gives you the ideal distance and position in the ideal situation. Be flexible. 15 feet makes no real difference if the acoustics and visuals are good. Don't stand too close, always give the person space to feel at ease.

And it you have to stay far... try to be at least within hearing distance and get a good vantage point.

PS: don't wear red if possible...

## LISTENING CLOSELY

Body language is "reading" but it is also "listening". "But listening has to do with words," you may argue. And you would be right – but not fully right. I know, I like puzzling you...

When you analyze a person's body language, of course you need to know what this person is saying. This you already know. But you also need to check for signals which are not just verbal... They are that step detached from being verbal and yet they come with the voice, with words and from our mouth.

Everything that accompanies a spoken word adds meaning to the word itself. So, pay great attention to:

- Intonation
- Volume
- Tone of voice
- Overall delivery
- Pauses
- Interruptions
- Anacolutha (it's when a person changes sentence or thought halfway through, the singular is anacoluthon and it is "something like – actually no" or "I took the car – I was going to..." They always show a change of mind or subject. It may be totally innocuous and proper, but sometimes this hides nuggets of gold for the body language analyst!)
- The formality of the words and tone chosen
- Even the person's accent may tell you a lot.

I'll give you an example with accents. People often use two accents, one is local, or of a particular community and the other is more standard and formal. Not everybody. However, imagine a person choosing to use his or her local accent when talking to someone from outside? It's a sign that the outsider is not very welcome, not very respected. And the more that accent is exaggerated the more it would show hostility. It's like saying, "We are not similar, we are not the same!" This, of course, assuming the person could use a more standard accent.

Also be aware of *non-verbal sound signals*, like little grunts, "mms" (when people agree), "ers", "tut-tuts", "eh-ehs" and of course laughter and giggles... All these are often far less controlled than the actual words they come with.

These offer a very good insight into what the person feels about the conversation and the person they are talking to. These also show you where the person wants the conversation to go. You can see if they want to change subject, or insist on a topic, for example.

We have gone a long way in what feels like a very short, and I hope enjoyable time. Next, we will dive very deep indeed. So deep that we will go under the skin of the person we analyze... Yes, I am teasing you – but it's sort of true!

# 8

# HUMAN BEHAVIOR AND THE
# MOTIONS OF THE BODY

D id I say that body language analysis is a bit like mind reading? Well, not literally. The truth is that it's more like "reading behavior" than the actual mind... You see, we don't hear the words that the person is actually thinking. That would be mind reading – I suppose. Instead, we are after particular behaviors and the reasons behind them. This is why I said we would be going "beyond" in this chapter.

## IT'S A HUMAN REFLEX!

Imagine you are driving along a busy road. Imagine you have a small head-on collision with another car. What do you do? I know it does not look related but bear with me... To start with, your car would physically bounce back. Next, you would switch into "defense mode" straight away... Third, you would immediately consider the other driver as a potential adversary (in psychology we say "position"... you *position* a person in a social role, e.g. as a buyer, as a client, as a friend etc.).

Ok, now let's change road... You are by bike now (bike, not motorbike!) and you are riding down a green road with trees on both sides... Someone comes up to you on the side and smiles... How would you position this smiling rider now? For sure you would not "bounce back". Secondly, you would open up to this person.

And now I will tell you a secret: they were the same person! Okay, let's abandon our vehicle metaphor now. Society is like this: in some situations, it puts us into a conflictual relationship from the start. Shop assistants and call center operators know it quite well: sometimes clients come with a complaint and the clash is inevitable. Other times, especially when we are free from worries and engagements, we can meet "side by side" and start on a different and positive foot.

Basically, society is the biggest "positioner in our lives". But let's focus on your reaction in these two cases... Why did you react in two different ways? In a way, your car explains it very well. If you bump into another car, your vehicle will recoil and bounce back. The very same dynamics are at play with social relationships.

Let's wind back a few chapters now and recall what we said about job interviews: the panel usually decides within 30 to 60 seconds. What does it mean? That it is during or just after the first encounter (a clash or a meeting of roads?) that we form *first impressions*.

I know, there are people who swear that their first impressions are always right. People make all sorts of claims, though. Instead, let's see what the actual science says...

To start with, that we form first impressions much faster than we actually thought. No, you don't even have those 30 seconds at job interviews. In fact, the speed we have in judging others is *counted in milliseconds!* It's not a typo. On average, we react to a facial expression (note the body language) in *between 33 and 100 milliseconds.* This has been found by psychologists at NY University J.K. South Palomares and A.W. Young in a study called 'Facial First Impressions of Partner Preference Traits: Trustworthiness, Status and Attractiveness' appeared in *Social Psychology and Personality Science* on Sept 19th, 2017. Wonder why politicians try to get the message across in the first line of their speeches...

What do we know about first impressions then? To start with, that we do change them. This may depend on the person, of course. There are those who will not move an inch from their first impression and those who will. Who is wiser? The second, according to Professor Alex Todorov from Princeton University. In his book *Face Value: The Irresistible Influence of First Impressions* (Princeton University Press, 2017) he states that most first impressions turn out to be wrong!

The reason is quite simple, and, in a way, you know part of it already. It depends on the situation, on society, on the moment... But there are other reasons too. One is that they are based on *superficial factors.* This is the main reason Professor Todorov gives. But I will delve a bit deeper... As we said, body language analysis is "reading behavior" and not "mind reading".

People can behave in a way for different reasons. If we could read these people's minds, we could then be sure about the reason. But as we do not, we can only suppose, suspect them, or even imagine them. We can use deductions to make our assessment to make it rational and reasonable. But it will remain a "very, very high probability" at best, never a "certainty" in scientific terms.

On a personal and professional development level, we need to realize that this applies to body language analysis too. *The professional body language analyst is always ready to change his or her mind and assessment if new evidence, new details come up or simply if a better interpretation is given.* It is a core ethical point of this practice. Basically, we need to be wise, and even wiser than untrained people.

Everybody is different, correct? But when we make quick decisions, like when we have a car accident, we use *"ready-made models and categories* to make our decision." Think about it. At work you are "productive" because you know how to decide quickly. And you do it using simple categories.

With people, these are *stereotypes,* and more often than not, these stereotypes are packed with social and cultural *prejudices.* There are very broad categories we use with stereotypes, for example:

- Trustworthy/untrustworthy
- Likable/not likable
- Strong/weak

- Masculine/feminine
- Extrovert/introvert
- Capable/incapable
- Self-centered/social centered
- Conservative/progressive and traditionalist /innovative
- Rational/irrational
- Old/young.

There are more, but just looking at "masculine and feminine" we realize that defining gender and/or sex is a much more complex matter than finding "the right box". Most people are gender fluid in some way. This does not mean that they necessarily have fluid sexual relationships. People can feel feminine or masculine in different situations. Men can have maternal feelings as women can have paternal ones...

So, an assessment made by quickly fitting a behavior or person into one of these categories is necessarily wrong. At least, let's go back to it and then see if there is more to say, or some shades and hues we need to retouch...

It gets even worse still. Very often, *prejudice sets in.* Linguistic studies in the UK show with no doubt that if you speak Standard English you immediately get the "trustworthy" stereotype but if you speak with a regional accent you get into the opposite box. Skin color is used by many people to people in one or the other category... Age is also a very determinant factor in stereotypes.

We get to the almost comical point in the business world (and white-collar working environment) that the suit color already places you into one or the other stereotype. Black is very self-important and harsh, blue is managerial, brown is old fashioned and maybe trade union sympathizer, green is for those who "want to look different" but no one wearing a green suit will expect to be taken seriously! Really?

So, keeping all this in mind, and always being ready to change our mind on these issues, let's look at a very core of body language and language as a whole: yes or no?

## Is It a Yes or a No?

Even in verbal language there are two types of questions and answers:

- Closed questions: where you can only answer yes or no (e.g. "Did you pick up the keys?")
- Open questions: where you can answer in many ways (e.g. "What do you think about Bach's music?").

When reading body language, *understanding yes and no signals is fundamental to direct all the analysis.* They are a bit like the points on a railway. They decide which way the conversation – actually, communication – goes.

Not only this... Imagine this as a cartoon strip... In your mind you have lots of questions which you don't verbalize, but – unbeknown to you – your body is asking them all the time. At the same time, your eyes are fixed on the other person to read her or his answers in her or his body language...

This means that you will need a "set of tools", a broad framework with clear yes and no signals that our bodies give off, more or less consciously.

- *Head nods vs. head shakes* are the clearest, most explicit signs of yes and no. Sometimes, we also do it unconsciously.

- *Open arms vs. folded arms* are again clear signs of yes and no. This gesture can be controlled rationally or at times it happens spontaneously, and this is an interesting distinction to find out when you read body language.

- *Raised eyebrows vs. lowered eyebrows* are a more subtle sign of yes and no. In this case, though it can be done consciously, in most cases these facial expressions are involuntary, spontaneous.

- *Lean towards vs. lean back* can be signs of yes and no. This is not a must though. Leaning forward is usually a positive sign, but leaning back can also be intended as positive, especially when sitting down, as it can mean "I am relaxed".

- *Eye contact vs. no eye contact.* This is possibly the most intriguing way to say yes or no. Do pay attention to movements and changes. A sudden break in eye contact may mean no. But do follow up. If the person comes back into regular eye contact, it may have been a distraction. If you, on the other hand, notice that after that eye contact is less frequent and "forced or unpleasant", then it most likely is a no.

- *Open vs. locked ankles* often show unconsciously if a person is in agreement or not. It is a yes or no with your feet, which, as we said, we are often unaware of. Because of this, it is one of the most interesting signs for body language analysts. The reason must be clear to you by now: it is unlikely that the person is faking it.

- *Open palms vs. fists.* This often shows openness or resistance. Not literally yes or no, but the fact that the person is receiving what you are communicating or, on the contrary, that the person is resisting it. Maybe it is just a sore topic, though, do not rush to conclusions.

- *Facing vs. turning away* shows that the person is within the conversation or that s/he wants to get away from it. We have seen it and it's another message that you can read in terms of yes and no.

- *Relaxed mouth vs. biting lips* isn't always what it seems. Okay, most times, if someone bites his or her lips it usually means discomfort, so, a no. But sometimes they may do it on purpose to tease you, especially in a romantic situation. So… check the person's eyes and overall body language.

- *Harmonic vs. disharmonic movements.* This may take some practice and experience to note, but it is one of the most consistent yes and no signs. If the listener's body moves to the beat of the speaker's speech, then it's a yes. By movement here we mean *any movement*: eye movement, feet, arms swinging, fingers tapping etc.… This is a clear sign of total accordance and ease. While if the movements are disharmonic, it of course means that the person is not "in tune" with what you are saying… take it as a "no" …

- *Relaxation vs. tension.* It is hard to say no. for some people (like me), it is almost impossible. If you are one of those, learn to say no, for your own sake... Now, moving on... Even people who like to say no (or they think they like it, but here we enter psychology and philosophy...) need to build a barrier between them and you... And that means creating tension. Signs of tension always show a negative attitude.

These are basic pairs of signs that will give you a yes or no reading. But there are some provisos, some "warnings"... As usual...

- *Always read the body as a whole.* We said it and here it's important to remember it. One little negative sign in a series of positive signs does not mean no. It may mean that it's not 100% yes, or that the person was distracted etc. We don't need to be "conspiracy theorists" all the time. However, sometimes conspiracies turn out to be true... So, it might just be that the person pretended to be in agreement but actually wasn't.
- *Observe for a length of time.* You don't want to end up with a first impression, do you? So, keep the observation for as long as possible and base your final assessment on the whole period and behavior. Sometimes it will be easier, sometimes you will have a short time. But *the longer your observation is the more accurate your assessment will be.*

We will come to ideas for giving positive body language signs in a few chapters; don't worry. This is as much a self-development practice as it is a book on reading others. But before we wrap up this chapter, we need to make a final point...

## JUDGEMENT VS. ASSESSMENT

Have you noticed that I used the word "assessment" when talking about body language analysis? There is a huge difference between judging and assessing, and this brings the chapter to a nice full circle.

At the beginning of this chapter we talked about how people judge based on first impressions. However, we should never really judge people... But still, the point with judging is that it has consequences. A judge passes a verdict and then if necessary a sentence (guilty, sentenced to community service, for example).

*Judging people means that we change our attitudes towards them as a consequence of our evaluations.*

Now, let me put you in the shoes of a psychologist, if I may. Psychologists hear all sorts of things. As do doctors, psychiatrists and psychoanalysts etc. But they *do not judge.* They do not put a "value judgement" of "good person vs. bad person" on what they hear. They *assess* instead. What does it mean?

It means that they:

1. *Analyze* (they collect signs, they look at each in detail, then put them together to make sense of them).
2. *Assess* (they draw a conclusion on what they have observed).

An assessment does not need to have consequences. If at all, it is used to help people and to improve situations, like teachers do at school.

We will be taking another dive into the depth of human behavior in a moment. But next, a little summary of all the different types of body language we have.

# 9

# CATEGORIES OF BODY LANGUAGE

Haptics, kinesics, oculesics... You have already learned a lot of technical words concerning body language. These three weird terms, for example, relate to contact, movement and eyes... There is virtually a branch, field or category for each part of the body, and they all have strange names! No, don't worry. I was joking. There isn't one for your little toe and they don't all have names that sound like Greek heroes...

Anyway, this is exactly what we are going to see now. We have seen some, and now it's time to complete the list. We will briefly also go through the ones you have met already, adding some information.

## KINESICS

You know that kinesics is the study of body movements within body language. What you don't know yet is that it too is divided into subcategories! All disciplines are like that, they branch out and branch out… It's simply because scholars discover new things all the time and they become more specialized.

And there are three of them, based on the *type of gesture:*

1. *Adaptors:* these are signs that come when the person needs to adjust his or her balance. They are *"balancing acts"* that often come from either discomfort or excitement. The jump you had when I went "boo!" is an adaptor. So are *many involuntary movements* like sighing, legs shaking, nervous responses like when students click pens in class before a test etc.

2. *Emblems:* these are *very easy to read because their meaning is conventionally agreed upon.* Things like the OK sign, or the thumbs up or thumbs down, high fives, etc. … These have a clear "sign – meaning" code and correspondence, like you find in a dictionary for words.

3. *Illustrators:* these are the signs we use to accompany our speech. You know, those typical gestures each person has when they speak? No person has the same set of illustrators as others. We all use different gestures. On top of this, illustrators in most cases do not have a meaning of their own. But ironically, we soon pick up "the code" the set of meanings of the illustrators of a speaker. Some, however, have positive and some have negative effects.

*Kinesics is also used to mean "body language analysis" as a whole.* People, however, including scholars, prefer the term "body language" to kinesics in this meaning.

## Head Movements

We have seen these, and they include:

1. *Head movements*
2. *Eye movements (oculesics)*
3. *Brow movements*
4. *Mouth and lip movements.*

There is a little trick I want to give you at this stage about facial expressions. You know that the left side of our brain is more rational and the right side more creative. Not "all rational and all creative" as popular belief would have it... Okay. You also know that the brain works in a very strange way. The right eye goes to the left side of the brain, the left nostril goes to the right side of the brain... There's an inversion of sides from the brain and the organs it controls.

Thus, the right side of our face is controlled by the left side of the brain (the more rational one), and the left side of our face is controlled by the right side of our brain (the less rational, more creative and intuitive sign).

Let's apply this to body language. What your left side of the face says is more likely to be spontaneous, not controlled or faked, more in touch with your real emotional state. So, people do wink, a very charming and at times irresistible sign. But the chances are that a right eye wink is "premeditated", and a left eye wink is spontaneous. The chances are – it is never a certainty...

## Facial Expressions

There is a difference between facial expression and head (face part) movements. The key note is in "expression". A movement is an easy, factual event to describe: "eyes left" or "head down". But facial *expressions* are indeed a complex system of movements and communication of feelings, even of changes in quality. Think about how you speak with your eyes... *there is much more than movement in the expressive quality of a person's* eyes. Even of a dog's eyes, to be fair.

What we need to understand is that there are some *general expressive areas.* These are *broad categories of expression* with inner shades and shades between them. Use them as the points of a compass, rather than boxes, when describing facial expressions.

- *Happiness,* which can be expressed with a smile but very often also with your eyes. Try the experiment of covering your mouth in front of a mirror and smiling with your eyes... then try smiling with your mouth and being sad with your eyes. Now you know how to spot a fake smile!
- *Sadness,* which of course is the exact opposite of happiness. It is often revealed by the difficulty of smiling, rather than its absence.
- *Focused,* which is an important state of mind to spot in body language analysis. From the physical and physiological point of view, it is often showed by eyebrows getting closer together. However, the trained observer will also notice the

focus in the speaker's eyes. Focus and determination are also closely connected. If a person looks focused, s/he will also look determined, active, convinced, ready to act etc.

- *Unfocused,* of course, is what you never want to look when you are taking a job interview. However, it is not necessarily negative. There is no "natural value" that says that being unfocused is bad. If you are dreaming, relaxing, imagining, being creative, letting yourself go, being unfocused is very normal indeed! In some cases, it may even show trust. For example, if you are having a romantic time with your partner, being very focused would actually be out of place. Come on, you are not discussing a bank loan!

- *Confident* is the best way to look most times, but even here there may be exceptions, for example, if you are asking for serious help. If you look top confident, you may well get a "no" for answer. A confident person will look centered, full of energy and the facial expression is usually accompanied by an upright and steady body posture. Steady eye contact is also a sign of confidence. Once more, it is a series of signs that gives us the final assessment.

- *Afraid:* people show it in their general body language and facial expression. They will look de-energized, the face will try to "shrink back" and avoid eye contact, of course no signs of happiness and confidence will appear on the face etc. When people become seriously afraid, their first reaction is to protect their face. Covering your face or moving it out of harm's way are typical signs. Notably, the scalp becomes tense when people are afraid, hence the saying "it makes my hair stand on end". This has a technical name too and it is called *"horripilation".*

## OCULESICS

Oculesics deserves a section of its own given its importance. Eye reading may even one day become its own discipline, as will "eye speaking".

The problem with oculesics for body language reading is that the reader (a.k.a. you in this case) often has limited access to the person's eyes. You will understand that there is a difference between looking into someone's eyes and "reading them" or standing at a distance and an angle and trying to read someone's eyes.

To train with eye reading, the best exercise is to look for videos. Find videos of people staring at the camera, and not from a distance, there are many politicians you can find, and even salespeople.

Talking about the last ones, forgive me the stereotype. Do you know those classical car sales adverts (furniture too has taken that path)? Look at their eyes... there is something missing, do you notice? They look at the camera, but they are not looking at you. And this is the trick with sales. Salespeople will look at your face, but their stare will stop short of actually looking into your eyes. They will look *at your eyes*, but they will never establish a *full bond, a full contact...*

You understand how delicate this type of reading is? Now, back to the videos... Choose a few and look how far the speakers "pierce the screen" ... What a weird thing that this phrase is no longer used very much... It used to be the "star quality" of actresses and actors...

Then think about your reaction. Which speaker gives you more trust? Which speaker do you feel more "familiar" with? I think we will agree on the answer...

Then there is another issue. We do notice if we are being observed. There is a wonderful book by Dr Rupert Sheldrake out, *The Sense of Being Stared at.* I think I told you already, but do you know that when police people, detectives and secret agents stalk someone they are trained "never to look at their backs". Do you know why? Because the person realizes it.

It's not hearsay, it is mathematical, and all evidence undoubtedly says that we somehow realize when people look at us. We don't know how, and Dr Sheldrake suggests it may be a defense mechanism... Back in the days, when we had to run away from lions, having this ability was an advantage. And zebras and gazelles do have this sense too.

But there is more... Again, all research statistically shows that if a security guard looks at the camera when someone is in front of it the person realizes it. So now they teach security personnel to look at the cameras with the corner of their eyes like they teach detectives to look at people's feet.

So, what's in it for us? That it is hard, in a formal setting and with live readings, to read people's eyes. True. But there is more... and good news...

*When you read people's eyes keep your focus as far as possible from the actual eyes of the person you are observing.* People realize if you look at their back, let alone if you look into their eyes. It is possibly the most invasive intrusion into someone's privacy before we border into illegality and utter crime...

So, *never look at the person directly into his or her eyes.* Try to keep that angle and look somewhere *in front of his or her eyes.* Note that in many cases you have an advantage: *people who speak know they are being observed... they expect a certain level of eye scrutiny.*

And this leads us to a very important point. This is a famous phenomenon and well researched by linguists...

- When people speak, they look less into other people's eyes than when they listen.
- Conversely, listeners look at the speaker, while the speaker will tend to avoid eye contact.
- However, if listeners fail to look at the person who is speaking, that shows lack of interest, lack of trust, disagreement etc.

... and this is gold dust for body language readers and analysts, both when our observed person is speaking and when s/he is listening... At a board meeting, for example, this may tell you an awful lot about what each person really thinks of what all the others are saying – again though, never jump to conclusions and, especially at board meetings, do factor in the fact that these (and the speakers therewith) are actually most of the time incredibly boring!

## HAPTICS

You know haptics by now. The *study of how people touch themselves and touch other people within body language.* You also know that it very much depends on the culture... In Italy men walk round the streets arm in arm (a tradition which I am told is disappearing) but in many other places it would provoke bouts of prejudice galore.

Yet, there is one other factor you will need to take into consideration with haptics: *age.*

Young people tend to touch themselves and each other more. Then, this gets stigmatized as a sign of "childishness" and even "lack of manliness". So, men especially will tend to stop touching others in affectionate ways.

The affectionate touching around adolescence becomes ritualized into a "mock fight" like slaps, "mock slaps", soft punches etc. This is a sign that these young guys actually *need* affectionate touching with their peer...

Anyway, at the same time, women touching themselves becomes "sexualized", by which I don't mean that *they* intend it sexually. I mean that society applies prejudice and sees these as "sexual hints". As a defense mechanism, many young women reduce self-touching (in both frequency and range, for example they avoid certain areas, like legs etc.). But women keep a healthy touching practice with their female peers, unlike men.

Then adulthood sets in and touching is reduced on the whole.

This trend, however, inverts when people are old. Old people usually turn back to touching others and people touch old people with fondness more often than they do adult people. Maybe the "authority challenge" of touching disappears; maybe the "sexual tension" is cleared; maybe people just rediscover their humane nature with old people... who knows?

## PROXEMICS

We have seen that proxemics is the *study of how near or far people stand, place themselves and move within body language.* And now we will look at some further information you will find very useful in reading body language...

Have you ever been on an elevator with someone else? How did you feel? No matter who you are, unless you are with someone you are very intimate with (family, close friend or partner) the experience is always the same. People "make themselves small", they look for an empty spot to stare at where they can avoid eye contact, they become rigid and even small talk like "Nice day, isn't it?" becomes a major difficulty...

Why is it so? The fact is that in an elevator you are too close to other people and there is no way this can change. People are "in your space" we say, and this is not just a metaphor. We have an area, like a circle (it's an ellipse on the ground, like an oblong bubble in three dimensions) centered in the middle of our body. This area is called *intimate space.* Any intrusion on this space is a problem.

But if you are in the open, you feel the other person's presence, but you have the option to look away, find comfort on the side. This happens all the time on busy sidewalks. But when you are, for example, talking to someone, not just passing them by, an *intrusion in your intimate space is always felt as very uncomfortable.*

Actually, I lied. We don't have one circle around us: we have four concentric circles (ellipses). *We prefer to have different relationships in the four different spaces, according to how familiar and intimate we are.* And scientists have actually measured these areas. Now, hear they are, and with the radius of the area for each person:

1. *Inner space:* from 0 to 1.5 feet from ourselves. We only allow very intimate people in this space for any length of time.

2. *Personal space:* from 1.5 to 4 feet is the radius of the area where we want normal, everyday (not affectionate) interactions without friends and family. This distance is measured by how far you can stretch your feet comfortably standing. As if we "marked our space" with our feet... like animals do (hold on to this thought; we will return to it soon).

3. *Social space:* from 4 to 12 feet away is where we want to have our everyday social activities with colleagues, people we meet, acquaintances, shop assistants etc. It's the "transactional" area, where we manage our necessary but not friendly relations. Go to your boss's office... Which distance will you keep? You will see that its's within this space.

4. *Public space:* 12 feet or more away from ourselves there is

public space, that space where we allow normal social things to happen freely, without becoming "our business", our concern. Normal activities of course. A man with menacing behavior is better kept a bit further off…

Basically, "our space" has a radius of 12 feet. It's a whole big room…

But here we come to another key principle proxemics:

## Territoriality

Did you hold on to that thought? Yes, we are a bit like dogs, wolves, or robins (but not so much cats): we are territorial animals. Not for hunting, but for personal and social relations.

When you are reading someone's body language and proxemics you will need this concept to see, for example:

- If a person allows another person into his or her space easily. You can find out a lot about their relationship from this.
- If a person keeps other people out of their space and who they keep out. You can see his "hierarchy" of friends or even actual hierarchies. Presidents, kings, queens and rock stars keep others they don't regard their peer at a distance, in the public space… It can be a power game.
- If someone tries to intrude into someone else's space. This can be quite annoying, and it may mean that the person is trying to gain something. This "something" though may depend. In some cases, it even feels "slimy", in a working

setting it may give away the careerist, but it might just be a request for friendship in other situations...

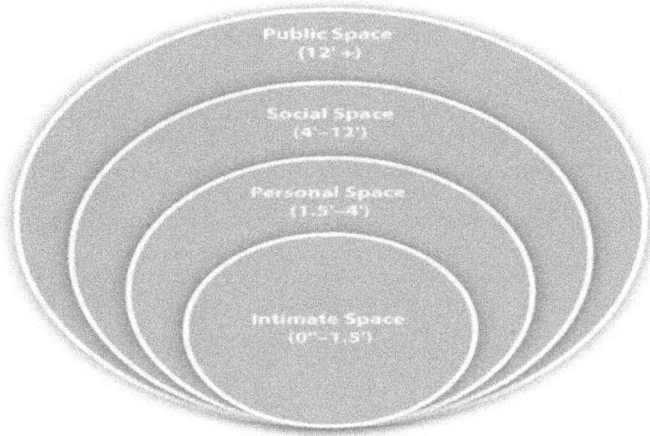

Public Space
(12' +)

Social Space
(4'–12')

Personal Space
(1.5'–4')

Intimate Space
(0"–1.5')

*Territoriality* again works on a cline, on a continuous line from "almost not territorial" to "very territorial" and it depends on three main factors:

- The relationship between the people involved (close or distant)
- The situation (informal, formal; private, public)
- The individuals (some people are more territorial than others).

When reading body language, you want to try to distinguish these three. For example, if the first two are set (a meeting between two businesspeople) and you see one of them being very territorial, then you know that this person is or is trying to be authoritative and dominant.

In fact, there is a direct link between being territorial and being dominant, being the alpha dog (I prefer it to alpha male…) or trying to exert authority.

## POSTURE

Posture is not technically a movement nor is it given by a single part of your body. Thus, we can see it as its own category within body language.

Posture is very important when training to read body language for many reasons:

- It is most often the *first thing we notice at a distance.* So, it is key to the notorious *first impressions* we talked about before.
- Most times, *we read the messages of posture subconsciously* and only sporadically consciously. This tells us that posture speaks directly to our subconscious.
- *Reading posture trains you to read the body as a whole.*

However, having said this, there is one part of the body which is very key to posture and it is in the middle of our body: our *chest*.

### The chest

The chest is key to posture as it is the "central part of our body". What we can say about the chest is whether it is:

- *Centered or off center.* If the chest is centered, so, not off to the left or right, it projects confidence and authority, on the other hand, when off center it may also indicate relaxation, friendliness, informality, intimacy etc.

- *Leaning forward, leaning backward or straight.* This shows attitudes towards what is being said. Forward means agreement, empathy, interest. Backward may mean diffidence, even worry, or repulsion. At times, it only means relaxation as we said, especially if sitting down. A straight posture means "I am in control", or even "I am fine with myself". Noble people (look at the Queen again) are taught to keep a very upright chest all the time to project authority and status.
- *Stretching or shrinking.* We can stretch our chest out or "make it small", and of course, it means "stability" or "nerves and uncertainty" accordingly.

We had not talked about the chest so far, but as you can see, it too matters.

### The neck and head

The neck too is important for posture. Forward, down, backward, sideways etc. positions give different signals. Let's see them.

- *Forward neck and head* mean interest and involvement.
- *Backward neck and head* mean distance and even self-protection.
- *Head tilted,* as we said, indicates deep thought, even creativity.

- *Head down* as we said is most often a negative sign, showing tiredness or shame or uncertainty, or in any case an unwillingness to engage.

## Legs and feet

The way we keep our legs and feet are too part of our posture. We will look at sitting positions later on, but for now we shall focus on standing positions.

- *Legs partly apart (one foot) and feet straight or outward,* the singer's position, as we called it, is a sign of *confidence, self-awareness and balance.*
- *Legs close together and feet too:* this can be a sign of worry or even insecurity or perceived threat.
- *Legs and feet spread out* (like resting on a step, sideways etc.) is a sign of great ease, confidence, a sense of security, informality and also self-confidence.

We already talked about how arms are used to "appropriate the space", thus they have a very important role in hierarchical relations, but now let's look at sitting postures.

## Sitting postures

How people sit is telling. Now, once upon a time, teachers actually taught *how to sit.* Then of course, most students never learned it. But in high society in the UK and Europe in general, sitting "properly" is a clear sign of "good upbringing" ...

But more than a sign that you went to an expensive school, it is also a way to project authority. Look again at the Queen and her mother. Examine how they sit. That is "sitting properly" and what does it translate into? Imperturbability.

They form perfect 90-degree angles with their legs and their abdomen. They look like geometrical figures if you look at them. The Queen Mother was noted by body language analysts for her perfect posture well into her old age, when she was in severe physical decline and needed to use a crutch... Still sitting perfectly upright.

The legs should be parallel but a small distance apart (a few inches) and they should form perfect vertical lines, no diagonals allowed...

This is the same posture you will find is used to depict pharos, kings, queens, popes, emperors and cardinals throughout history. Why? You know the answer: it projects authority.

Any deviation from this may tell the observer quite a few things, for example:

- *Feet back, with calves retracted under the body, or legs bending backward.* This is a sign of "self-protection". The person is not fully confident with what is happening. There may be some nervousness and even anxiety. If to this, you add...
- *Crossed ankles,* which always means a closure, then the sign is that the person wants to disengage. S/he does not seem at ease at all and is trying to "get out of it" most probably. This

"it" may just be a difficult question, not necessarily the whole situation.

- *Leaning forward and backward,* as we have already said, mean "engaging" and "not engaging" or "relaxing".
- *Parts of the body off symmetry,* like chest off center and leaning, legs over the armrest, resting on one elbow etc.... These are signs of informality, of a friendly attitude, of relaxation and "feeling at home", but they may also appear rude in some situations, especially in formal settings and with people that you don't know well.

There are also cultural influences. In the USA, people are on average more relaxed with posture than they are in many other countries, including Europe and Asian countries. You will never see a Japanese CEO with his feet on the table... he may even get fired for it.

## HOW YOU SAY IT MATTERS

We said that body language analysis is not language analysis (that's another science) but there are obviously overlapping zones. And we said that all those "mm's" and "er's" are in this overlapping zone... As are accent, intonation etc. Now we shall see exactly what these categories tell us in terms of body language analysis.

And yes, you guessed it, there are categories and subcategories here too!

## Paralanguage

This is what we say but is not verbal. So, all those grunts, mm's and er's. These are fairly easy to understand in most cases, but we just need to remember that we do need to take note of these.

But there is more, and we are getting to it straight away...

## Vocalics

Vocalics is the *study of the vocal quality* of speakers. And this is huge, actually. Let me tell you a few facts...

Not everybody has the same range, both in pitch and expressiveness (actual quality of the voice), but we all have more than one *register* or *voice*. Let's hear your "child voice"! You see, you too have different voices. Now, give me your "scolding voice"... You got the point.

Thing is, some people have a large repertoire of voices. Imitators for example, but also many actors and other people. You can actually train to get new voices...

And then there is the actual range: some people can go up and down the scales like singers... This is what we call:

### *Pitch*

Exactly the same as with singing, and exactly the same with singers. Some singers have many notes, others have fewer... So do people. Some men can get their voices to reach the soprano, range also when speaking, others, on the other hand, always sound like a bass or baritone.

We use exactly the same categories as for opera singers. In the end, when we speak, we use notes too. And pitch is very telling...

- If a person has a *flat pitch*, this may indicate boredom, disinterest, tiredness, or even (hear, hear!) depression. Yes, one of the first signs of depression a psychology notes is a flat, monotonous pitch.
- A *low pitch throughout* tends to project authority, severity and seriousness.
- A *higher than usual pitch* may indicate the opposite, so things like playfulness, empathy and informality or even vulnerability, but sometimes it is used to mock the other person (we will see that in the "tone" section).
- A *varied pitch* will usually carry the meaning properly and, unless exaggerated, it will project competence and interest at the same time. That's the pitch of a good teacher or public speaker in general.
- An *exaggerated pitch* may tell you that the person is not fully in control, maybe simply due to excitement.

But the most important thing is that the person *adapts the pitch to the circumstance.* You don't use the same pitch playing with a child or speaking at a board meeting or at a drunken birthday party and at a funeral, I hope!

### Tone

The tone of the voice is one of those things that is not mathematically measurable, like many things in music, for example "andante con brio". And that is tone when we speak. But we all understand it. There are so many key tones, and areas in between, so, again, use them as the points of a compass rather than rigid boxes.

- *Factual*
- *Serious*
- *Playful*
- *Annoyed*
- *Enthusiastic*
- *Warm*
- *Cold*
- *Cynical, sarcastic, ironic*
- *Doubtful*
- *Threatening.*

These are things you need to take into consideration, a bit like the subtitles to films… They are not actually fully part of the film, but they help us understand it…

### Functions of vocalics

These are functions of communication. Let me explain… Function is a term that comes from grammar and it means "why do we use this form". For example, a verb has a function, which is to express an action or a state. Similarly, a past tense has a function, which is to talk about something that happened in the past etc.

But when we talk, we help each other out, we contradict each other, we interact all the time. So, we need to see how we do it, and *with which functions*. And these are the main ones:

- *Accenting* is emphatic, it serves to underline, stress and even agree or make a point.
- *Regulating,* which means that when we speak we give signals to the other person about turn taking or waiting. These are signs about the conversation itself, a bit like road signs... But they tell us the intentions of the speaker. Lowering the voice or slowing down at the end of your turn (followed by eye contact). Or raising your voice to say "I am still talking" etc.
- *Contradicting,* this is when you use your intonation to say, "I mean the opposite". It means "contradicting the verbal message, the words you are using" not the other person.
- *Substituting* is when you use nonverbal sounds to replace words (like the famous "er" to mean "hold on I need to think").
- *Complementing,* which is whenever you add meaning to a word (any meaning) using your voice. This is the most general term. For example, you can say "I would love to go to Paris" with "love" pronounced "loooave", then you are expressing a yearning, strong desire. So, you are complementing the word itself (not contradicting it but adding to it).


## CHRONEMICS

Timing is also important, and chronemics (another Greek sounding word) is how we use timing when speaking. Of course, this too is part of both language analysis and body language analysis.

Going fast or slow, speeding up or slowing down, taking pauses are all important elements of speech and body language.

The general idea is that:

- *If you go slow you are confident and in control.*
- *If you go fast you show lack of confidence, interests or a tine that you are trying to "get it out" rather than "get it understood".*
- *If you slow down, you mark something which is important.*
- *If you speed up it may mean that you are not too interested in it or you want to get over it, leave etc. (or maybe the bell is about to ring).*

Then *pauses* are important:

- *Regular short pauses show confidence and competence.*
- *No pause at all or short and infrequent pauses show the opposite, lack of confidence.*
- *Long pauses show drama, importance and a sense of great control.*

And this last point leads us to an important observation. *You should read all these in conjunction with body language signs.*

For example, let's take the long pause. It's a very difficult thing to achieve. Holding attention when being silent is a thing only phenomenal actors and actresses can do for more than very few seconds.

But if during the pause the speaker looks calm, has a confident posture and may even look around, then that shows the speaker has the audience literally charmed...

If during the pause you start fumbling with what you have in your pockets, if you look down at your papers etc.... I bet the audience will be left with a totally different impression...

And this leads us straight into the next chapter... Sometimes yes means no and no means yes even with words. But let me ask you a question: is it the same with body language?

# 10

# POSITIVE VS. NEGATIVE

Good vs. evil, love vs. hate, light vs. darkness are all archetypes of how we think and how we see the world. One needs the other to define itself and yet it is the opposite. The story of thought on positive vs. negative goes back to early Greek philosophers for sure (Epicurus, e.g.) in the West while the East has a whole school of thought based on it, represented by the Tao, that symbol of opposites that has amazed generations.

Grand starting paragraph, but what does it mean in practical terms and body language? Sure, we have already touched on this topic a few times in this book. That's natural because it is very basic but also far reaching and all-permeating. But now it is time to explore it fully. What is more, this chapter will be useful for two areas of your body language studies:

• How to read positive and negative body language.

- How to keep a positive body language.

Now in fact you have learned quite a lot about reading body language and only a few things about controlling your own body language. In the coming chapters we will turn more closely towards the second...

But without further ado, let's get into the thick of it straight away!

## HOW TO TELL POSITIVE VS. NEGATIVE BODY LANGUAGE

There are *two main ways of saying if body language is positive or negative: the body language itself and contradictions.* Let's see them.

### The body language itself

There are *body language signs that are clearly, solely, or primarily negative or positive.* The head shake for "no" is maybe the clearest and most recognized. But even saying no with your fingers is common. Or putting your hands forward showing your palms.

These are either *emblems* and *adaptors* and even something in between, like the palms forward gesture. These are usually easy to tell. But remember that the "ay or nay" meaning is only *at face value.*

What do we mean by this? That we need to remember that we often say the opposite of what we mean. It's the literal (and literary, but linguistic too) meaning of *irony: saying one thing but meaning another.* And we do it with our body language too! Like the mother shaking her head but smiling we saw a few chapters ago...

Yet, the key point to take home here is that *we can only use irony with voluntary body language.* So, when reading body language, you really need to pay a lot of attention to which signs are voluntary (and the meaning can be willfully changed) and involuntary ones (adaptors for example, but also as you know eye movements, breathing etc.).

To understand if a sign has had its meaning changed, however, we need to use the second method:

### Contradictions

Whenever there is a contradiction, one of the two terms must be positive and the other negative. There's no escaping this... What we need to determine then is only which sign is positive and which is negative... That looks straightforward in theory, but in practice it is not that easy... Why? First of all, *where can you find contradictions?* The problem is not that it will be hard for you to find them... It's that there are too many in most cases!

You will, in fact, need to look at contradiction between all "communicative means" and "factors" ... Let me explain:

- *Contradictions in body language signs within one person.*
- *Contradictions in body language signs between the participants* (the observed person and the others s/he is interacting with).
- *Contradictions between body language and what people say verbally.*
- *Contradictions between what people say and how they say it.*

- *Contradictions between the body language and the topic itself* (talking about children with a sneer can show a contradiction between a topic we should find pleasant and positive and the body language…)
- *Contradictions between body language and the context as a whole* (informal body language in a formal situation… Just imagine a soldier who picks his nose, or just yawns while receiving a medal… It's a stupid image, I know but it does show you how far we can go from what the situation expects of us).

Thus, you will need to find where a sign clashes with another sign and look everywhere for it. But then your task is to find out which of the two signs, positive or negative, represents the position (meant as mind, idea, opinion or feeling) of the person you are analyzing…

But to learn this, you will have to wait till the next Chapter!

Now let's turn to ourselves, let's apply what we know about positive and negative signs to ourselves.

## HOW OFTEN DO YOU SHOW POSITIVE AND NEGATIVE BODY LANGUAGE?

We are far less aware of ourselves than we usually believe. Most people are convinced they know exactly what they look like, how they are appearing to others… If only they could see themselves on camera! Did I tell you about slouching? Do you know that I was not aware of it until an opera singing teacher told me? I was an adult by then already... This means that I spent about 30 years or so not knowing about my own negative body language...

Look around you, take a walk in the streets... Look at how many people give off negative body language and how many people give off positive body language...

Actually, let's try a little experiment... Go to a busy road near where you live and check positive and negative body language at rush hour on a weekday. Then go back there at the weekend and do the same...

Most probably, you will find that the rush hour walk gave you an overwhelming prevalence of negative body language and the weekend one gave you more positives...

## NEGATIVE BODY LANGUAGE

There are many factors that make us give positive or negative body language (and this is a matter of "prevalence" not total exclusion of positives or negatives):

- *Personal health* (the most obvious explanation in many cases)
- *State of mind*
- *Context* (pleasant vs. unpleasant, stressful or relaxing...)
- *Activity* (a leisurely stroll in the park vs. being late for work)
- *Even the weather will bring out positive or negative body language...*

These are factors I am asking you to note down for the next Chapter, which is strictly connected with this one... For now, however, this should prove one thing, namely:

- If of all these factors, your intention is only part (and not even the whole) of one point, "state of mind", most of the positive and negative body language signs are determined by factors independent of our will!

But there is another corollary to this, another conclusion we can draw: *if you display negative body language, don't feel guilty about it.* It is not "your fault"; the context, repeated activities etc. literally train our body to give off negative body language signs. Slouching being maybe the most exemplary once more...

A slouch is usually developed over years. Day in day out, you use a negative posture until it "feels natural and neutral" to you and you don't even realize that you are doing it. Instead, it will always appear as negative to people who see you...

Imagine now you are starting an acting course... We'll start with "wiping the slate" or "clearing the space" ... Before we start correcting our body language, we need to eliminate negative body language... And in order to eliminate negative body language we need to become aware of it.

Now, take the time you need. But this time I will ask you to get a small notebook and a pencil and keep them with you all the time. For a week or any time you need. In this notebook, I am asking you to *note down all your negative body language habits.* To find them out you can:

- Record yourself, or ask a friend to record you, especially at a time when you are not aware of it.
- Look at yourself in mirrors and shop windows when you walk in the street. Try to "catch yourself unaware" ... I mean, whenever you see a mirror, just look at yourself as if by surprise, without correcting your posture etc.... I did it, and I still do it a lot... This is really handy also when you are correcting your body language.
- Every now and then, stop; shift your focus from whatever you are doing to your body, and scan it for negative body language signs (especially posture with this exercise). Don't do this when you are driving though!
- Ask friends or family members. Do tell them to be honest. Sit down and explain, "You need to be a real friend. Honestly, tell me the truth..." then ask about posture, facial expressions etc.... go through the whole list and note down things that may be negative. Here, then use your discretion. Your friend may well also tell you things that get on his or her nerves for personal reasons, but they are not necessarily negative body language.

After you know which signs you need to eliminate from your body language, we can move to the next phase... eliminating them.

## Eliminating Negative Body Language

As you may guess, this can take some time. So, the sooner you start, the better.

First of all, *start with the most prominent one.* In particular start with *posture.* You know by now that it is the most noticeable body language sign. And your best friend here is a *mirror:*

- Every day when you wake up check yourself in the mirror and take a correct, open and upright posture.
- Set yourself reminders to check on your posture during the day (use that ringtone).
- When you get home at night, again, go to the mirror and correct your posture.
- Doing some stretching and physical exercise can help a lot with correcting your posture.

You should notice that *once you correct your posture, many other negative signs should disappear.* In fact, lots of them are consequences of it, including your gait, the way you look at people (straight, from below or from above...), how open your gestures are etc.

Then, pick on a sign in turn, choosing the big ones, or the ones you dislike most. One by one spend a few days correcting it with a similar method, till you feel confident that you can move to the next one.

Once you have "leveled" the first few major body language negatives you habitually display, it is time to move to the next phase, *introducing and displaying positive body language.*

## POSITIVE BODY LANGUAGE

To start with, developing and building positive body language does not mean being "dishonest". In most cases, it means *aligning your body language with your actual personality.* Most of us *are* positive people, but we just don't look it.

Yet again, *start with your posture!* If you have followed the exercises so far, you have already started correcting your posture. But there is more to correcting than just eliminating negatives...

Shall we look at two concepts that people often confuse, to make this point clear? "Confidence" and "being bossy". Once you have eliminated the "non-confident" signs (like slouching, making yourself small, avoiding frontal positions etc.) you can build a new "image" of yourself. Unfortunately, especially in the business world, the idea of "bossy" has become a replacement for "confident".

You can even see this in a general shift among politicians... They used to stand and look confident, in control, authoritative *but not aggressive.* Instead, among many politicians nowadays the attitude you see is that of the bully (which as you know is all but confident in reality). Lots of "chest out ready to fight" and fists and closure to the audience...

*You need to choose which image of yourself you wish to project.* It is literally like building a character for an actor or actress... You see, good actresses and actors "level their real personality off" and add all the traits of the character they need to embody, perform and bring to life.

Study how actors and actresses change their gait, posture and even facial expressions with each new character. I am talking about professionals here.

But this leads us into another trick... Choose a person you admire. This could be a famous person or a friend or family member... *Study that person's body language:*

- How would you describe it in a few words?
- What is/are the key trait(s) of his or her body language? Choose a handful.
- Can you try to imitate them?

Imitation is a very profound learning method... We learn to speak by imitating our parents. What I am asking you to do is to choose a *body language role model* and *introduce some traits of his or her body language in yours.* Not all – we are not in the cloning business here.

Also do keep in mind that what may look good on a person may not on another. So, be self-critical and be ready to change in case...

For facial expression, the really best exercise is to *pull faces in the mirror.* Even facial expressions are habitual, and we reduce the range of expressions when we are stressed, we have a monotonous life, we are always being judged (including at work or school!)

The fact is that a person with a wide and free range of facial expressions will go far... And as usual, I don't just mean business, but also personal relationships. Pulling faces is like "stretching for your face". It exercises the muscles we then use (often unconsciously) to produce facial expressions.

Bold and expressive facial expressions become simpler and better marked if you train and build the very muscles that produce them. This at the same time has a "backdoor effect", which means that you will at the same time become more confident. Expressing yourself with confidence literally builds your inner strength.

Then choose a few major body language signs you wish to introduce and work on one at a time... Again, the mirror is your best friend here. Play little scenes in front of it, and if you do it regularly, you will *internalize this gesture.* So, when it comes in handy in a normal, everyday situation, it will come out naturally.

A few signs are enough to change the overall perspective that people have on you, and in any case how you project your personality...

## Positive and Negative, True and False

Coming to a conclusion, you now know how to tell positive and negative apart but also how to build a more positive body language for yourself. And this is closely linked with what is coming up next: a whole chapter to develop your skills in telling lies and appearing truthful.

# 11

# LIAR, LIAR, PANTS ON FIRE!

P ants are actually *not* a reliable way of finding out if someone is lying to you... Trust me, there are much better ways, and you know some already. Most importantly, we said that lies are not detected by a single body language sign (like touching your nose, that's a myth) but by reading many signs in context and matching them against the words spoken.

The true/false dimension of our communication (both verbal and non-verbal) is so big and complex that we need a whole chapter to explore it. And this is exactly it!

## WHY DO WE LIE? IS IT ALWAYS INTENTIONAL?

Most of us have lied at some stage in our lives. Most of us will do it again. Lying is regarded as "unethical", "wrong", "disgusting" and even "a sin" in religious terms, but it is so widespread and common that, behind this public condemnation, *most societies, especially Western ones, actually condone lying (to a certain extent) behind the scenes.*

Currently lying is even being promoted. Only a few years ago, a politician caught lying even on a minor issue would be forced to resign. Nowadays politicians lie openly, and some people even esteem them for this; the idea that all that matters is "getting to the top" and "outsmarting others" has really had major negative effects on our moral compass.

So, why do we lie? There isn't a specific reason, but we can start with a facilitating factor (rather than motive): *it is implicitly condoned by society and it is becoming even more so.* But while this may give the "all clear" to lie to some people, it does not tell us why they decide to lie in the first place...

And the reasons are many... To start with, *when is lying actually lying?* I've not lost my mind... Let me give you an example:

- Is a child telling a story lying?
- Is a writer writing a fiction novel lying?
- Is a teacher giving a simplified explanation to make it accessible lying?
- Is recalling "creatively" filling in the gaps of your memory with "what you think happened" lying?

On the first one, I think we can agree... But this habit can keep going till you are an adult, and some people may then end up *literally not being sure about what is true and what is not.* For these people telling a lie is like saying the truth. These are *pathological liars.* Of course, they are not (that) many and they suffer from a very serious mental condition.

But people can convince themselves that what they are saying is true every now and then... It happens, either because you don't remember well, or because we actually do sometimes lie to ourselves...

It happens very often when people's life compass, their very basic beliefs, their ideology etc. are challenged. Imagine the famous Bishop who refused to look into Galileo's telescope. You see, for him the choice was: change all you have ever believed in or lie to yourself this once. It's not a conscious choice though... it's subconscious. And most of us do it quite often.

This leads to *cognitive bias,* which means that there is a difference between what you subconsciously know is true and what you consciously say is true. Most *prejudice can be read as cognitive bias.*

Even in this case, most people are not even aware of lying, because they are lying to themselves.

But there are many more reasons why people lie, even much more practical ones:

*We lie to fend off interest,* for example. If some stranger asks you, "How much have you got in your wallet?" You are most likely going to reply with a lie, especially if you happen to have a big sum. Why? You are *"giving a red signal" to the other person*; you are saying, "This is none of your business".

This is very common in stores and shops. Many people reply with a lie to an insistent shopkeeper or shop assistant. "Come on, buy these socks, they are on sale and high quality!" What would you say? "Stop bothering me you fool!" or a more innocent (but false), "No thanks, I have them already!" A creative and cheeky liar may say, "I never wear socks, thank you!"

In these situations, the lie is detected. You don't even expect the shop assistant to believe you, do you? You just want to give them a cul-de-sac in the conversation, an "access denied" sign...

*We lie to help people, and these are white lies.* Most people think that white lies are the only acceptable ones. But "acceptable" is a socio-cultural value, and I would say that society accepts the previous type of lies too.

*We lie because we are afraid.* This is a habit we pick up at school or as children anyway. We are afraid of the consequences of telling the truth, and so we lie. "Did you eat the slice of cake I left for your sister, Charlie?" and of course the answer is "No, a mouse came and took it away!"

This just becomes more sophisticated, better honed, more "professional" but for many of us it remains a *survival technique* well into our adult and especially professional life. The fact that in many places your workplace is a very competitive environment, such lies become very common.

Not just this, but because we often see that *those who lie have fast-tracked careers in many places, lying itself even becomes an advantage!* People lie to make money. Quite simply...

Here we certainly reach the opposite of those who lie compulsively. People who lie out of selfishness do it fully consciously – at first! Like all habits, it then can become *internalized and naturalized and therefore become subconscious.* And then you become a compulsive liar. It's a circle.

But there is more... How about our last case, the "filling in the blanks" with a bit of imagination? Is it lying?

It certainly is if you are giving a witness statement in court. But this is a legacy of our childhood experience, when telling stories (imaginative ones) is part not only of growing up, but of finding your place in society.

Think back to your early years at school, at elementary, or primary school... Do you remember that friend who always had amazing stories that now sound like fairy tales? Do you also remember how popular s/he was?

There are people who keep this liking for "coloring" their stories into their adulthood, a bit like comedians do when they tell a joke... Again, how far is this acceptable? It's hard to put a general rule on this...

Importantly, there are also clinical problems. People with any form of *dementia* may use this very method of *"filling in the gaps"* to make sense of what they are recalling and saying. If you know anyone with dementia you will have noticed it. They say something true then insert something that's completely false. This is of course acceptable.

But it leads us to another case: *people lie because their memory is wrong.* With irrelevant episodes but also with painful ones, time plays a little trick... Over years, it starts changing our memory. In most cases, we tend to remember things in a "better version" of the reality. This is a self-defense mechanism with painful memories... Sometimes, however, the opposite is true.

A very curious phenomenon is that people often remember being on the right side of an argument while actually they were on the wrong side at the time... A sort of "I told you so" in retrospect...

And then there are cases when *people lie without actually knowing why.* The lie just comes out of their mouth, often when answering in a hurry or under pressure. They realize that – well, it's as if someone inside of them has beaten them to the answer and told a lie... And what can they do? In most cases they are taken aback, realize they lied and pretend nothing has happened. More rarely, people correct themselves.

Then of course, you have those who lie to you out of evil intentions, like getting information out of you, getting money out of you, stealing your ideas etc. And these of course, are the main ones we need to look out for.

So, no, lying is in many cases totally subconscious. In some cases, people think they are telling the truth (but is it lying), in other cases people lie but they are not aware that it is wrong, and there are then those who lie because they just want to...

## 7 WAYS TO SPOT A LIAR

As usual, we need some theory to see the big picture, but we also want some practical tips. However, before we move forward, at the risk of sounding repetitive... we are going to see 7 signs that can *make you suspect that someone is lying*. But importantly, *none of these on its own will tell you that the person is lying.*

Be professional, look out for these signs but then *always look at body language as a whole, collect as many signs as possible and base your assessment on the whole, not the individual sign and finally check the signs against the actual words of the person.*

1. **Lack of eye contact;** this is by far one of the best ways of finding out if someone is telling the truth or lying. But beware! Some people may actually be shy! Or maybe they don't trust you?
2. **Sudden change of head position;** this may signal a sudden change of thought. Matched against what the person is saying, it can reveal a contradiction. This sign is especially useful in readings, lectures, presentations etc.
3. **Rigidity;** a very stiff, nervous and static posture may indicate lying. Lying in general makes us tense, and that means physically as well. Lie detectors in fact monitor muscles as well... But remember to read everything in context... If we took this rule as absolute, we would conclude that our old acquaintance the Queen has never uttered an honest word in her life!
4. **Covering your mouth;** this is an instinctive reaction when

you realize that you said something wrong, and it may come out when someone is lying. But again, beware, *it does not only come out when you are lying.* It can also express uncertainty, even concern, or a closure to the speaker.

5. *Tense lips;* tense lips usually show, you guessed it, uneasiness with the words you say. And the most detectable sign of this is when *people curl their lips.* Once more, it may also mean that it's a difficult thing to say, not necessarily a lie.

6. *Sudden change of breathing;* breathing is often involuntary, and if you become suddenly nervous, anxious etc. you will need more oxygen to calm yourself down, and your breathing accelerates automatically. This however, needs to be quite sudden or it is more likely to be due to other reasons. What is more, breathing can change pace due to other factors: general anxiety, stress, heat, dehydration etc.

7. *Frequent jitters;* this seems quite non-specific, but actually it is. All sudden changes of behavior, movements, little twitches and signs of nervousness are clear signs of worry, and they may be signs of lying.

You see, the point is that we usually feel at ease with the truth and the average person worries when lying. But there are pathological liars who lie "with a straight face" as we say informally. Luckily pathological liars are comparatively rare, and even they give off signs to expert observers. Politicians, for example, may avoid facing the audience with their breast, and turn it sideways... That could indicate awareness of lying.

In fact, as a bonus sign...

*Covering vulnerable parts;* the politician hiding his or her chest is trying to protect a vulnerable part (his or her heart and other vital organs). Similarly, people cover their neck, sometimes eyes, belly etc. when they feel threatened. Lying and being caught is a threat, isn't it? Yes, because you will be judged etc. So, the expectation of being judged and caught makes you protect a vulnerable part.

## IDENTIFY THE KIND OF LIAR YOU ARE FACING

We have seen that there are many reasons for lying. Surprise, surprise, there are also different types of liars. The categories of liars (taxonomy of liars, if you want to impress your friends with a technical term) partly depend on the reason for lying but they are also determined by behavioral patterns when lying.

These may include factors like how often they lie, how easily they lie etc.... All in all, we can group them into 6 categories.

**1. Compulsive liars;** these are the hardcore liars, people who lie consistently and with an attitude like they don't even care if you find out that they are lying. For many of them, the important thing is that you listen to their lies. Some politicians are like this and many conmen: on a large audience, they know that someone will believe them. They don't care at all if the others find them out.

Having said this, *compulsive liars are easy to spot. They display a wide range of body language signs that suggest lying.* They will avoid eye contact; they tend to turn away from the people they are talking to etc.

What is more, they are also easy to find through what they say: their stories don't add up and often become implausible. Actually, the more people give them positive feedback, the more they exaggerate their lies.

There are two types of compulsive liars, *narcissistic liars* and *habitual liars*.

> ***a. Narcissistic liars*** do it because they want attention. These are usually story tellers and they add and embellish their stories with false details. They basically are like those children who are so popular with peers because they "tell tales" – only they are adults and they should know better.
>
> ***b. Habitual liars*** are simply people who will lie all the time out of habit. We change and we can learn any bad habit if we "train" (even unwillingly) long enough. And these are people who have been brought up lying all the time and just find it natural to, like for a dancer it is natural to do the splits and not for us... With habitual liars it is very difficult to trace the reason why they are lying. In fact, in many cases there is none...

**2. *Pathological liars*** are not compulsive liars because they don't do it all the time out of habit or attention seeking. They *respond to stimuli by lying*. They lie constantly, but not indiscriminately.

Of all liars, *pathological liars are the most difficult to find out*. This is because they have become so accustomed to lying that they display very few signs. These are the ones who "lie in with a straight face".

They often keep lying undetected for long periods of time, and they will use this to their advantage.

In fact, they will often have good careers in competitive environments. You can surely guess how... by lying to your boss and lying to you... And by keeping that straight face that hides all their lies for years...

There is a beautiful technical word for this *pseudologia fantasica* (Latin for "fanciful false thinking" or "fanciful false argument") ...

**3. Sociopathic liars;** these are dangerous! They too tend to be pathological liars. However, they are classed as sociopathic liars because they fall within a much more serious mental condition: sociopathy (psychopathy is similar), which means that they have *no ability to feel empathy*. What does it mean? That they do not understand other people's feelings at all. These can literally watch a person being tortured and they feel *nothing at all* in grave cases.

Sociopaths and psychopaths also lie a lot. They do it because they only see people as "objects", or "things to exploit" and they are incapable of thinking about other people's good. They do it to profit themselves.

Unfortunately, they will feel nothing when lying apart from risks for themselves. Let me explain... They do not become tense because of the very fact that they are lying, and they are uncomfortable with it. They don't care about it. For them you could even die there and then. They are only afraid that you may catch them.

This means that they may not have all the signs of big liars, despite being super big liars themselves. But they may display more "protect vulnerable parts" signs, like turning sideways etc.

But there is a trick to find out of you are dealing with a sociopath or psychopath... *Check their reaction to emotions. If they have none, that's a very clear indicator.* Look at reactions to emotional stimuli... They will either fake concern (and they are bad at that because they don't understand it), or even cut it short and show uneasiness with "being put in the spot".

And if there are no signs? Throw a little trap! Tell them you are very uncomfortable with something they are saying and observe them. You will get no body language sign of real emotional involvement... And remember, these people are seriously dangerous. It's no hyperbole. They will ruin anybody's life with no remorse.

**4. *Careless liars;*** this is another bad category of liars. They are often the cause of broken relationships... I hope you have never had a story with one of them in your life, but if you have, I am sure you already understand what sort of person we are talking about.

These people will lie, in fact, carelessly, as if it did not matter at all. They often even have moral values in life, but when they need to lie, they suddenly feel nothing about them. These are the typical people who will lie to you about extramarital relationships for example. Or those that may lie to you about where they have been etc.

Despite lying carelessly, they do display signs. For example, they will become nervous (fidgety, closed posture, even raise their voice) and even restless or aggressive as soon as you probe their lies. You see, they lie to you and they think they got away with it and you should just believe them. They don't expect you not to trust them!

**5. *Occasional liars;*** these are *usually bad liars,* but they are also very common. We all occasionally lie. The fact is that *they repent about lying most times and very quickly.* Actually, it is virtually impossible that an occasional liar will not have second thoughts and moral issues about his or her lie, even if small.

They are very easy to spot because they will display generously that they have lied with their body language. But what is more, just like with fibbing children, after lying both their body language and behavior will usually change.

**6. *White liars*;** I wanted to close on a positive note. White lies are good lies. And white liars do it for your own good, so, maybe together with some lying signs, you will also see signs of *empathy and even protection,* like a warm look, palms towards you, etc....

Good white liars, if you want to become one, also have a steady, comforting but "refracting" eye contact. I'll explain, they know in their heart that they are doing it for you, so they will look into your eyes and they will express love and care, but at the same time, they will invite you not to probe too far. Just repeating to yourself "I am doing it for you" when looking into the person's eyes will have an effect.

However, this effect may end up being that the person understands you are lying, but that you are doing it for her or his sake... You can't lie with your eyes...

# THOSE WHO LIE BEHIND THE SAFETY OF A SCREEN

The issue of fake news and disinformation could not be more topical. It may well be one of the biggest problems that the democratic world is facing right now. We are not here to make a full list of reliable and unreliable sources, though I suppose you already have your own favorites and least favorites.

But this topic partly merges with our field... To start with, *you cannot analyze the body language to someone who is writing an email or a Facebook post.* Or even a newspaper article to be correct! That is a disadvantage.

What is more, as the title suggests, *lying behind a screen is easier. People just feel safer doing it.* You may wonder why...

- The person they are lying to is not present in person.
- They can double check what they write, while if you lie face to face you just get one chance...
- People often read these posts and messages very quickly.
- The platform itself (social media etc.) gives the, credibility... the "I read it on Facebook" syndrome...
- With modern technology, that can prepare fake evidence (photoshopped images or even links to other lying sources).

So, what can we do about it? I will answer this with another question: are these people totally exempt from that "lying shame" that appears in body language?

The answer is that in most cases they are not. You see, they feel protected, but they still feel a level of uneasiness!

And this will then translate into behavior. Okay, it's not body language but it is related, contiguous in a way… And here are a few things you can look out for:

- *How credible is the account itself?* An account is not a person, but many of the fake news spreaders also use fake accounts. Some are easy to spot. Some don't even have an account pic. Some have one function. Some repeat the same words over and over again.…. But this is mainly for small accounts. These have one function only, and it is "to make mass". Bigger, leading accounts will look more credible.

- *If the account is real, is it trustworthy?* There are famous accounts that spread fake news. If you are a social media user, you will know quite a few by now. If you are new, be very careful when you join them.

- *Does the text use the first-person pronoun?* Even when writing, we feel uneasy when "putting ourselves in the lie". So, many liars will avoid saying "I" and "me" and at times even "my" and "mine" ("my" is a possessive adjective, not a pronoun to be exact…) This will be more common with less experienced liars though. Very experienced ones may even suffer from the opposite. Why? They know that these pronouns inspire trust.

- *Do they repeat some key words?* By this we mean, are they just spreading a hashtag? Or a key word to pass on a message? Some even repeat the exact text as others, but when you see that someone is repeating a phrase over and over again, that account is trying to drill it into your brain... That is in itself a sign of dishonesty.

- *Are they specific or general?* Sometimes, the statements are so general that they will prove very little. But you will see the one that tells you about his cousin who... They have become smart, you see? They know that this will look trustworthy. Probe them then. Ask for more and more details until you find contradictions.

Then again, with the written word, the key strategies remain the old-fashioned ones:

- *Check the logic behind the text.* You need to find mistakes in the logical processes, contradictions, false reasoning etc.
- *Check with other sources.* Look at opposing views. They may enlighten you a lot!
- *Check the source or origin of what is being said.* Someone tells you that there is water on Mars? Check with a scientific source about it (by the way, there is and even on the Moon!)

Finally, use commonsense. No, it is very unlikely that a distant relative in a country none of your family has ever even mentioned has left you a fortune! Yet many people did fall for those emails...

Never trust people who make first contact and propose a deal or ask for money...

## FROM LIES TO EXPRESSION

So, we looked at reasons why people lie, different types of lies and liars. But we also looked at how you can spot lying people and even which type of liar you are dealing with. And we also dipped our toes into a sister field, linguistics as applied to lying with written words.

Next, we will delve even deeper into the realm of body language... Ready to dive into what your body manifests?

# 12

# SPEED-READING PEOPLE

Have you ever heard about speed-reading? I am talking about words here. If you read word by word, as many people do, your speed will be limited to about 140 words per minute. "Not bad," you might think – but wait till you hear how fast the fastest reader in the world can read... Howard "Speedy" Berg is in the *Guinness Book of Records* for reading (and understanding) ... 80 pages in one minute. That's about 25,000 words!

And the first concept of speed-reading is to read whole sentences in one go rather than individual words. The same applies to body language reading... If you read a sign at a time, you will be much slower than if you *look at clusters*. And I have given away a "trade secret" of body language speed reading.

The difference may not be as big as with words, but we'll never know... Guess why? Most body language speed readers work for the intelligence services...

## WHY SPEED-READ PEOPLE?

The fact is that Police personnel, army personnel, secret agents and border agents are all trained to speed read body language, simply because they need it in their jobs... Now, imagine if you have to identify a possible terrorist or threat in the time you go through the customs at the airport... You don't have all that time you would at a conference, a board meeting or a political rally...

You really have minutes, actually seconds, sometimes on camera, to read body language. If you have seen how body language speed-reading has been used in emergency situations you would've been blown away.

There are two things that strike you:

1. With what speed and precision, they can pinpoint even a small tell-tale group of signs, out of what would appear to most like normal behavior.
2. The professional trust their colleagues and superiors give them. They don't ask why or what exactly. The reader points and they jump into action.

Of course, then they need to find out if it was actually true. A body language sign is not enough to incriminate anybody... But it gives you the idea that body language reading has developed with skills and "tricks" to the point that it is constantly and routinely used for security and safety reasons.

And speed-reading is a great advantage.

## DEVELOPING YOUR SPEED-READING

Of course it will take time, but little by little, you too will develop your body language speed reading. Let's get straight into it actually...

Now you do know quite a lot about analyzing body language, you have a little "tool kit" you can use to read even quicker, but first of all remember:

- *Be ready to change your reading, your assessment, especially with speed reading.*
- *Keep in mind that speed-reading is more limited than a full analysis...*
- ...but it is useful in emergencies or when you have little time.

Don't get me wrong now... I'm not asking you to go out and come back with generic "first impressions" ... We know all the issues with them.

I am asking you to go out and come back with *clues, a lead, a possible reading angle...*

So, ready? Take a very short time... Go to a busy place (a park, road, a shopping mall). Look around randomly and only note down the body language that strikes you. Let your eyes choose why and what... Five minutes maximum!

Quick? Okay, now make a list of the body language you noticed.

Done? Now, not all of them, this is a "snapshot", but... for some of them, can you give a sketchy interpretation. *And sketch is exactly the word we are looking for.*

What's so special about sketching? It is fast, okay, it is not a finished work of art. But above all, it is open to corrections... You see, you can hardly correct an oil on canvas painting, but you can use your eraser with a pencil sketch...

So, for example... The woman who was swinging her arms visibly (I am guessing what you might have noted). What could it be? She had some happy news, maybe? She just left work and is going to meet someone she likes a lot? Or maybe she's a bit tipsy? That's the sort of sketch we are looking for.

Now I will ask you for a reverse exercise...

Go out, again, for five minutes and in a busy place... This time I'm asking you to find, as quickly as possible:

- A happy person
- A sad person
- A confident person
- A distracted person
- A tired person.

Choose some of your own if you want but give each spotting a super short time. As short as you can.

Now, go back home and tell me: what *cluster of body language signs* told you that the person, was happy? Sad? Etc.

Now you see, do this exercise over and over again and you will become *faster at spotting clusters of body language signs.*

Note that these *clusters are flexible.* Not everybody has the exact same body language... But after you do it a few times, you will start developing general (and flexible) clusters, or groups of signs that immediately tell you a lot about the person you are reading...

Training and exercising are the best ways to develop speed-reading – like all skills indeed! Quick, easy to do exercises like the ones I have just given you are ideal. In fact, the key is in the repetition. When you do one of these exercises first, you will develop some skills, even improve your speed a bit. The more you do it, the faster you will become.

But are there any tricks of the trade? Of course there are, and here they are for you!

## 5 TECHNIQUES TO SPEED-READ PEOPLE

You guessed it; these are all tricks that come from FBI agents and the like... Do keep in mind that speed may go to the detriment of accuracy in some cases. This is simply because you have a "snippet" to go on. It's like reading a whole book fast, with verbal speed-reading, and there you will get a very good understanding, or simply reading a page but fast.

So, you can use speed reading even if you are observing a five-hour long speech (poor you!) and in that case, you will get a very precise analysis. But if you speed-read a person for a minute, then you will get a partial picture anyway. Still, you will get more than if you used normal reading.

## 1. Look for clusters of signs

We have already said it, and luckily enough, this chapter comes after the one on micro-expressions. You see why this is handy? You have learned micro-expressions as clusters, groups of signs. If one is missing in a cluster, you still get the idea that the emotions expressed is that... You only need 3 out of 4 or 4 out of 5 to say, "This is the cluster of micro-expressions for happiness," right?

The same applies to subconscious reading. We don't need all the signs of sadness to understand that a child is unhappy. Sometimes, we can't even see them all from where we stand. But when you see large tearful eyes you will also expect all (or most) of the other micro-expressions, like eyebrows raised in the middle, pouting lower lip etc. ...

You do have clusters already, and they are often centered on the emotion or state of mind they express together rather than a precise sign on its own. So, take the key archetypal emotions and states of mind and make a quick list of all the signs you know about them. Those will be clusters. These clusters can be very large, including 20 or 30 signs at times. But you will only need a handful to make a fast but accurate analysis.

So, complete the list as you wish, but don't forget happiness, sadness, anger, discomfort and frustration, negativity, positivity, aggression, honesty and openness, dishonesty, and a closed attitude.

Make a list for each then go out with one cluster in mind and spot the first person that displays enough signs for you to make a reliable assessment.

Do it again and again with all archetypes and you will see great results with your speed reading.

## 2. Know what you are looking for

Imagine you are an FBI agent and you are watching CCTV to spot a criminal walking in front of it after a crime. What would you look for? Maybe a hurried step, maybe someone who looks around a lot, maybe someone who is hiding his face, any signs of a fast heartbeat if you can etc.... You surely would not be looking for a skidding child, someone helping an old lady cross the street, someone walking with her or his heard in the clouds, would you?

The same as guided reading with words, fast reading is very focused from the start. Now, look for the word "sketching" in this Chapter. Found it? How long did it take you? Did you read all the words to find it? No, you exclude any word that does not look like it.

The same is when you are looking for specific traits. Try it out now... Go out and find everybody who is hiding his or her hands... Find all those who are focused on the destination of their journey, those who want to get somewhere. Then find those who are lost on the journey itself, like enjoying the view etc....

## 3. Do your research

If you know the person or sort of person we are talking about, start with possible scenarios. Going back to our intelligence agents, the more they know about the person they are looking for, the faster they can recognize them.

Anything can come in handy. Are they married? What sports do they play? Which TV programs do they like? In our case, however, as I don't think you are taking an entry interview for the CIA just yet, you may want to know some information about your clients, for example...

You see, if you know the client is a young and informal person, you may expect a very relaxed attitude and any signs out of it can be quite telling. On the contrary, if your client is an old and very formal person, any sign that shows lack of control may come from a strong internal negative reaction.

You see, you will be looking for very specific signs if you know your chickens. With friends, we can already expect a very clear set of signs, and we notice any small change...

## 4. Focus on discrepancies rather than individual signs

The previous tip leads us straight into the current one. The formal person having an informal sign. The informal one having a sign of stiffness. The manager showing a sign of fear. The speaker fidgeting. The bride looking at another man... Okay, the last was a joke but it gives you the idea.

*Look for something that is not in line with what you would expect from that person, in that situation and at that stage.*

## 5. Check what people are trying to hide

People use body language to project what they want you to see. So, make a clear distinction between:

- Voluntary body language
- Involuntary body language

Go out for your usual walk and find 5 clear signs of voluntary body language, and try to find 3 of involuntary body language... Again, repeat as necessary. Do it again and again until you feel that you are quick at dividing these.

Next, focus on involuntary body language. Sometimes, people don't mind about it. But if people are aware of it and try to hide it or control it, then you are on to something. That's a key indicator for those who are trained to spot the criminal, like border agents... The person who wants to *look calm but is not...*

## MAKING FAST ASSESSMENTS OF BODY LANGUAGE: THE 5 C'S

There are two stages however with speed reading body language. One is being quick at spotting relevant signs and clusters of signs. The other is being quick with the conclusions, or better with the assessment.

Use these 5 C's to guide you in your analysis, and yes, we have seen them already (some in detail, one, "culture" will have its own chapter soon). But now is a good time to make a point and a summary of them all. And they all start with C.

1. *Context*, something we have talked about at length. Look for signs and clusters that look out of context...
2. *Clusters*, so... don't get side-tracked by the odd sign, focus on the groups of signs. Having said this, do keep the odd but unusual sign in mind... Come to it later and you may make great use of it... As you will find out from the bunch of flower story (I'm teasing you again!)
3. *Congruence*, which of course means that you need to look out for *congruence between what people say and what their body language says.*
4. *Consistency,* by which we mean that the person is consistent not just with the words, but with his or her personality, the situation etc. Try to get a baseline behavior you expect from a person and work from there. And this is why studying the person beforehand is very important.

5. ***Culture.*** Please take into consideration how culture affects
   body language… We have talked about it a lot in theoretical
   and general terms (nature vs. nurture again?!) and have seen
   some examples, but this is so important that we'll come back
   to it in a lot of detail.

All these, as you see, are practical and useful strategies and tips to
speed-read people. But maybe nothing matches a particular quality
you may have (or will develop!) *emotional intelligence.* And this is
what we are going to see next!

# 13

# ARE YOU EMOTIONALLY INTELLIGENT?

There are things no amount of mathematical computations can solve. Like, what do we feel looking at a child crying? It's like there are two worlds out there: one made of "things" that we can "count" and another world made of "feelings" which we can hardly describe...

Both are real (at least the emotional one is real, we are not sure about the physical one, but this is philosophy). But one is very much prompted by society (maybe because "things" can be sold for other "things" called money) and the other is at best underestimated, at worst repressed and criminalized.

I remember studying "the condition of women in Victorian Britain" at university and under the pretense that they were "innocent" and "angels of the hearth", there was a big prejudice: *women were seen as emotional and irrational.* That meant that women "were not fit to run the country, the economy" etc. – actually, not even fit to vote!

Yes, things have moved on, but what does society propose when we think about the word "intelligent"? A mathematician? A physicist? Whatever – we think about a *rational person.* Then I could keep complaining and say that actually the highest IQs are in categories where rationality is at least on a par with emotional intelligence... Writers for example... I could complain that Einstein, the world's "epitome of rationality" displayed clear signs of a very deep emotional intelligence and he did say that he used a lot of irrational thinking. In fact, like another giant of physics, Dr. Micho Kaku, Einstein spent most of his time meditating, like a Buddhist monk, not scribbling long formulas on a board, like they show us in *The Big Bang Theory.*

Do tell me to stop moaning – but not before I say the last thing... How many people are not regarded as intelligent only because they are not primarily rational? Sorry, mine was a crusade against injustice...

Nowadays, however, the importance of emotional intelligence is becoming clearer and clearer...

Even talking about body language, the emotional intelligence side of it is quite important. You see, we have broken down body language signs to the smallest bits, really... But there is always that "something" that does not add up rationally. And because I am stubborn, I am going to explain it to you.

Let's copy Einstein and make a thought experiment.

A means B, okay? So, a yawn means that you are tired or bored.

And this is correct, and we can read it rationally.

But if this is the case, why do people also understand body language signs they have *never seen?* Especially facial expressions are a wonder of this field and a great puzzle. There are some we can break down into clear signs, into "body language words" but there are so many facial expressions that it is as if you are "reading a new language" every new face you meet. And yet all studies show that we don't need to learn the new language to understand it, at least subconsciously.

That's because *even with body language we do not read and interpret everything rationally.*

So, the question now is...

## WHAT DOES IT MEAN TO BE EMOTIONALLY INTELLIGENT?

Our mind works on different levels. Actually, the mind is not the brain, and the brain is not even all in our head. We have at least another brain in our heart (neurons) and one in our intestine (more neurons).

Then again, the brain does not follow a single method when understanding the world. You see, rationality and deduction are ways of thinking and understanding the world. So, if I say that A means 3 and B means 4, and I ask you, what is A+B then? You would use your rational mind to say, "A+B is 7!"

That is logic, that is rational thinking.

But when I ask you to explain what you feel when you hear Beethoven *Ode to Joy* you will not go down a logical process. You can't say the note D, followed by the note F etc. gives me happiness, uplifting feelings, ecstasy etc.

Yet you do have an answer, but to give it, you need to use your *emotional intelligence.*

There are many theories about why and how we use emotional intelligence... At a very visceral, if you want ancestral level, if you need to work out all the logical processes when you are running away from danger (say a lion)... the chances are that before you end solving the "equation" you have become a delicious meal for the lion.

Yes, because rational thinking may be exact, but very often it takes a lot of time.

We could even get to a long technical analysis of that beautiful piece of work that is *Ode to Joy,* but after years and years, we still would need to use emotional intelligence to say what we feel about it...

So, you are emotionally intelligent if you can "read feelings" and "think intuitively" (as opposed to deductively). But there is a bit more... You are emotionally intelligent if you can express yourself creatively.

So, to recap, emotional intelligence has three main elements:

- *Understanding feelings*
- *Using intuition*
- *Being creative.*

But note, *there are many levels of emotional intelligence.* Some people have impressive levels, we don't even realize it many times. I used to know a man, I am not joking, who would literally feel a sad person walk into a busy disco club. Impressive and I still regard him (he was a man, a gay man to be exact) as the person with the highest emotional intelligence I have ever met.

What is more, *you can improve and develop your emotional intelligence,* just like you can improve your memory and your rational intelligence.

Finally, though *the three elements are related, you do not need to have all three at the same level.* In my experience, it is hard to develop one to very high levels without having the other two at sound levels too...

Great artists can express themselves so well because they also understand feelings and they are intuitive, but maybe their intuition is less developed than their creativity... See what I mean?

Not everybody has good emotional intelligence, though. You may remember sociopaths and psychopaths. We met them when we talked about liars, big liars and manipulators in fact. These people, you may remember, have a very serious psychological condition, a pathological disease if you want: they do not understand that other people have feelings. They may "know" it, but they have no sense of *empathy.*

Right, in their case, their emotional intelligence is low or non-existent (there are, of course, different levels of sociopathy and psychopathy). So, one thing is sure... *Not having emotional intelligence or having a very low level is a serious pathology, a disease.* Actually, it is a disease that makes people dangerous for society.

## 9 SIGNS THAT YOU HAVE HIGH EMOTIONAL INTELLIGENCE

But how would you know if you have good, or even excellent emotional intelligence? We are about to find out. Again, take these signs as general guidelines, and each will have different levels, degrees, even development stages. And you do not need to have them all, nor all at the same level, to have good emotional intelligence.

One thing though: *people with good emotional intelligence are naturally good body language readers, and reading body language develops your emotional intelligence.* It's a virtuous cycle.

These are the 9 signs that tell you that you have good or even above average emotional intelligence.

### 1. You are easily moved

This is the most straightforward, telling and indisputable sign of emotional intelligence. Being "emotional" was once seen as an insult, as a flaw... and it still is for many people. However, if you watched *Schindler's List* and you were not moved, then your emotional intelligence needs improving. While your friend who starts sobbing even during a comedy – well, he or she has a very, very high level of emotional intelligence...

### 2. You identify easily and with people who are different from you

The ability to understand people who are not similar to us (in age, class, education, skin color, sexual orientation sex etc.) is a clear sign of emotional intelligence. Actually, when I say people, I mean also four-legged people, like dogs or cats... or six-legged people, like bees and ants...

Put quite simply, a very emotional intelligent person may even feel for the fly trapped on a windowpane. I know, many people would regard this as "silly". But that is a very emotionally intelligent person. At the same time, a person with low emotional intelligence may even find it hard to understand a puppy's eyes. Similarly, a person with low emotional intelligence may empathize only with similar people to him/her. An intelligent one will empathize with a wider range of people, if not all.

### 3. You are often unsure

Strange, isn't it? There's a myth that intelligent people always know everything... Not true. Even a rational person will need to doubt before s/he reaches a decision. Otherwise we would confuse arrogance and cockiness with intelligence. If to this, you add the fact that *you feel the impact of your opinions and choices on the world and others...* Then you will see why an emotionally intelligent person often has big moral dilemma and doubts.

If you are the one who sat at the back of the class waiting to give your answer, because you wanted to be 100% sure. If you did it even because you knew that a bad answer has emotional consequences (even for yourself), you likely have a high emotional intelligence. I would like to write a pedagogy book on how the school system actually represses emotional intelligent students, and you are having an insight right now…

## 4. You forgive and forget

It may sound counter-intuitive that sensitive people forget and forgive more, but all studies and statistics show they do. And by a measure. Psychopaths, on the other side of the scale, do not forgive. But that's because they see people as "objects to manipulate".

On the other hand, if you understand that you not forgiving someone makes that person suffer, you will try your best to put your feelings behind and make their life better.

## 5. You sometimes feel vulnerable and protect yourself

The relation between "feeling for others" and "feeling for yourself", the outside vs. inside world may well be one of the biggest leitmotifs of psychology as a whole. So, we can't go through it fully here.

But... it looks like feelings and emotions are what goes through this barrier quite freely... People who display a sense of care and love for others also often feel vulnerable themselves. People who don't care about other people's feelings also tend to underplay their own feelings. It's the macho thing, in simple words.

You can see yourself as a permeable membrane... You feel for others when they suffer but you are also easily permeated by feelings when others act in a way that affects you. Put simply, you feel sorry for people when something bad happens to them, but it also takes less for other people to make you feel bad.

Very sensitive people often (but not necessarily) show signs of shyness, embarrassment, and you will every now and then need that "time to yourself" or "away from all of it" ...

## 6. You are very susceptible to positive and negative

I know I am talking to an emotionally intelligent person because you thought, "But who isn't?" I read your mind again! (Only joking, of course!) The fact is that not everybody is severely affected by positivity and negativity. Some people are actually quite indifferent to it.

I'll reduce it to a very simple example… A beautiful color and an ugly one. People who are sensitive to the positivity or negativity of colors have high emotional intelligence. So, look around at what your office colleagues wear, and you'll find out that quite a few people are not *that* emotionally intelligent (it's a partial joke, but you get the point).

## 7. You have a complex relationship with criticism

This point is not as straightforward. What it means is that:

- *You give constructive criticism* (rather than using criticism for put downs). And this is easy to understand.
- *You can respond well to criticism.* But… you can also be offended by it. It all depends on whether it is *positive* and the way it is delivered. If someone criticizes you with malice, or with strong words, or in public, you may take badly to it.

## 8. You naturally mirror people's body language or language in general

We have talked about mirroring and we will get back to it in a few chapters. But it's like when someone sits one way, you too sit that way. When someone smiles, you smile back naturally. If someone speaks informally, you immediately switch into informal language...

These are all very strong signs of empathy and emotional intelligence. But this does not mean that you do it all the time... You will do it easily, but only with people you get on well with.

## 9. You have a good relationship with nature

Research shows that emotionally intelligent people appreciate nature at a very deep level. If you are one of those people who look at a sunset and you feel your heart swell... Then you are emotionally intelligent. If you feel at one with nature when you are in a park, you are emotionally intelligent...

Compare with people who only see nature as a resource... Do you worry if they cut down a forest to build factories or do you think, "Well, I can find another forest if I really need one for a picnic"?

I am sure that now you are starting to see why emotional intelligence is important to analyze body language but also how *it helps you project body language that makes you appear authentic and reliable.* "How," you may ask? Well, for this, you will have to wait a little bit... But not too long – promise!

# 14

# NEGATIVE PEOPLE: PROTECTING YOURSELF AGAINST DARK INFLUENCE AND MANIPULATION

B ecause you're emotionally intelligent, you'll be very sensitive to people with negative influence on you. You know, the person you have a gut feeling about? That colleague "your skin" tells you is bad news? That neighbor you have the impression has ulterior motives? But how about those your emotional radar does not detect?

I am not trying to scare you. Not everybody is out to get you. But there are negative influences and even "dark", hidden influences in your life. If you don't find them out early, they may develop into "toxic relationships" (there are other factors too for such relationships...)

What is more, clearing your social world (professional and personal) of negative people and influences will make you a happier person, a more successful person and a person with fewer problems. Finally, if you want to become an influencer, or a person who wants to lead others, this is a necessary step to start this path or career.

In a board of directors (or any place where decisions are made and there are many people, like parliaments, school boards etc.) negative people will tend to lead to in-fights and repression outside. Now you understand why so many countries have bad politics...

If you want to set up, for example, a YouTube channel, you need to have honest collaborators, people who work for *your good*, not against it.

We will soon move into developing your body language profession-ally, to use it in your job and even become an influencer or a public speaker. But if you have negative people around you, even trying to manipulate you, no matter how much you work, things won't go as you would like them to. So, first of all... Let's see how people influ-ence you negatively.

## HOW DOES DARK INFLUENCE AND MANIPULATION WORK?

If you think that we are going into "conspiracy theory" when we talk about hidden influences and manipulation... Really, these have been used, studied and even taught (especially at university) for decades, actually, for sure for more than a century.

You may remember Ivan Pavlov, the man who did those famous experiments with the bell and the dog? The founder of that psycho-logical school, known as *behaviorism?* Basically, you know that if you associate a sign with a positive stimulus, people sooner or later mix the two and at the sign they react as if they had the positive stimulus.

We're not that different from dogs! Pavlov's dog salivated when he heard the bell, because he associated it with food, even when there was no longer any food with it. People still smoke cigarettes many years after they realize that they don't look like James Dean... And why do vodka ads have to include some nudity? Nothing to do with Siberia, I guess... They associate two types of pleasures to do what? *To influence you into buying vodka.*

*The whole of marketing can be interpreted as manipulation.* So, you see, it has gone much further than we think. And there is a lot of body language in marketing... From the salesman shot from the waist up with a smile, facing the camera, wearing work or business clothes, a middle class haircut and the product in his hands (usually he was a man) to the celebrity witness, body language is used every day to tell you, "Buy this and buy that!" And most of us obediently comply...

If it works for television, it will work in face to face interaction – what do you reckon? And in fact, it does. Salespeople do it every day. If they were not good at that, they would not have a career... Politicians of course do it all the time too... But there may also be your "friend" and your "colleague" among them.

So, what are the key principles of manipulation?

We have already seen one:

# 1. Repetition

Why are ads repeated over and over again? They become even unbearable at times. But they don't care, do they? No, because the more you repeat a message, the more it sounds true. This is actually a manipulation of what we think is reality.

What's the best pasta brand? What's the best whiskey? The best milk? Water? Most of us will have a "clear" idea about these questions. But it's not even "their idea" and it is not "clear", rather it is "stubborn" ...

This happens also at a personal level. *People who manipulate you will repeat the same message over and over again.* And by "message" I don't only mean "verbal message". The Don Giovanni who steals hearts to "use women for a night" will do it with a very attractive body language, with many nonverbal signals with a clear message. One will not do the trick, and patience is, of course, one of their great qualities!

## 2. False personality

You see I remember everything? There was a very famous case among secret agents. The CIA was after a spy... But you know, double agents learn how to act, literally. They change the way they talk, walk, their body language and true, sometimes even use disguises... But this one was very good...

One day though, a CIA agent saw a little clip of him, and he was carrying a bunch of flowers... They arrested him, and on arrest, he said, "It was the flowers, wasn't it?" Do you know what happened? He bought a bunch of flowers and carried it with the flower heads down... Simple, we usually hold them up in the West... In fact, he was from Eastern Europe....

This is an extreme case, but it shows you how deceit and manipulation works. Good manipulators put on shows, create characters, and they make sure that they are credible. Don't get me wrong, these are skills one can learn consciously (like for double agents) or not... Some of them just find it natural to "change mask" ... In a way, we do it every day as well. You don't have the same personality with your partner and with your bank manager, do you? They see it as an extension of this normal behavior. But while we do it just for social norms and to a limited extent, they do it to manipulate and very often at very high levels.

## 3. Thomas's Theorem

This is a sociological theorem, and it is used by manipulators... The fact is that *a manipulator wants you to act upon a stimulus*. He or she wants *you* to buy that rusting car... They want *you* to help them with their career etc.... So, they need to *convince you to do something*.

And here Thomas's Theorem comes in handy. It says, "If men define situations as real, they are real in their consequences". Basically, you *only need to believe that something is real to react to it with real actions*. You only need to "think you need a new smartphone" to buy one. You don't actually have to need it for real...

You see this is at the core of advertisement but also of manipulation. So, *manipulators will convince you that you need to do something*.

They will need to *convince you of an untruth*, therefore. Or at least they would need to *overstate a problem to get the answer to it that they want from you*.

## 4. Reverse psychology

The idea of reverse psychology is to pretend to want something, knowing that the person who needs to act will do the opposite of what you want. So, if you convince them that you want the opposite of what you actually do, you end up getting the person to do what you wanted in the first place.

Yes, it sounds like one of those speeches Sir Nigel Hawthorne gave as Sir Humphrey Appleby in *Yes Minister* and *Yes Prime Minister.* In fact, the character is Machiavellian. And by Machiavellian, we mean people who will stop at nothing, including lying and cheating but, above all, manipulating others in order to achieve their goals.

## 5. Seeing people as "objects"

If you want to manipulate a person, you need to treat that person as an object, as "instrumental to your aims". Politicians treat whole sectors of society as such, very often. And here we come to some old "friends": sociopaths and psychopaths.

These people are manipulators like few others. In fact, very sadly, sociopaths and psychopaths often make amazing careers in business and politics. For them, you are like a washing machine, something to use till you are useful. Then throw away.

These people and manipulators do not see you for your intrinsic, emotional or social value... No, they see you as an "investment". Even when your friend, who actually does see you as a human being, uses you for something, at least in that situation, she or he has seen you as an object. And this is why we then "feel used".

## 6. They move you by degrees

Do you remember that famous evil manipulator, Iago, in Shakespeare's *Othello?* He's the primary example of how a manipulator works. And he follows all our steps. He pretends to be a friend of the Moor, he uses reverse psychology, he repeats his lies etc.... But he also moves Othello's mind step by step...

Manipulators move your position on a topic by dint of little, almost imperceptible shifts. This way, once you realize you have "moved to the dark side" it is too late, if you realize it at all. Many psychological and sociological studies about how Nazism came along show that people did not even realize that they were changing their position and embracing outright evil.

So, if you hate video games on a matter of principle and they want you to buy their own brand... Well, they will slowly move you into "not being that disgusted by video games", and "maybe not all are bad", and "some actually have some good features", then "even if I try one I will not like it," but "I will try one", to "it's not my cup of tea but it was better than I thought" and then with a few more steps you will wake up in the morning saying, "I can't do without you" as if you were a chain smoker...

## 7. Time!

As a consequence, manipulation takes some time in many cases. People who want to manipulate you, first of all will need easy access to you. Then they will need constant access, and time, of course.

## DEVELOPING A DISCERNING EYE

Most of us have been fooled, conned, grifted and cheated upon in life. Now, you have seen how manipulators act. It's a very unpleasant topic, but you should look on the bright side, actually on the bright sides:

- You now know how they work.
- You know about body language, and this will help you spot them.
- You are going to learn how to keep them at a distance.

And there is more... Maybe your best tool to spot a manipulator is your emotional intelligence. You must have had that friend who "always knows from the start if a person is trustworthy or not"? Well, that friend, if s/he is right, has a very good emotional intelligence.

And of course, you need to look out for clues, and develop a discerning eye:

- *Look out for differences in the way the person behaves to you and others.* It is amazing how people sometimes are blind. They think the boss who butters them up but is horrible to others is doing it because the boss likes them? Keep dreaming.... They are just being used.
- *Look out for unnatural, contrived behavior.*
- *Look out for excessive kindness.* By this I mean excessive according to the person, your relationship with the person, the culture and of course, the situation. The man who

screams about how great your average shoes are has something else in mind, most likely.

- *Look out for sudden changes of behavior (and body language) when he spots you.* For example, if you walk into the room, or if s/he suddenly sees you etc.
- *Look out for insistent behavior.*

## 5 WAYS TO PROTECT YOURSELF

So, what can you actually do to protect yourself from toxic and manipulative people? Here are a few tips for you!

### 1. Control your emotional involvement

This is very difficult, especially in personal relationships. But even there, as soon as you start realizing that a "friend" is using you, *start a journey of emotional distancing.* Start coming to terms with the idea that you may not be friends much longer… Start going out with other friends. Start "filling in the emotional gap" that your breakup will cause.

For colleagues and people you work or deal with, this is easier. However, emotionally intelligent people will still suffer quite a lot. There are people who do not get emotionally involved with colleagues, for example. That may be necessary sometimes, especially if you work in a very unpleasant and competitive place. That's where manipulators concentrate.

### 2. Do not try to change them

In most cases, these people will not change for you. Do not get taken by the "good Samaritan" calling to save a person who is using you. To start with, the risk is that they will work out that you are trying to change them, and they will use it as an excuse to keep close to you and manipulate you even further.

Sociopaths and psychopaths especially will. And they will even think you stupid for wanting to help them...

## 3. Do not confront them face to face

That would be a waste of time in many cases. Furthermore, after denying the whole story, some may want to take revenge on you. Remember, not everybody has your moral compass, and if you have stumbled upon a dangerous person (again our antiheroes, psychopaths and sociopaths) the fact that you know about them will be seen as a threat by them! And they may want to render you harmless, maybe by discrediting you with others, lying about you etc.

## 4. Push them away slowly but steadily

Invent some excuses as to why you are not acting upon their trigger, so, why you are (no longer) falling for their trap... Then, little by little, cut off all meetings, all contact and all communication.

The more carefully you do this, the less s/he will realize what is happening and try to counter your move. Not only, but the less s/he will take offense, and as you know, these can be vicious people sometimes.

## 5. Go slow with relationships

There are friends you will trust with your life... How long have you known them for? A decade? Two? Five? The fact is that because we have good friends, we may be fooled into thinking that another person who, for some traits, reminds us of them is as trustworthy...

Instead, it may be a chance or, if you have met an experienced professional grifter, like those who marry rich partners to then steal their property, that person is actually imitating your friends' body language, personality, language, style etc. to gain your confidence.

Go slow and go safe. This is by far your best defense against manipulators.

## KNOW WHO YOU ARE FACING AGAINST

Once you realize that there is something "fishy" about someone, start working out:

- Their real personality (key and hidden traits, like greed, envy, careerism)
- Their motives, their aims
- Their tactic and strategy.

Try also to assess *the gravity of the situation.* I mean, it can literally go from a dishonest shopkeeper to someone who wants to marry you to then bankrupt you... In your business life, it can go from a person who just wants a small advantage to the one who has decoded to end your career.

Beware, again, of sociopaths and psychopaths. Do throw in the "empathy test" like telling him or her that you are not comfortable with something. Do it even more than once… But if you get the idea that they don't feel anything. Steer away from them as fast as possible. And remember, they are not good at faking empathic feelings because they don't actually know what they are…

## SPOTTING A PERSON WITH CONDESCENDING ATTITUDE

Very often, manipulators and toxic people are condescending towards their victims. I'm just watching an impressive six-part docu-film on Totò Riina, the most horrible mafia boss in history. I am amazed at how condescending he was, and he showed it, as a way of showing his power…

Here are some body language signs that the person has a conde-scending attitude you can group into a cluster to help you:

- *Chin upward and forehead moved backwards.* This is a very typical sign, so much so that it may even be voluntary.
- *Chin thrust.* This is when the person thrusts his or her chin forward. It is a sign of lack of respect for you, lack of consideration.
- *Sideway glance.* Looking at you from a three quarters position with the corner of their eyes, they are showing you that they do not trust you and they look down on you.
- *Literally looking down on you.* Lifting the head or moving

it backwards to look down on you is another sign of condescension.

- *Nostril stretch and sneer.* Making a sneer with the mouth so that the nostrils are stretched out is a sign of disgust and condescension.

Sometimes, they may try to hide them, so, look for these with great care.

## RECOGNIZE THE BODY LANGUAGE OF AGGRESSIVE BEHAVIOR

Things may get bad and out of hand, and you may end up being threatened, not only physically. Many bosses use threatening body language just as a way of establishing their power. Some politicians do too.

What is more, people who are trying to manipulate you or harm you may, every now and then, show signs of aggression which they do not notice or control. In the end, manipulation and aggression share many traits, and are even the same thing from some points of view. They are a way of using others, in both cases the victim is seen as inferior and even dehumanized etc.

So, here is what you need to look out for. Again, see them as a cluster.

- *Chest pushed outward towards you.* This, at all levels, is an aggressive sign.

- *Shoulders out.* Especially if visible, they may be a threatening position.
- *Belly out.* This too, unless the person has eaten far too many beans, may mean that the person has negative intentions or a negative attitude towards you.
- *Fists and stiff arms.* That's what boxers do before they start punching, so, not a nice sign from someone who is in front of you.
- *Mouth tips visibly turned down.* That is a sign of displeasure, but it can also show anger. in fact, ...
- *All signs of anger and condescension* we have already seen.

Phew! This was a hard chapter in many ways. I know and I understand you. It is never nice to talk about negative things, and especially people. But we had to do it and I thank you for getting through it.

As they say, "bad things happen" (okay, they use another word!) What we can do is be prepared for them and move on... and, talking about moving on... Next we will talk about how you can use body language to become the person you want to be... Something very positive indeed!

# 15

# BECOME AN INFLUENCER

D o you want to run your own vlog or podcast? Or maybe you actually want (or need) to become a public speaker? Maybe you have a political career in mind? Or perhaps you are a teacher and you want to improve your presentation skills? And what's a manager giving a presentation in front of a board if not an influencer in suit and tie (metaphorically, especially if you are a woman...).

All these "activities" and "roles" rather than necessarily jobs, are *influencers*. You see, in life, even in most jobs, we switch from *influenced to influencer* regularly. A teacher is an influencer in class but not necessarily when talking to colleagues. This is why we should see it more like a role than a job.

Having said this, there are now famous professional influencers. Social media have made it possible for many people to launch their own channels, and they all need to use their body language correctly, even professionally, to become one.

## HOW CONFIDENT ARE YOU?

Confidence comes back again and again in this book. We have seen how you can develop your confidence, and here we want to step back for a second and look at this topic again.

What we want to assess here is how "naturally" confident you are. Naturally is not really correct (nature vs. nurture again!) What we mean is *what is your baseline confidence level*, because more than natural reasons, what makes people confident or not are social and personal experiences (nurture). We do not have a "confidence gene" ...

This means a lot, as you may understand. But it does not mean that you can or cannot be an influencer. If for example your answer to this question is, "I am very, very confident," you may think that you can start working as an influencer straight away. But it may not be very wise! On the other hand, if your answer was, "I am not confident at all," you may even think you are not cut out for this role, while I would suggest that you start straight away!

No, you have not stepped into a parallel dimension! The fact is that people who are sure about their confidence may fall into three categories:

- Those who think they are more confident than what they really are.
- Those who are so confident that they appear arrogant.

- Those who actually are confident.

It is quite hard to assess one's own confidence. A dictator would say that he (most times, but theoretically she) is very confident. In reality most psychological analyses of dictators show that they have major psychological problems and they confuse arrogance with confidence (which often they lack!)

I am not saying that you could be a tyrant... But many bosses fall into this category. And they think they are confident, but to you, they appear as "bossy" or even "bullish".

The risk for people with this tendency, once they become influencers, is that their "cocky" and arrogant side comes out more visibly. How many famous people, especially journalists, commentators etc. start off as "confident and competent" and after a few years on TV they are outright arrogant and insufferable? I won't mention names because I don't fancy being sued, but I am sure you have plenty examples of this.

*If you already are very confident, you need to avoid the "confidence back feed" you get from being an influencer.* Do *you* remember Pavlov and the dog with the bell? Well, getting positive rewards and feedback for being an influencer can really affect your ego... you get used to it and then you take for granted that people owe it to you. Like the dog with the bell and food, you will expect the food (metaphorically) every time you hear the bell (post your vlog, make a speech etc.) ... And that very expectation of recognition is arrogance.

If you fall into the second category, you risk being very disappointed and even "wounded" if things go wrong. You need to understand that "losing face" in front of people is much harder than most people think. There are famous politicians who think they are confident just because they are on a winning streak, but as soon as they get criticized, they take it personally, badly, and even reject the criticism… That's no sign of confidence…

Keep in mind that if you have a vlog and something goes bad, you will have people annoying you for a long time, potentially forever. If you are an actor and you get heckled or booed in public, it will stick with you far longer than the end of the show. It will even be difficult to go back onto the stage. If your boss puts you down after a presentation with your colleagues, you will have to work with them after that.

And how about if you are not confident? That's a reason more to start practicing!

In all cases, what you need to do is *start small! Start on a small scale, with a small audience and build from there.* Whether you are confident or not, you will have a chance to correct yourself. *Keep modest if you are very confident and boost your confidence if you are not as you go along.*

What is more, *start with a friendly audience.* Even if you want to just run a vlog, start circulating it among friends, maybe, or on a small and friendly platform…

Finally, *take criticism constructively.* Your best friend is a *critical friend* who tells you honestly what you need to hear… People who surround themselves with yes-men sooner or later find at their own expenses that stroking their ego was not a replacement from doing a good job.

And what about your body language? *What is the "right" body language for an influencer?*

Hold on, we need a whole section on this…

## THE CORRECT BODY LANGUAGE FOR AN INFLUENCER

You know the question. Now the answer: *it depends!* Disappointed? Maybe but you know we are going to find out… What does it depend on?

- *The topic*
- *The audience*
- *The format*
- *Your persona.*

You will want to look *confident, competent and in control all the time.* For all these variables… But in different ways.

Now, make a little film in your mind (a mind experiment like those Einstein used) … Faduma wants to become a businesswoman and she decides to run an online vlog on "how to run a business". What will her body language look like? Jot down a few ideas (even mentally).

On the other hand, Sam too wants to run an online vlog, but the topic is hip hop music… Fine, now, what will Sam's body language look like?

You see, even with the same format, the different topic calls for different accents, levels of formality, typical gestures etc.…

The audience is often strictly related to the topic. You may expect Faduma's audience to expect a more "canonical, institutional and contained, mainstream" type of body language than Sam's.

Similarly, nowadays there are many online influencers who specialize in wellbeing, spirituality and self-help. You will expect them to project calm, health, peace, serenity etc.… More akin to the Dalai Lama than a car salesman or a politician (don't correct me; I know the Dalai Lama is also a politician, but not your typical one…).

Here too, *try to put yourself in your audience's shoes...* What would you expect? What would you find "grating" and out of place? Try to match your viewer's expectations.

But this is not the whole story… Now, Faduma is making her vlog for university students and young entrepreneurs. That means that her body language can afford some informality and friendliness. But now, Faduma has been asked to present the exact same topic of one of her vlogs in front of a board of an important international corporation. Do you think she should change her body language?

I would think so. Most boards are run by older people to start with. They are also fully focused on the topic, and they don't need anything to keep them engaged. They also tend to be very formal, and in many cases, even very aware of their social position…

*Once you have achieved the right formula with topic, audience and format, you can add some traits that set you apart from others, and make stand out, but without looking out of place.*

You would look very silly if an estate agent opened a speech or video with the "Latin kings" sign (the horns with the fingers rappers do) ... That is extreme, but it shows the point...

On the other hand, to make sure you are recognizable, and you stand out, use:

- *Signature signs.* These are signs that people use to start or finish a speech or video etc. They are used by viewers to *identify the influencer or speaker.* Look at professional influencers and they all have one... it can be a wink, a sign with the hand, a small gesture... But it is always the same, accompanied by the same words (greetings) and moderate but clear.
- *Cultural signs.* These may refer to your culture, if you wish to project it, but also the culture related to your topic. For example, many healers and spiritual guides online use the "namaste" sign quite often (hands with palms together, like praying). That immediately tells the audience, "We have the same cultural background, we believe in the same things."
- *Personality signs.* These may be small personal identifiers that you scatter through your performance, rather than at the beginning or the end... Again, these should be moderate and in harmony with the topic and your personality.

## INFLUENCER'S MOVEMENTS

Take a topic you are really passionate about. Get your smartphone out, and improvise a speech about it. Now watch it... I bet the first thing you notice is that you keep moving...

We move spontaneously when we speak, and the more we are engrossed in the subject, the more we move. Unfortunately, this works at times, but it will not work most times. The odd politician who shows great passion may stand something to gain. If it becomes a regular habit, that politician may end up looking deranged (like Hitler, Mussolini etc....).

This, to be honest, has its trends too. Recently, we have seen a trend in favor of politicians looking "engrossed" at the same time as we have seen a radicalization of politics. The two things go together, and politicians most often fake being engrossed in the topic when they shout and scream and beat their fist in the table... It's a show.

This is also very tiring for the audience and after a few years we go back to more "boring" body language from politicians, who nevertheless look more in control and tire the audience less. It is physically and emotionally demanding to watch an agitated person who keeps moving.

So, back to your video... One of the key things to learn especially when videoing (but also on stage) is to *keep still in front of the camera*. That does not mean completely still, or you would become boring. But:

- *Try not to move your chest.*
- *Try not to touch your face* (it's not a problem of looking dishonest, though some viewers may even see it as that, do it and watch it: it just is annoying).
- *Try not to move your head too much and especially not up and down.*
- *Focus movement in your eyes, hands and arms, and keep it slow and contained.*
- *Try not to move parts of your body (hands etc.) out of shot.*

As you can see, there are quite strict rules when you want to make a video and you also want to be taken as a professional influencer. Look at all the famous ones and check it out: they all follow these rules.

You will be relatively freer at a live event. But if you are being videoed, then again, you will have to *play to the camera and not to the live audience.*

## CLOSE OR TOO CLOSE?

How close should you stand to the camera or your audience? It's an important point, very often neglected or underestimated... To start with, we need to understand the concept of *distance.*

*Physical distance also indicates interpersonal and social distance.*

You will see pop stars who get away with amazing close ups. But the relationship between a music star and their audience is incredibly intimate. They really have a love bond with their audience, who knows everything about them, feel they are friends and even family members. That's why it works for them. Similarly, your aunt or sister may send you a video with a "big face" and that would be okay.

Now, imagine being on a video conference with your boss and colleagues and they had the same "big face" as your sister's... No way! You would feel embarrassed, too intimate, uncomfortable.

So, we go back to our proximity zones, intimate, personal, social and public... *The distance from the viewer, spectator or camera will depend on the relationship you have with them.* In most cases, even with a camera (I am really thinking about your vlog), keep a *social distance.* That, as you know, is between 3 to 10 feet approximately.

In a monitor, you should aim that when you see your face, on a landscape image is between 2/3 and 1/3 of the height of the frame. Even there, look at the huge difference there is between a face that takes up 2/3 of this height (quite intimate, string eye contact, high emotional impact) and one that takes up only 1/3 (more impartial, respectful if you want, and detached).

This too will depend on what sort of podcast or speech you want to give. Even HM the Queen has different shots in her New Year Speech (to mention an old friend...) Very often, the camera starts from a distance and zooms in when there is an emotional touch. A closer face has a stronger emotional impact.

So, even Her Majesty's cameraman seems to follow our rule.

## BODY LANGUAGE TIPS FOR INFLUENCERS

For an influencer, body language is an essential skill. Few people have actually made it in the public sphere without good body language abilities. Some, maybe extremely talented scientists or artists, buck the trend. But they are few and they do have exceptional skills in other areas. For most people, even with very good skills in their "trade", body language is a determining factor of success.

You are now learning how to use your body language skills. And we have seen some important principles. Now, it's time to "hone your skills" with some practical tips... Here they are!

## 1. Always get a "third person opinion"

You never actually fully appreciate how you "appear to others". Especially at first, get a friend to check on how you appear live, how your speech sounds and looks, or how your video impacts the viewer.

Actually, real professionals will do it even when they are at the top of their career, like singers take singing lessons even when they are at the top of the charts... If you know someone with some experience in "the trade", treasure their opinion. I am talking about actors, directors, drama teachers, public speakers, media experts, photographers, camera operators and the like.

## 2. Develop slowly

You will need to build your repertoire of body language slowly. But even once you are professional and established, *keep developing and improving your body language, but do it step by step and slowly.* A "sudden change of character" may strike your audience as odd, unfamiliar, even suspect... Don't risk it!

## 3. Learn from experts

Keep watching and observing other people in your field and influencers in general. *Read and analyze their body language.*

*Experiment by mirroring and incorporating some of their body language into yours.* Before you actually "make it public" and use it in a speech or vlog, please:

- Check with a friend if it works.
- Make sure it fits in with your persona, theme, topic, audience etc.
- Only use it once you feel you have "made it yours". It's like driving a car, you need to feel it is natural before you can drive one.

## 4. Be ready to change

Developing your body language does not just mean "adding signs"; it also means "eliminating signs". In the end, you never know how your audience is going to respond to signs... Even signs you think are great may end up being a total flop. Don't take it personally and get rid of them if necessary.

## 5. Never make the step longer than the leg

This is an Italian saying, which means that you can only bring changes that are well within your abilities... Remember when Theresa May, the former UK Prime Minister tried to look young and trendy, to give herself an image make up by dancing while walking on stage?

Why was it a disaster? Because she is not a very "smooth dancer"? Yes, that too. And a politician is not usually seen as the person you would dance with… So, she pushed it too far and did not have the skills to do it. Let's learn from other people's mistakes…

## 6. Use your mirror

We said that your mirror is your best friend. So, use it! Even if it will never give you the eyes of a viewer, even if it will never be the same as the camera, rehearsing in front of the mirror is excellent practice.

It will give you an immediate feedback loop from you do to what you see. This way, you can correct yourself immediately, without the risk of naturalizing, or internalizing a sign, a gesture, or a move, which would then make it difficult for you to correct it.

## 7. Strike a balance between rehearsal and spontaneity

However, sometimes we look at a speech, a video, a presentation and we say, "It does not sound real." On the surface, however, it looks "perfect". So, what is it that strikes as "perfect but not real"? It's the lack of spontaneity.

The sales agent that repeats the rigmarole to perfection, even with the right gestures, but fails to look like it's the first-time s/he has ever said this has few chances of getting your interest – let alone your money!

In a way, there is a big concept from the theatre we need to keep in mind here: *no matter how much you rehearse a play, you need to remember that each performance is a unique event in time!* It's not like re-playing a movie. It's a here and now event, with its own presence and you need to make your audience feel they are witnessing a unique event.

Don't worry if you will use it almost exactly the same tomorrow… as long as they "feel" you were not just repeating words…

And so, you see that body language is central to the role of influencers, but that what matters is that you build your own personal style, that fits your field, your medium and, of course, your audience.

But how about if your vlog or speech is meant to be seen in the UK rather than the USA? Or how about if you are doing a video for your Japanese customers? How would you need to change your body language?

# 16

# CULTURAL DIFFERENCES IN BODY LANGUAGE

Let's take a coffee on a terrace in the Sorrento Gulf, near Naples, Italy... Wonderful scenery, amazing sea and impressive sunlight. The food is great, and the people gesticulate like they are putting on a show! Quick flight to London, not that far, and we go to a tearoom... There, you will see, the Sun – well, it's gone – the furniture is lovely, but people seem to be hiding all their gestures. Actually, the more you look like a marble statue, the more you fit in.

Yes, you guessed right! We are back to the nature vs. nurture leitmotif... Cultural differences (nurture) can really affect body language, to the point that you can recognize a person's nationality but not only (also class etc.) from the way s/he moves, gesticulates, stands, underlines what s/he says etc.

Keeping in mind your possible aspirations as an influencer, the *culture your audience mainly identifies with is also important to develop your body language.*

Similarly, if you ever happen to have a job where you need to deal with people from all over the world, you will need to be aware of gestures and body language that is (and, above all, is not) appropriate. This does not just include international negotiators and salespeople, even TEFL teachers will need that, or maybe if you decide to go traveling and you want to fit in…

## IS IT APPROPRIATE?

We have seen that there are things that look "normal" in a county and may get you fired in another, for example putting your feet on the table (okay in the USA, not in other places). But there are also smaller signs that may not put your whole job at risk, but they may "give the wrong impression" especially subconsciously. And you know what that means…

To start with, let's state a general rule:

*Less is more when it comes to body language and different cultures.*

What do we mean by this? Especially if you are on a business trip (or similar) the idea is to "level your body language to a minimum" to avoid misunderstanding. Every unusual gesture would stick out like a sore thumb.

This, of course, does not mean that you should become a robot, that would make you appear boring, artificial and even give the impression that you are hiding something. However, try to reduce the size and frequency of your gestures.

### Keep within your intimate zone

This is quite limited, but look for example at a Japanese businessperson... They will take up as little space as possible, keep their hands and arms to their sides as much as possible; they will sit upright and avoid stretching their legs out...

Asian people are very much aware of other people's spaces. This is due to a culture that values the "awareness of the other", and it does it much more than most western cultures. There is also an awareness that "space is shared". That's why they can live in small (but very tidy) spaces compared to Western people... But this also means that *taking up excessive space is regarded as utterly rude, inconsiderate and bad manners.*

If you are having a meeting with people from all over the world, *use the minimum denominator*: small gestures, little space taken etc. as a form of respect for everybody.

Looking at body language at these meetings will also show you how it is going once you get experienced with these things.

### Be adaptable

Having said this, we need to look at the other side of the coin. *A stiff and very restrained body language can be taken as "untrustworthy" in some cultures, for example Mediterranean ones (including South America).*

Spanish, Italian, Portuguese cultures as well as many African cultures have a very expansive form of body language. Contact is common even with strangers, they easily go beyond the intimate zone, actually they tend to move almost freely into the social zone. Their gestures are more accentuated, and they welcome creative and unusual body language.

So, if you are dealing with people from these cultures, you may wish to be a bit more relaxed with your body language, however…

### *Do use mirroring but don't turn it into mocking*

Mirroring, as you well know, is a key body language technique. But be careful... Use it in moderation and if you feel comfortable with it, or the result may be counterproductive.

Imagine if you kept bowing (as some Asian people do) at a meeting... On the one hand, it may be taken as a form of respect, on the other it may look like you are making fun of them. You see, you can *show respect for their culture, but you cannot appropriate it and you need to show respect for it with your body language. Remember that it is not your culture; it is theirs.*

### *Don't use signs and gestures you don't know the meaning of*

They say that the Italian dictionary is in two volumes: one for words and a bigger one for gestures... It makes them very interesting for body language analysts, and you may feel very drawn to it. However, keep in mind that these many gestures have a very wide range of meaning, and some are downright rude and negative – actually, quite a lot of them.

Passing your fingers under your chin, stroking it with the tips of your fingers outwards, for example, looks innocent enough, does it? Unfortunately, it means "I don't care about what you are saying," and you can add an expletive after "care" to make the meaning properly correct...

### *Careful with feet*

Feet are so important to body language, for many reasons:

- We are not very much aware of them.
- They have a strong connection with the ground, with the soil.
- They have strong cultural implications.
- They are often seen as unpleasant, and their use can be rude.

For example, in many Asian countries (Philippines, for example), showing the soles of your feet is at any time absolutely rude.

In some countries, however, like Arabic countries, people point with their feet, not their hands.

In some countries you need to take your shoes off indoors. This happens in most Asian countries but also Scandinavian ones. In other countries, like in Spain, taking off your shoes even indoors is rude... Keeping them on in Japan is rude...

So... Know what is expected of you. And the habit of taking shoes off indoors is spreading in many Western countries, but especially among "non-conventional" people, like liberal minded nature lovers etc.

Avoid touching people with your feet.

Avoid raising your feet above the knee. That is like a "borderline" of decency in many places.

In countries like India, feet are regarded as dirty, and touching the feet of the elders is a sign of respect, on the other hand.

In business situations, it is usually wise to avoid bringing attention to your feet.

On the other hand, a pop band will sit on the sofa with feet clearly in sight; that is informality, it makes them look at ease and "with friends" and it also draws attention to their sneakers, which, as you know are a cultural identifier.

There is a level of relativity in everything, including in body language and how you use it in different cultures.

## What Do We Mean by "Culture"?

So far, we have mainly looked at cultures along one of its most common, easily understood and important determinants: origin, nationality, regional belonging… But culture moves along many lines:

- *Origin*
- *Age,* the cultural distance between generations reflects in body language too.
- *Education,* in fact, even within the same town the educational divide can be very marked.
- *Ethnicity,* which, in terms of body language, can mean different idioms altogether.
- *Cultural affiliation,* by which we mean every cultural variant, from what type of music you like to your political, religious, spiritual and ideological inclination.

All these are factors that you need to take into consideration, in all circumstances, and, in particular, if you are trying to close an international business deal.

## SUCCESSFUL INTERNATIONAL BUSINESS DEAL

International business deals, like deals between states, are a master-piece of body language skills deployment. Look at the official photograph of an international deal between countries and you will realize how staged to the least detail they are. Where people stand or sit, who is on the right and who on the left, the handshake etc.... All is decided to give a precise signal.

On this point, for example, you will know that in the handshake, the man in the right always has the "upper hand" (yes, it's a pun) ... They look more powerful because you can see the back of their hand in the photograph, while if you are on the left, your hand disappears behind the other person's, and you look less important... What is more, the person on the right shows the outside of her or his arm, the strong part, the one on the left shows the soft inside of his or her arm, the vulnerable part...

This is just to show you that it's a delicate business when we talk about international deals. Now, for example, at a business deal with Asian people, should you shake hands or bow?

This has changed over the years, as the position of Asia has changed. Especially when you are in Asia, nowadays the accepted protocol is to use both. Once upon a time, when the West was very dominant and the language of business was mainly US-UK centered, so was its body language. Nowadays, however, Asian economy is becoming more and more important and even business transactions are changing face, flavor, style...

US business style is fairly informal, and, in some cases, showing some arrogance is even encouraged. That is unacceptable in most countries all over the world and especially in Asia. It does not matter what kind of deal you are working on, if it is fair to both, if you are "shredding the competitor to bits" or on the losing side...

In international business deals there is *a very strong sense of formality. It's as if the behavioral rules were always the same. It's like a ceremony, with steps set out in advance that you will follow whatever the deal turns out to be...*

Hand shaking is usually ritualized; it will happen at the beginning, as a greeting, on agreeing the deal (that is actually a "let's shake hands on this") and it will also happen at the end, on parting, as a sign of friendship and a promise to keep the deal.

But this is not all... There is a very rigid sense of hierarchy and relative standing in these meetings. The most "powerful" person is the first to give the hand for shaking (in fact, with people like the Queen or the Pope, it is actually rude to initiate the handshake).

If you are meeting a senior businessperson and you give your hand first, you will look very ambitious, determined, and even careerist... To some people, this may even be a plus, but for most businesspeople that would usually strike as an affront, an insult to their senior position.

Similarly, seating is also very formalized; always wait for the host to indicate that you can sit down, and always try to sit down after the more senior people are present.

If there are Asians, do keep in mind that *seniority is extremely important for Asian people, and this includes age seniority.* Sitting down before a person who is older than you is a huge challenge to their seniority, while you are expected to bow first and lower. That can make the whole difference between a successful deal and a total disaster.

Sex can be a major issue in international deals... *In many countries, women are yet not considered equals to men.* This means that for women it is much harder to find a place around important international business tables and that even if they do, they will have stronger opposition, problems with prejudice etc. Their body language is very often scrutinized, so they need to be very good and careful indeed.

Apart from the general rules and setting of international business deals there are many things you need to be very aware of.

To start with *never show any signs of being nervous, restless or bored.* There is no tapping your foot, clicking your pen and fidgeting with your papers if you want to strike a good deal...

The "watching the time" gesture is really dangerous too. It is a sign that you want to get out of there, or that you are in a hurry. True, it is allowed, but only if done by the "chair", or the person who needs to call the meeting to a close. If anyone else does it, it may really give the wrong signals...

You also have to *avoid any signs of aggression or arrogance.* Leave Hollywood movies with cocky businessmen or women on the DVD shelf... They don't represent reality. Dealing with other businesspeople means trying to get the best out of them. They have something to offer to you, otherwise you would not be there. So, *respect is the key word.*

*Nodding is generally seen as an agreement sign.* You will have seen foreign secretaries and even presidents nod when a foreign politician was talking – in their own language... Of course, they didn't understand a word of what was being said... still, their nodding was taken the way it was meant to: as a general sign of agreement, more like a bonding sign than a commentary on the point.

So, do nod regularly, even if you don't understand what they are saying. But regularly does not mean all the time, or you will end up making a fool of yourself. *Try to understand when the person is making a point and nod.* Again, keep everything underplayed: a small nod, just a hint at a nod, not like at a heavy metal concert!

Finally, and above all, *never shy away from eye contact.* In fact, try to keep your eyes up, avoiding looking down (apart from checking on your notes). Let your eyes move around the room or place but keep them at the other people's eye level (roughly). Looking down can be taken as a sign of defeat, or a sign that you are in trouble. Looking up may give the impression you want to get out of there. Looking back, too, is a sign that you expect something different or something to happen or that you are seeking help.

Try to be ready to engage in eye contact and absolutely try to disengage at the same time as the other person. Interrupting it too early is a sign of lack of confidence and even dishonesty, staring at a person's eyes after s/he has moved away can be a challenge, appear insistent and even aggressive.

So, working on an international business deal is a matter of fine and delicate balance. You will really need to use all your body language skills to walk away successful. And now, to be honest, you are quite an expert of body language. But the good learner is the one who knows how to better himself or herself, and that's why the last chapter of this book is meant to help you become an independent and always improving body language reader and user...

# 17

# APPLYING WHAT YOU LEARN

L ook back at the journey we have made together... You have learned so much! From the basic principles of body language to shaping and developing your own body language, even at professional level...

But as you know, we never stop learning. In truth, people who become passionate about a topic keep studying it, updating their knowledge and becoming more and more professional well after their formal studies are over. And, who knows, new things may come to light even in our field...

So, this is not the end of your journey. But my duty is to make sure that you keep learning, that you keep developing your skills and that, from now on, you can do it independently.

*The key principle of personal and professional growth is that you apply your skills, and even experiment them, in different areas of your life:*

- *Everyday life*
- *Relationships*
- *Public speaking*
- *Work*
- *Negotiations.*

So, off we go!

## EVERYDAY LIFE

You will have noticed that all our exercises only take up a few minutes and you can do them even when you are shopping, during normal everyday activities. There is a reason for this. Actually, there are many... To start with, we are all busy, and few of us have whole hours to dedicate to our self-development. Next, it is easier to learn something by small but regular efforts. Small mistakes also have more manageable consequences. Finally, it is by getting confident with the subject that you learn it best, so, by using it in your everyday life.

*Keep using your body language reading skills on the bus, when you go shopping, when you are at work etc....* That practice is so essential to your development that it's like breathing or drinking water for us.

*Find readings on the topic.* It is fairly popular, which means that you can find articles online etc. However, in many cases these are not professional articles. A quick online search has brought up more urban myths than truths. But… There are professionals (and I will give you a reading list). To start with, doubt anyone who tells you "this sign always means this" … Follow the core principles in this book and you will find it easy to tell a charlatan from a professional body language reader.

Make sure you use reliable magazines but above all, *watch body language readers in action.* These are always very insightful and great source of knowledge and information.

*Set aside a few minutes every day to study and improve your body language.* And give yourself breaks. Maybe five days out of seven, or even three would be fine. When? Find one of those blind spots we all have in our lives, those useless times like going to work, time spent in the bathroom, waiting for the bus etc.…

*Keep in mind that your body language must primarily suit you.* Don't give in to pleasing others too much. Strike a balance; by all means try to improve yourself for your family and friends, but don't assume that you should do it uncritically.

## RELATIONSHIPS

Reading body language can help you make wide choices when it comes to social relationships. Developing your own body language can help you improve your social relationships.

However, keep in mind the key principle: *a hurried assessment is most likely a wrong assessment.* Which is our old "don't jump to conclusions."

At the same time, *try not to use your friends and family as Guinea pigs.* Reading a bit here and there is fine, but always keep in mind that their value is as people, that they are important parts of your life and that you should never objectify them.

*Prefer people you don't know well to read their body language.* To start with, you will start with a clearer, less prejudiced mind. Secondly, you will not risk changing or even ruining important relationships. On the whole *avoid body language analysis with significant others.* This is not a "you mustn't"; it is, as it says, an "avoid".

If you do *use body language reading with significant others, then tell them that you have and what you have found out.* Body language readers sometimes use their skills in disagreements; well, after doing it, they should table a chat on equal terms about it.

In terms of improving your body language, social relationships can be a light on the one hand, or a cause of chaos on the other... Put simply, *you cannot change your body language to suit each and any social relationship individually.* You may have a repertoire that allows you some change, but you cannot tailor it to each individual.

You *need to keep a steady baseline with everybody.* If you change too much, people will notice it and you will appear fake, deceitful and untrustworthy...

Also remember that if you *experiment your body language with relationships, do it in small doses and small steps.* Do not face a friend with a huge change all of a sudden, or s/he can be disoriented, and your relationship may suffer.

## PUBLIC SPEAKING

Public speaking is an art... I am thinking, some comedians are great in a play or TV series, but then you go to watch their standup comedy performance and it's a disappointment. This means that even trained professionals find standing in front of an audience on their own and speaking quite tough...

On this, a very quick tip: *timing is of the essence.* I can often see comedians deliver great jokes but then there's a split-second mismatch with the punch line and it does not work (or not as well). So, this means that public speaking is hard, but that you need to *keep working on your timing.*

*Do not try out something that does not suit you in public speaking.* It would be like the Pope telling a dirty joke. No matter how good it can be, it will never work.

Here, hitting *the right balance between being serious and cracking the odd joke* can make the difference between a good speech and a disaster. US Presidents on average have done that well. UK Prime ministers have traditionally failed.

In many business speeches, it has now become almost a format to start with a joke. Most *Ted Talks* start with a joke. And on average they are good ones... But make sure you *rehearse your intro joke to perfection and that it is a good joke!* Also, make sure it is a joke everybody can understand, but at the same time one that sounds original and not desperate.

Do not laugh during your joke but *freeze your face at the end.* That's the trick, you see... That is the nonverbal clue that the joke is over, and you are expecting the audience's response. Choose that freeze frame very carefully.

Of course, *watch as many public speeches as you can.* In fact, Ted Talks are excellent practice; you have a range of different speakers, topics and styles. Not all are super professional and not all are as successful. But that is an advantage, because you can see where you may go wrong, which is more difficult if you only watch great professionals. Add political rallies, business presentations and, of course, standup comedy!

*Keep in mind that the audience is always different.* Some audiences are very hard indeed. Don't panic, and *don't exaggerate your body language if the audience is hard and hostile.* That is a gut reaction but also a mistake. If they are hostile, they will read your exaggerations as buffoonery, and most likely they will not appreciate them.

## WORK

Most of us spend the vast majority of our waking lives at work or in work related activities. This means that the body language we use at work can make a huge difference to our quality of life and even improve (or damage) out career chances...

So, some final tips on how to go about it...

First of all, *focus on your stamina.* You know that old employee who comes in every day at the same time and leaves every day after a hard day and yet it seems that he has made no effort? You know the young employee who comes in, runs around all day and goes home looking like a wreck?

Okay, the first has built physical stamina (PS: all studies show that old employees are more productive and there is a difference between activity and efficiency!). But if s/he gives you the idea that s/he can go through the fay with little or no effort it is because... Look at his or her shoulders! They stay up all day! So...

*Improve your body language when leaving work.* Do you think your boss does not see you leaving the office? Do you think that s/he does not notice that you feel the weight of the day on you? Now, do you think that, with a promotion to offer, your boss will choose someone who appears to sail through their days or someone who is already in difficulty at 5 PM every day? And your boss does not need to be a body language reader: remember that most of these ideas are formed subconsciously.

*Control your body language as you progress in your career.* If you have ever been to a canteen or staff room and heard the comments on people who have got a promotion you will know... Most of the comments, if negative, focus on the person's change of "attitude" (and body language).

Do not show your "former peers" that you feel superior. Good managers in fact will establish egalitarian relationships with the people they manage. That little lack of respect of appearing superior not only will cost you friends, efficiency and production. It may come back to bite you later on, when you are more vulnerable.

*Pick times in the day to correct your body language.* You see, you may start the day with a perfect posture, but as time goes by, you start slouching, bending over your desk etc.... So, I would suggest you focus on your body language when leaving home, when entering the workplace, at every coffee break, when you go to the toilet, every time you enter your boss's office and when you leave.

*Pull the string.* A simple trick that opera singers use is to imagine they have a string that falls to the ground from the very top of their skull, in the middle of the crown. You pull that string and align your body to it, and that gives you a perfect and upright posture. Like a puppet...

## NEGOTIATIONS

Negotiations can be part of your work, but also of your daily life. Every time you go to a store or market you negotiate (maybe not on the price, but on the choice of items etc....) And we need to negotiate even in our social lives... You want to go to the cinema but your partner wants to stay home? Well, you'll have to negotiate it!

Negotiating is another difficult set of skills, maybe even an art (metaphorically). For this reason, body language is key to success. And here are some tips to help you develop it.

*Use some regular negotiators.* Try to have deals with the same people now you know how to read body language. This will allow you to see patterns of behavior and even small signs. You see, if you change partner every time, you only have a chance to see major signs. But if you want to hone your skills, you will need to analyze the same person many times.

*Only experiment when the post at stake is low.* If you are haggling over the price of a kilo of potatoes, do play with different body language signs etc. But if you are negotiating to get the job of your dreams, better safe than sorry.

*Play games where negotiations are core.* That will give you a chance to improve your body language when negotiating in a safe but educational way. Some card games have a lot of negotiating (and body language) in them. Monopoly and similar games too have the same elements etc.

*Study great negotiators.* There are now some TV programs that show negotiations but be careful. These are often faked and distorted. They have the "Hollywood narrative" of the tough and arrogant world. It is tough, and it is arrogant – don't get me wrong. But you don't want to be arrogant to someone who can give you a deal or give it to someone else…

That arrogance that exists (unfortunately) between boss and employee becomes kindness and even false servility when it comes to getting a deal you need.

*Study different cultures.* For example, Arabs are wonderful negotiators. On the other hand, they train for it… You go to a megastore and the price is fixed. Even at the grocer's the price is fixed. Well, in the Arab world the center is the market, where everybody haggles over the price all the time. It's expected; it's normal. So, even a child doing his or her mother's chores starts learning how to negotiate…

## FUTURE DEVELOPMENT

Body language is a now a fully-grown discipline, which means that it will keep growing, but maybe at a smaller rate and with lesser "big discoveries" than in the past. When disciplines become "adult", they tend to specialize rather than go through revolutions.

But new things will come along, and you will need to know them. And, while we are at it, maybe you can keep a good diary of how your body language progresses, both in terms of reading and of your own development...

# CONCLUSION

It looks like yesterday when we started this journey together. Personally, I feel it has been a very rich one, with so much to talk about, so many twists and turns along the road. For you, I hope it has been an enjoyable one and, above all, a useful and informative one.

Looking back, we have gone from the very principles of body language, how it came about and how it developed at the beginning to very advanced uses of it, including how to use it professionally...

Along the way, we kept swinging like a pendulum between reading body language and applying it to our own personality, how we present ourselves. A bit like reading and writing when it comes to verbal language: one is the "passive skill" and the other is the "active skill" as teachers and educationalists call them.

We have explored all the different fields of body language: kinesics, proxemics, oculesics etc. we looked at each part of the body in detail, from head to toe, literally, and many times... We also now know that reading what people communicate through their body is not a matter of "adding up discrete signs"; it's a holistic activity. You need to read individual signs within the general perspective, the overall appearance, a bit like reading words within a paragraph...

We have also applied our knowledge to many different areas of life: from private life to business, via social relationships, you now have a good toolkit to read what people actually mean with their body. What is more, you now have a wide and growing repertoire of body language signs and "idioms" to use for yourself.

Along this journey, as you well know, two words have cropped up regularly, "nature" and "nurture". This is not strange though... It has been a big dichotomy (or two ways of reading and interpreting reality) in philosophy and science since the times of the ancient Greeks.

And when it comes to nurture, we have seen how different cultures greatly influence how we express ourselves with our bodies. And with a world that becomes metaphorically smaller by the day, understanding these cultural differences may well make the difference between a bright and successful international career or ending up in a provincial office with no prospects of a better future.

And in fact, I hope you have appreciated the balance of theory and practice I tried to strike within this book. I apologize if I had to introduce (at times even advanced and complex) theories. On the other hand, thinking about it, I hope you have enjoyed it, because it is the theory that gives us those broad lines, we use to make sense of the world around us.

The many real, practical and I hope at times colorful examples of this book, however, may well be what will stick to your mind best. They are the "coloring" of this book. And we have had a few chances to smile and even giggle along the way.

And the exercises I proposed, I trust, were all easy to do and never took up longer than they had to. As we are about to part ways, maybe till our next book, do keep in mind that your improvement as a reader and as a user of body language will come from many, frequent and regular sessions and exercises, not from big chunks of time every now and then. It is a bit like learning a new language or mathematics: ten minutes every day are better than two hours once a week. And I wish I'd followed my maths teacher's advice on this when I was at school, maybe I'd be a famous physicist now!

It's also been nice to "fly" all over the world and see how different cultures use body language in different ways... We have traveled east and west, always with respect, and we have seen how even greetings change all over the world. And, along the way, we discovered that our feet, those often-forgotten parts of our body, can make a huge difference if we want to integrate in a foreign country, find friends from that country or strike a deal with people from abroad...

And we have also met people from all paths of life, from poor people and the way rappers use their hands to Her Majesty the Queen and the way she uses body language to project her authority... Because body language is also a manifestation of class, social values and even musical taste!

All has been "spiced up" with a lot of psychology and sociology, as these are the founding sciences behind body language analysis. And the parallels with linguistics, another science that informs our field, have been many and revealing indeed... But because our life is a kaleidoscope of experience, along the line we also ventured into art, music (classical and pop), literature and, why not, quite a bit of philosophy... All within the perspective of that "mother of humanities" which is history...

And if at the beginning of the book you were wondering whether body language analysis was a "quackery" or a real science, I trust you are now sure that it is a fully valid and "adult" scientific study. However, like with most fields, be aware that there are urban myths and misconceptions about it, especially online.

And we finally came to the point where you have to fly the nest... Maybe, and I hope so, we will meet again on the pages of another book... But if we do not, I wish you all the best in your personal, social and professional life. Now that you have made it to the end of this book, however, I can leave you with a calmer heart, because if you have made it this far, you *really* have learned a lot, and you *really* *have all the tools and skills to read body language correctly and in depth, and to use it to make your life a happier, richer and more successful one – on all fronts!*

# RESOURCES

And if you want to explore this fascinating topic even further, here are some great reads for you to check out!

Cooper, B. (2019). *Body Language Mastery: 4 Books in 1: The Ultimate Psychology Guide to Analyzing, Reading and Influencing People Using Body Language, Emotional Intelligence, Psychological Persuasion and Manipulation.* Independently published.

Cooper, D. (2020). *Decode People Personalities: How to Analyze People by Knowing Body Language Signals & Behavioral Psychology. Understand What Every Person is Saying Using Emotional Intelligence and NLP.* Independently published.

Edwards, V. V. (2018). *Captivate: The Science of Succeeding with People* (Reprint ed.). Portfolio.

Goleman, A. (2020). *Manipulation, Body Language, Dark Psychology: How to Analyze and Influence People, Read Body Language, Avoid Deceptions, Brainwashing and Mind Control. Discover 9 Secrets to Stop Being Manipulated.* Diamond Mind Ltd.

Houston, P., Floyd, M., Carnicero, S., & Tennant, D. (2013). *Spy the Lie: Former CIA Officers Teach You How to Detect Deception* (Reprint ed.). St. Martin's Griffin.

Lowen, A. (2012). *The Language of the Body.* The Alexander Lowen Foundation.

McGray, P. P. (2020b). *Dark Psychology and Manipulation: How to Leverage the Secrets of Mind Control, NLP, Brainwashing, Hypnosis, Body Language in Dating, Relationships, and at Work.* Independently published.

McGray, P. P. (2020b). *Dark Psychology and Manipulation: How to Leverage the Secrets of Mind Control, NLP, Brainwashing, Hypnosis, Body Language in Dating, Relationships, and at Work.* Independently published.

Navarro, J. (2018). *The Dictionary of Body Language: A Field Guide to Human Behavior.* William Morrow Paperbacks.

Navarro, J., & Karlins, M. (2008). *What Every Body Is Saying: An Ex-FBI Agent's Guide to Speed-Reading People* (Illustrated ed.). William Morrow Paperbacks.

Rouse, S. (2021). *Understanding Body Language: How to Decode Nonverbal Communication in Life, Love, and Work.* Rockridge Press.

Segal, I. (2010). *The Secret Language of Your Body: The Essential Guide to Health and Wellness* (Reprint ed.). Beyond Words.

Williams, J. W. (2020). *How to Read People Like a Book: A Guide to Speed-Reading People, Understand Body Language and Emotions, Decode Intentions, and Connect Effortlessly (Communication Skills Training)*. Independently published.

# DARK PSYCHOLOGY AND MANIPULATION PROTECTION 2 IN 1

DISCOVER HOW TO ANALYZE BODY LANGUAGE
& INCREASE EMOTIONAL INTELLIGENCE TO
PROTECT AGAINST DARK PERSUASION, NLP,
NARCISSISTS & MIND CONTROL TECHNIQUES

# INTRODUCTION

We are living in a world that is intrinsically dark and scary. What you see is a fraction of what happens in the dark, far hidden from the naked eyes or, at times, beyond human comprehension. Reports have it that some marketers, businesspersons, religious leaders, cultists, even our so-called friends and relatives can engage in dark psychology to manipulate, mind control, coerce, persuade, and influence us in a way that makes it very easy for them to take advantage of us and get whatever they want from us.

This problem has relatively got out of hand as there are so many books and different forms of instructional media out there teaching people how to use dark psychology to manipulate the others for their own selfish gains. However, the good news is that an equally large number of people, who have now woken up to the realization of these evil practices, are seeking for ways to protect themselves against manipulation, persuasion, and dark psychology.

This book, a practical guide, is specifically written to offer the much-needed help so that people can avoid becoming victims of dark psychology, manipulation, hypnosis, unfavorable coercion, and deceitful persuasion.

In September 2015, a tragedy struck at my former workplace, one of my colleagues—my best friend ever—had committed suicide inside one of the workshops adjacent to the main administrative building. Big Alistair, as we used to call him, did leave a suicide note. "I have let everyone down," he regrettably stated. More enquiries into the cause of this gruesome incident revealed that he had met a dashing, young lady on one of the online dating sites. The strange lady, we learnt, had taken control of Big Alistair's life, coercing him to act on all occasions against his wish.

The comprehensive investigations by the police revealed that my former colleague, following the strict orders of his newfound lover, had emptied all his savings, estimated to be about £45,000, and handed everything to her. However, her demand for money didn't abate until she had forced him to borrow from friends and family members. When Big Alistair couldn't find someone to lend him money due to his inability to repay those he was owing, he turned to stealing from our company's coffers—he was one of the accounting officers. He embezzled a total of £200,000 from our company, giving it all to his eccentric girlfriend!

It reached a point that he had no money on him, no one to lend him any, and he knew that the time to do the annual auditing of our company's financial accounting was fast approaching. He realized he had had no apparent option than to kill himself. So sad he ended his life that way, without even letting his family or friends know! Finally, the news broke out that the weird lady had been manipulating him, using all kinds of dark psychological powers to hypnotize, control, and order him around like a baby.

It is the story of Big Alistair that led to the development of this book. We cannot afford to wait for the next victim to come up before we do something about it. It is quite unfortunate and bewildering that an increasing number of people are still learning hypnotism, dark psychology, and neurolinguistic programming (NLP) for the singular purpose of harming other people. A search on the internet will turn up hundreds of schools and institutes offering NLP courses for whoever wants to learn it. This reveals that the enormity of this problem is bigger than what we had previously envisaged.

What will you do in the face of all these mounting life challenges and risks? Will you just sit down and fold your arms, doing nothing? Well, many people are truly clueless about how to address this very serious issue. This is why this book is designed to help people in that situation. It will not only make you to be fully aware of the things happening around you, but it will also empower you with the right amount of practicable knowledge that you can utilize to protect yourself from evil-minded people.

After the eye-opening circumstance of Big Alistair, I was able to timely intervene and prevent one of my own cousins from going down the same drain. He had madly fallen in love with a lady he also met online and the lady, using some dark psychological powers on him, had requested for his ATM card and its PIN number. I sat him down on the Christmas Eve of 2018, just one day before he could hand over everything to her so that she could go on a shopping spree on Christmas Day!

In another but closely related situation, a successful steel company owner discovered that one of his customers often asked him for goods on credit, even though he was still owing him a lot of money, around £100,000. But the most surprising aspect of this story was that the businessman never had the courage or energy in him to say "No" to his Oliver Twist customer. After asking the steel company owner some thought-provoking questions, I discovered that his so-called customer had been using some dark powers to persuade him. Such an evil customer will keep requesting for more steel products until the amount runs up to, say £1 million and then he would suddenly disappear. After holding series of consultations with the businessman, we were able to confront the customer who later confessed to his evil deeds. He was handed over to the police for proper prosecution.

You will discover, in this book, all the necessary things you need to do to better protect yourself. It is counterproductive to wait until you find yourself in a difficult situation or falling victim to some evil people's machinations or devious actions before you keep yourself and your loved ones safe.

When you are dealing with a manipulative person, the extent of what you could lose is infinite. People have lost valuable possessions, including their own precious lives when they did not quickly realize how dangerous the person they were dealing with was. However, identifying a manipulative person and escaping from his/her firm grip are two different things. Armed with the knowledge in this book, you will be able to quickly detect the traits of a manipulative person as well as doing everything in your power to set yourself free from his/her self-centered persuasion, coercion, and destructive manipulation.

Congratulations that you are one of the lucky people to be reading this! It is now in your power to help someone else by sharing some of the topics that you will learn from this book. Help your friends, relatives, colleagues, and even your neighbors stay abreast of the latest information about the danger of NLP, dark psychology, hypnotism, coercion, and damaging persuasion. You will be happy you did if you could help save just one person's life.

# I

## PREPARE YOURSELF

## IT STARTS WITHIN

Overcoming the tricks and traps of hypnotists, heartless manipulators, and wicked practitioners of dark psychology requires some strategic preparations. And it all starts from within.

### ARE YOU READY?

Freeing yourself from a cruel person or a group of mischievous people who want to take control of your life for their own personal gains or gratifications is comparable to fighting a war. Unlike the physical one, this battle requires you to be mentally strong and determined. And are you ready?

Asking this question is very important because you won't achieve any tangible victory against those callous manipulators and hypnotists if you are shoddily prepared for it. Do you know what being ready means?

It entails that you are no longer going to be:

- Destroyed by self-pity or getting depressed instead of taking your fate into your own hands
- Blaming others for your problems, but you have already made up your mind to fight it to the end
- Fearful and indecisive about it
- Postponing when to act, for there is apparently no room for being lazy about dealing with an enemy that is coming after everything you have, including your dear life, if you don't act NOW!

## MENTAL HEALTH IS INVOLVED

This war requires that you exercise your mental muscles, not your physical muscles. You must exhibit sound mental health to ward off the subtle advances of manipulators and practitioners of dark psychology. What does it mean to have sound mental health? Very simple. You must demonstrate a high degree of emotional, cognitive, and behavioural well-being. You must absolutely be in charge of your emotional and behavioural reflections so that you are capable of handling all stressful and disturbing circumstances that come your way without demonstrating any signs of mental disorders or breakdown.

The adage goes like this: "A disturbed soul is a conquered soul". If you want to be able to stand your ground and frustrate every trick of the manipulators, you must make sure you are not the type who breaks down easily under any pressure. There will be some socio-cultural and psychological pressures, partly instigated by the actions of the cruel manipulators or practitioners of dark psychology whose primary goal is to first destabilize your life before pouncing on you.

## Some Early Signs You Should Watch Out For

If you are showing any or all of the early signs of mental health problems described below, you should immediately work on developing your mental health or seek professional help:

- Irregular eating habits
- Suffering from insomnia or sleeping too much
- Extreme social withdrawal
- Lacking adequate energy to carry out the normal functions at work or home
- Occasionally feeling numb or too tired
- Suffering from migraines or other pains
- Periodically experiencing a state of helplessness or hopelessness
- Intentionally abusing substances such as drugs and alcohol in a large amount
- Displaying emotional imbalance characterized by intense anger, confusion, forgetfulness, or irrationally feeling scared
- Showing uncontrollable domestic violence to friends and family members
- Demonstrating extreme mood swings and inability to maintain good relationships
- Entertaining self-demeaning thoughts from time to time
- Stubbornly doubtful of the realities

- Hearing voices and experiencing blurred visions
- Troubled with the thoughts of committing suicide or harming yourself or someone else

Paying attention to the signs mentioned above may help you detect any mental issues in time and find ways to quickly ameliorate it before the enemies strike. If you see another person displaying any of the characteristics of mental-health problems highlighted above, you could be the savior of such a person by directing him/her to seek timely intervention before the problems get out of hand.

You will soon discover later in this book how difficult it is dealing with hypnotists or manipulators when you are mentally unstable, who usually exert social, psychological, and economical pressures on their victims. The truth must be told: A broken person is as powerless as a deflated ball because the air it uses for power has already been sucked out of it. You do not want to be in a powerless situation or see any of your loved ones in that pitiable state. This is why it is imperative that you develop your mental health.

## DEVELOPING YOUR MENTAL STRENGTH

There isn't any other way around it, you must take decisive steps to develop your mental strength, making it difficult for those who want to manipulate or extort you through hypnotism to do so. The very first thing you need to do is, with the help of your physician or licensed mental health professional, is to identify the probable cause of your mental health problem(s).

## Three Possible Causes of Mental Health Problems

- **Biological factors**: Some people exhibit mental health illness due to their genetic compositions or certain chemical reactions in their brains. This may be caused by some diseases or disorders such as type 1 diabetes, chromosomal abnormalities, Autism, and others. These biological risk factors can also be triggered by several environmental conditions. The brain usually functions improperly when there are certain levels of chemical imbalance in them, or there is dysfunction in the neural pathways responsible for dispersing these chemicals in the brain, such as in the case of anorexia nervosa.

- **Difficult life experiences**: People who go through some difficult life experiences do display some kinds of mental health illnesses. Trauma or past abuse can impair someone's mental sharpness and cause him/her to behave erratically. Take for instance, those who have been homeless for a long time may express some certain asocial attitudes normally seen in a mentally unstable person.

- **Hereditary**: People who come from a family lineage where signs of mental instability are common may exhibit certain levels of mental health problems. When looking at hereditary causes, it is important to trace back the family tree to as many generations as possible.

## 7 PRACTICAL WAYS TO DEVELOP YOUR MENTAL HEALTH STRENGTH

If you are in doubt about how to proactively develop your mental strength, which you seriously need to prevent instances of being manipulated, hypnotized, coerced, or abused, the following 7 tested approaches for strengthening your mental alacrity will be of special interest to you:

1. **Declutter your mind:** When confused, disturbed, and perturbed, human mind is comparable to a messy gutter through which run some dirty water, rubbish, and particles. You need to systematically declutter your mind. Take every precaution to identify those negative, self-limiting thoughts in your head and gradually remove them from your mind. You can never feel great and enjoy great mental health if you often doubt yourself or put yourself in a position of constant fear.

2. **Be positive:** You need to empower yourself with great positivism. This entails that you should live a positive life, only embrace positive things about yourself and others, and put out positive energy, because whatever goes around comes around.

3. **Coping strategy:** Do not aspire to be the person that runs away from challenges. You should rather be a person that withstands pressures of all kinds but always emerging victorious, successful, and confident. You need to develop some inner coping strategies you will need to handle external

challenges. This is because tough situations won't last, but tough people do.

4. **Be productive:** There are so many blessings associated with being super productive. In addition to helping you focus on the right thing at the right time, it also takes your mind away from useless, negative thoughts. Working hard will help you realize your full potential and become a source of motivation if you succeed at whatever you are doing.

5. **Life-enriching relationships:** It is counter-productive for anyone suffering from any kind of mental health problems to put himself/herself in relationships that will drain their energy and turn them into powerless individuals. Take it upon yourself to start or be in relationships that will build you up. Energy-sapping relationships if they don't kill you, will render you powerless for a very long time. Do something good for your communities and positively connect with others. One good way to remain mentally alert is to help others; You can help those who you perceive are in danger of being manipulated or psychologically attacked by practitioners of dark psychology. By doing this great human service, you are also automatically strengthening your own mental health.

6. **Taking care of your body:** You should get enough sleep and take good care of your body hygiene. Health is wealth, because if your body suffers some illnesses for a long time, it could consequently affect your mental health. Kick bad habits such as excessive drinking, smoking, and nightlife

7. **Get professional help:** When you have done all you can

to strengthen your mental health, but you are still feeling drowsy or down, you can seek help from qualified health professionals. Do not be shy about it; it is better you are outright about it and empower yourself by doing so. Psychotherapy and medications are some of the medical approaches for treating mental health illnesses. Your physician or an experienced mental health professional can gradually guide you through a process of recovery and rediscovering yourself. It may or may not be long, but it is surely worth doing. You will thank yourself later.

## PROTECTING YOURSELF

You have accomplished something tangible if you have taken all appropriate measures to develop your mental strength. However, maintaining one's mental health is not just a sprint; it is a marathon. It is something you have to do from time to time.

Surprisingly enough, it is not something you can do on your own. You need a kind of support system to keep your mental sharpness intact. Some people are so lucky surrounding themselves with good friends, relatives, and colleagues who are able to motivate, encourage, and assist them in their daily mental health development. Unfortunately, not everyone is that lucky; some are surrounded by vampires sucking their energy from time to time.

If you belong to the latter group, you will find this book very helpful, like a companion, to constantly guide you in the process to keep your mental health in good shape. You will unearth a lot of information designed to give you that emotional backing that you long desire. More so, you will identify ways to spot manipulators so you can escape from their traps.

It is very important that you constantly learn how to protect yourself from various unseen psychological attacks. It is like learning physical self-defense tactics you can use to knock your enemies down. In this scenario, you are just focusing on the strategies that will equip you with all the necessary information you need to protect your mind from external manipulators, many of whom are close friends, associates, relatives, or even your neighbors.

# 2

# DELVE DEEPER INTO YOUR EMOTIONS

This is the most important secret you need to be aware of: Cruel manipulators, hypnotists, and practitioners of Dark Psychology often target their would-be victims' emotions. They tamper with people's emotions for the purposes of altering, controlling, and subduing their thinking, realities and, of course, their actions.

Your sole chance of outmaneuvering manipulators begins right in your mind, realizing how powerful your emotion is. If you can prevent any wicked hypnotist from taking over your emotions, you are already victorious.

## UNDERSTANDING THE HUMAN EMOTION

So, what are emotions? Many scientists and psychologists have struggled with perfectly defining what an emotion is. Some believe it is just a human feeling, a kind of reflexive response to a specific condition or experience. Others have proposed that emotion embodies both the feeling and bodily reaction to both external and internal stimuli. Whichever definition of emotion you embrace, the fact remains the same that emotion plays a significant role in your ability to live a healthy life, enjoy robust relationships, be in control of your senses, and maintain your personal dignity.

There are six fundamental structures or kinds of emotions: **Anger, fear, disgust, surprise, sadness,** and **joy**. Each kind of these emotions can make or mar you, depending on how capable you are at controlling it. What a manipulator does is tap into your apparent weakness in handling your emotions and deftly use them against you, to decimate your psyche and literally take over your senses or subconscious.

This anecdote will better show you how crafty hypnotists or manipulators work: Mr. A is always full of anger. He often shows anger in his words and reactions to external stimuli. When he comes into contact with a manipulator, all the manipulator needs to do is to amplify his anger in a way that Mr. A will lose his senses, making himself vulnerable to a deceitful manipulator who does not mean well for him but just to use him for his/her selfish purposes.

To further illustrate how humans experience emotions, scientists came up with two mutually exclusive properties of human emotions. They call it **valence** versus **arousal**. In other words, they describe valence as the degree to which an individual feels good or bad, while arousal expresses the degree to which a person feels excited or calm. When you feel extremely good about yourself or your achievements, your emotion is at **high valence**. However, when you are sad and dejected, your emotion is at **low valence**. In the same way, your emotion is considered to be at **high arousal** when you are extremely excited, but it turns to **low arousal** when you are calm and confused.

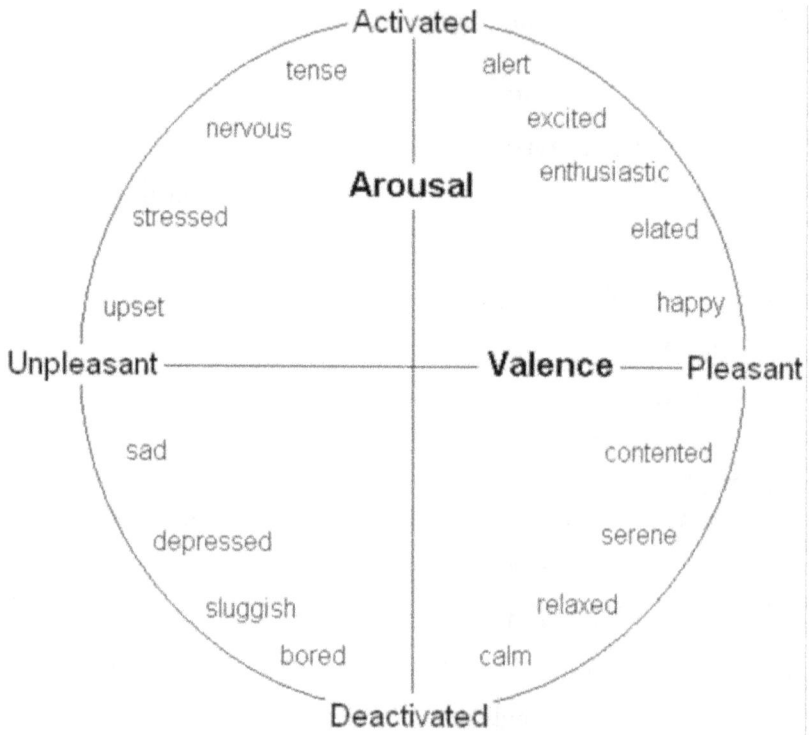

## Valence and Arousal: Properties of Human Emotions, diagram obtained from ResearchGate

As indicated in the diagram above, a person tends to become obviously **deactivated** when he/she reaches the state of high valence of emotion. As demonstrated in the anecdote, Mr. A will virtually become deactivated and lose his total composure or consciousness when his anger reaches the highest level. At that stage, it does not take a manipulator any extra effort to dangerously influence or run his life.

**Here is the greatest warning**: The same evil manipulation can be achieved with high arousal, positive emotion. Take for instance, a man who often loses himself when he is in a company of an incredibly beautiful lady can easily fall victim to any pretty female hypnotist.

You can now see how dangerous the situation is, that both your negative and positive emotions can be used to coerce, control, manipulate, or hypnotize you!

## WHAT CAUSES EMOTION?

Normally, emotions are our ways of responding to an experience or event that happens to us or around us. Almost all scientists and psychologists who have studied about human emotions agree that showing emotions, whether sadness or joy, is normal and expected. In fact, they outlined three main categories of emotional triggers in human beings.

**1. Common causes:** People commonly express their emotions because:

- **They are humans**—every human has a heart that can feel the good and bad, hence they respond exactly to what they feel.
- **Genetics**—some people are more emotional than others.

This is due to their inherited genes. Although environmental and social factors may also play some significant roles.

- **Insomnia**—sleeplessness or lack of adequate sleep can make someone depressed and affected by anxiety. These conditions weaken the immune system and can make an individual so emotional.

- **Tardiness**—not doing enough exercise can make your mood swings dangerous. Good exercise is believed to be helpful in stabilizing one's moods and emotions.

- **Unhealthy diet**—Scientists believe that consuming an unhealthy and unbalanced diet can weaken someone's immune system and make them susceptible to emotional outburst from time to time.

- **Being too sensitive**—Part of humanity is to show love and concern to the others around us. If you are too sensitive, you may find yourself expressing your emotions a lot within a short period of time.

**2. Health and emotions:** It is not surprising that the state of your health may be one of the reasons you are quite emotional. The following health factors are fundamentally responsible for expressing emotions in humans:

- **Hormones**—Hormones are wired in a way that they can cause both physical and psychological changes in your body and emotions when they are imbalanced. Some of the health issues that may alter the balance of hormones in your body include stress, thyroid problem, PCOS, menopause, birth control, PMDD, and PMS.

- **Depression**—is a typical mood disorder that affects millions of people across the globe. Those who are deeply depressed exhibit high levels of negative emotions. On most occasions, they may feel hopeless, sad, empty, and angry.

- **Anxiety**—like depression, anxiety brings a great deal of fearfulness and anxious feeling into the lives of people suffering from chronic anxiety. They may be tense on most days and have their emotions heightened. They are usually angry and show deep apprehension frequently.

- **Personality disorders**—those who are experiencing personality disorders often find themselves in a situation where it is difficult for them to control their emotions. They are quite sensitive, their moods swing every time they are criticized.

- **ADHD**—Those who are affected by ADHD are known for their hypersensitive and emotional behaviors. They apparently find it difficult to control their focus, feelings, and attitudes.

**3. Situational Causes:** Certain situations in your life can cause you to experience emotional fluctuations. Sometimes it may be beyond your power to immediately rectify the situations. For example, your emotion may be caused by:

- **Uncontrollable stress**—Stressed people often demonstrate quick mood swings. They are so physically and mentally tired that they sometimes, unintentionally, show their emotional side.

- **Grieving people**—when grieving about a loss, people do not necessarily make any attempt to control their emotions. They will just let their emotions take the best of them.
- **Eventful events in life**—If you are getting married, giving birth to a baby or getting a divorce, your emotions may run high. Several big changes in people's lives largely affect the way they feel and how they reflect on their experiences.

To a certain degree, culture, which is a set of beliefs, norms, values, and attitudes seems to have an overarching influence on how people perceive, receive, process, and display emotions. Why some individuals in certain cultures may shed tears when an elderly person passes away, that may not be the case in another culture. So, all the emotional triggers described above may not be usually applicable to people from different cultures.

## DIFFERENT LEVELS OF EMOTION

Individually, we operate at different levels of emotion. What does this mean? Haven't you seen twins that were born on the same day by the same mother displaying different types of emotions when witnessing the same events? This explains the undeniable fact that humans display different levels of emotion, even though they are going through the same experiences.

There are three unique levels of emotions, and they are described as follows:

- **Not showing adequate concern for others:** There are some people who don't necessarily feel concerned about what others are going through, whether good or bad. Even the Bible says that we should rejoice with those who are celebrating and mourn with those in troubles. Have you ever witnessed a ghastly accident where precious human lives were lost, and people were crying? There would be someone there who didn't feel moved by the outpouring emotions around him/her. Such a person had not affinity or chemistry of emotion with the victim. This is exactly how manipulators and mind-benders do; they derive maximum joy in seeing their victims suffer or be in pain because they simply cannot relate to the hardship, they had intentionally thrown them into. Expecting a manipulator to be considerate is like expecting the Devil to become a Saint overnight. It will never happen! Knowing about how callous and evil they are is your only weapon to protect yourself from their tricks and manifold wickedness.

- **Demonstrating extremely high concern for others:** This is the second level of human emotion. I think you can find this outpouring of positive emotions of joy, love, appreciation, encouragement, and the rest from your immediate families and loyal friends. However, you still have to tread cautiously when dealing with people; those who are your loyal friends today might turn into your sworn enemies tomorrow. The bottom line is that you don't want to put yourself in a position that any Dick and Harry can take advantage of you, using you the way they like.

- **Lacking good emotional coping skill:** A person who is too gentle and feeble is considered to be lacking the good skill for dealing with his/her own emotions and those of the people around him/her. You don't want to show the whole world around you that you are weak, feeble, and incapable of managing your own emotions. Manipulators, like a roaring lion, scout around for their next victims, and it would be a grave mistake on your part not to present yourself as a person with a strong personality.

How do I successfully manage my emotions then, you may ask? The first thing you need to be aware of is that your emotions are not only about your physical response to events or happenings around you, but they are also the outcomes of the chemical reactions going in your brain. Millions of chemical reactions occur in your brain, and they could affect your overall emotions. These chemical reactions occur as a result of synapses in your central nervous system. To be precise, emotions emanate from the arousal of the central nervous system. When something happens, neurons in your central nervous system transmit the message via neurotransmitters in your body. Then this will bring about a certain feeling that you will then display as your emotion.

How much control do you have on these chemical reactions that dictate which emotions you will display physically? That's an important question! There are some chemicals in your body that are responsible for these chemical reactions. The main chemicals are dopamine and serotonin.

Dopamine ($C_8H_{11}NO_2$) functions primarily as a neurotransmitter, and it has a huge impact on mood and emotions. If you have plenty of dopamine in your body it can lead to unexpected behavioural problems characterized by mood swings. Dopamine is not man-made; it occurs naturally in your body.

Like dopamine, serotonin ($C_{10}H_{12}N_2O$) is also a neurotransmitter, it mainly works by regulating thinking, mood, emotions, and impulse control. If you have adequate serotonin in your body, it can make you feel optimistic and happy. But if you lack enough serotonin in your body, you can be exhibiting signs of depression, anger, and anxiety.

While dopamine cannot be produced by man, serotonin can be artificially manufactured and injected into the human body when required.

## THE TENDENCY TO HIDE

In certain situations, people tend to hide their true emotions. Why do they do that? Culturally, people have different responses to circumstances. In Japanese culture, people are taught from their childhood to suppress their emotions. The main reason behind this kind of practice is that being overjoyed in an environment where others are sad might arouse jealousy, anger, and even unfavorable physical reactions. This is supported by a common saying in Japan that "a nail that raises its head above the other nails risks being hammered down!" So, you will normally see Japanese acting homogenously, avoiding standing out, even if it involves not expressing one's true emotions in the public.

Apart from the cultural undertone discussed above, there are other reasons why people hide their true feelings, which include but are not limited to the following:

- Ashamed to expose personal pain, failure, and sorrow
- Not willing to appear rude or disobedient for challenging rejections, maltreatment, sexual harassment, and so on
- Unwilling to be seen as "too needy" for protesting against disaffection or not being loved by people around them
- Unable to complain against some displeasure or embarrassment so as not to appear foolish and weak
- Not willing to hurt people around them.

In fact, psychologists believe that a lot of people hide their feelings so as to remain loyal to the group, society, or community they have found themselves. Take for instance, a secretary in an office may not be willing to show anger or irritation against a boss that has abused her verbally and sexually for years, just for the purpose of not drawing the anger from her colleagues who might think she wants some financial gains from the experience or pushing to destroy the boss' image and career. The secretary may even be afraid of losing her job if her complaints are not taken seriously by the company.

Unfortunately, hiding or suppressing one's emotions has some negative effects on us. For example, people tend to be so angry and always full of resentment, because there is something or some issues burning in their hearts that they cannot divulge.

Suppressing one's emotions may have a debilitating impact on one's health. It can make your blood pressure spike or cause you to lose focus on other things you are doing for a long time. It can cause some socio-economic problems such as losing one's job, having bad relationships with people, and not being able to live a happy and peaceful life.

Manipulators usually make it difficult to express their true emotions in public. How do you expect someone who was tricked into pornography, whose naked pictures have already been taken by the manipulator to come forward and tell the whole world what he/she has been going through?

All these pieces of important information are being released to you so that you can be better armed against any hypnotist or manipulator who may want to take advantage of you or your loved ones.

II

---

# WHAT YOU'RE UP AGAINST

# 3

# THE PEOPLE WHO WISH TO HARM YOU

You cannot adequately protect yourself if you don't know the nature of the people that wish to harm you. The first sensible thing to do is knowing who your real enemies are. This chapter reveals the categories of people you should consider as your potential enemies and do everything within your power to avoid.

## People that You Should Be Wary Of

For simplicity purposes, here is a list of ten (10) kinds of people that you should be wary of:

1. **Those who hate your guts for no apparent reason:**
   Naturally one can make enemies among colleagues, friends, and family members due to bad relationship or other reasons. However, there are some people in this life who genuinely hate you for no reason. You are neither their

business associate or partner nor share an apartment block with them; they just hate you for some reasons known only to them.

2. **Those naysayers:** Naysayers don't believe in your capabilities. They can also go out of their way to discourage others from believing in you. They spread cynical rumors about you and make others disregard your worth.

3. **People who lie about you:** In their evil minds, they fabricate lies about you and make it their business to spread calumnies about from one person to another. They instigate gullible others to treat your name disrespectfully, even though those people cannot say emphatically what you had done wrong.

4. **People who envy you too much:** There is no way you can appease someone who is quite jealous or envious of your achievements. Every time, their hearts are burning with anger that you have achieved what they would never attain in life. Even the former U.S. President, Theodore Roosevelt had this to say about envious people: *"The vice of envy is not only a dangerous, but a mean vice; for it is always a confession of inferiority. It may promote conduct which will be fruitful or wrong to others, and it must cause misery to the man who feels it."*

5. **Those who use and dump you:** You should stay away from anyone who is interested in just using and dumping you. For instance, if your business associate is only excited about using you to get new deals, but immediately shuns you after the deals have been successful, avoid such a person.

6. **People who drain all your energy:** Life is too short to hang around leeches and vampires who suck creative energy out of you. All they want to accomplish is draining you and then leaving you wimp and powerless.

7. **Bad influencer:** Most friends and partners who happen to be bad influencers in our lives are actually manipulating us for their own gains. So, why would you want to allow such discouragers to stay near you.

8. **The grumpy old friend:** Old friends are those we share the past with but, unfortunately, many of them don't deserve sharing in our present life. Why not? Grumpy old friends will be the ones to remind you how poor, unintelligent, and careless you were before. They are too engrossed in your past failures that they are not capable to appreciate your present good life or life achievements.

9. **The disloyal ones:** No matter how kind you are to disloyal people, they will eventually show their true colour— which is betraying you when you needed them the most. They are the ones who will craftily expose your dirty secrets to the whole world and come back to sympathize with you in the misery they had put you in.

10. **The Never-do-well:** This kind of person is lazy, but he/she will be the first to criticize your great work. They can never attempt to start a business, but they will come around to dissuade you from doing so.

It is clear from all indications that the different kinds of people described above can use dark psychology to take advantage or control others if they have access to it. They are likely to harm and take advantage of others when the opportunity presents itself to them.

## WHY THEY DO

Manipulators and hypnotists are not just out for something, they are out to rob you of your precious time, tangible properties and, if possible, take your life in the process. The truth is that they never approach you because they have good intentions towards you. No, never. Manipulators come to you because they have some set goals they want to actualize. Hence, when they discover that they cannot naturally carry out their evil plans, they resort to using Dark Psychology to get the job done.

In recent years, some manipulators who have been apprehended and prosecuted confessed that they took Dark Psychology for the following purposes:

- To gain the upper hand in a relationship/situation
- To overpower the subconscious of their victims
- To destroy their victims' self-esteem and willpower so that they will not be able to quickly recover from their hypnotism and evil machination
- To confuse the reality of their victims while misleading them
- To take a revenge against their victims for whatever wrong they had done in the past

## LET'S FACE IT

The truth is hard, and the truth is that many of our closest friends, relatives, colleagues, and neighbors are those who, on most occasions, attempt to psychologically and emotionally harm us the most.

Even the Holy Bible reckons that the most dangerous enemies people have are those of their own households.

This is why you should take this issue very seriously. Empowering yourself with the right amount of knowledge about the tricks of hypnotists and manipulators will place you ahead of them.

# 4

# WHY DARK PSYCHOLOGY?

.

You probably have known why some mischievous people embrace dark psychology from the warnings already dished out in the preceding chapters. In this chapter, efforts are made to explain, in details, what constitutes a dark psychology, why it is different from the usual "psychology", the dark side of it, and why you should do everything you can to perpetually stay informed and protect yourself and your loved ones.

## PSYCHOLOGY AND DARK PSYCHOLOGY, WHAT'S THE DIFFERENCE?

You should not confuse "Psychology" with "Dark Psychology". The American Psychological Association defines "Psychology" as the scientific study of mind and behavior. It is a multifaceted discipline that has been applied in various areas such as in sports, health, clinical procedures, human development, for understanding cognitive processes and social behavior.

In contrary, "Dark Psychology" can be succinctly described as the science and art of mind control and manipulation; it also studies human conditions as they relate to their psychological nature so that they can master their minds and routines for the singular purpose of preying upon others.

Even though the two types of psychology involve a scientific study of human minds and behaviors, they are so different from each other in the ways they are applied. One could differentiate one from the other by calling "Dark Psychology" a bad or negative psychology while the normal psychology as the good or positive one.

While the good psychology studies human mind so as to identify any attributes of human character that requires further development and improvement, the dark psychology analyses human mind for the purpose of discovering how it works, its apparent weaknesses, and routines in order to devise evil approaches for preying on people.

Emphasis must be laid on the differences between these two forms of psychology so that you don't mistaken one for the other. When you visit a hospital, the psychologists there are those practicing good psychology; so, you shouldn't be scared of them. On the other hand, the practitioners of dark psychology can be anywhere; they can be your relatives, friends, business associates, marketers trying to sell you something, or even your religious leaders. It takes a great deal of discernment to quickly identify these evil doers. This book is specifically written to help you spot them long before they strike and turn you into their hopeless victims.

## WHY IS THERE A DARK PSYCHOLOGY?

This is an important question everyone is asking. Unfortunately, dark psychology has been in existence for centuries, even before our modern world was created. It was an ancient practice that has been adopted by people of all races, cultures, and religious affiliations. Take for example, the Jewish and Greek necromancers were early practitioners of dark psychology, invoking the spirit of the dead to manipulate the living. God, in His holiness, spoke volubly against necromancy, sorcery, casting of spells, and other detestable dark psychology practices. You can read about this in the Book of Deuteronomy 18, 9-12 (NIV): *"When you enter the land the LORD your God is giving you, do not learn to imitate the detestable ways of the nations there. [10] Let no one be found among you who sacrifices their son or daughter in the fire, who practices divination or sorcery, interprets omens, engages in witchcraft, [11] or casts spells, or who is a medium or spiritist or who consults the dead. [12] Anyone who does these things is detestable to the LORD; because of these same detestable practices the LORD your God will drive out those nations before you."*

It may interest you to know that the Book of Deuteronomy was written in 7th Century BCE when King Josiah (reigned 641-609 BCE) initiated widespread religious reforms in Jerusalem. Surprisingly, dark psychology has been in existence far before good or positive psychology came into being, it was invented around 1879 (19th

Century) when German scientist, Wilhelm Wundt set up a laboratory that was wholly dedicated to the experimental study of Psychology in Leipzig.

You are not given all these facts to scare the hell out of you; it is just an eye-opener for you to be fully aware of the long-life evil you are up against.

So, to answer this rhetorical question, "Why do people practice dark psychology?" These answers may shock you. Again, the goal is not to shock you, but to give you the unique opportunity to reassess your life and discover if you have been or will be a victim of dark psychology practitioners.

You may have probably read on the internet or heard from the others why dark psychology is being embraced by so many people and used against others. For simplicity sake, I list them by categories in this book so that you can fully grasp the extent of the wickedness perpetrated against others.

1. **Use of dark psychology in relationships:** If a guy or a lady is in any form of relationship with someone who practices dark psychology, he/she will be subjected to a number of things that do not exist in normal, loving relationships. For example, the dark psychologists will control the other partner in a way that he/she cannot refuse. The manipulator may use sex, money, mere words, and other influential things to keep the relationship going, even when the dark psychologist knows for sure that the relationship will not end as expected. You may have seen one

or some of your friends engaged with or in a relationship with a manipulator, they will just stay in the relationship for years (some are in it for up to 10 years) without any promise of marriage or common-law partnership. At the end of the day, the other person realizes that his/her time has been wasted. On a more serious note, a manipulator can push his/her boyfriend or girlfriend over the top. You will have read of people being introduced to cocaine and heroin by their lovers or conjured to borrow huge amount of money because they are so deeply in love with someone else. Those are examples of harmful effects of allowing dark psychologist into your life.

2. **Use of dark psychology in Politics:** Politicians are not only sugar-mouthed individuals who promise their electorates what they know that they can never fulfill if elected, but some of them also actually embrace dark psychology to primarily create a cult-following. A shrewd dark psychologist politician will tap into the subconsciousness of their supporters and use their grievances to make a string of incredible promises that will sweep them off their feet. Adolf Hitler came on the scene promising envious Germans that he would help them flush Jews out of their country. At that time, Jews were the most successful people in all fields; they excelled in science, business, politics, education, you name it. All those Germans needed was a country devoid of Jewish competitors. Similarly, Donald Trump presented himself to the Americans as someone who will help them drive out the Mexicans he supposedly referred

to as drug traffickers, rapists, and murderers. He captivated the Christians by promising to overturn any LGBTQ legislations that threatened American morality and strongly opposed funding abortionist organizations. Many American Christians easily fell for his manipulations without necessarily questioning Trump's personal Christian convictions as revealed in his personal life.

3.  **Use of dark psychology in business:** If you are having some business dealings with a dark psychologist, it is a very dangerous thing to do. Why? His/her eyes are always on the prize—the money—and how he/she will defraud you and have everything for himself/herself. He/she doesn't mind going to any extent to actualize his/her desire. A business partner who practices dark psychology will manipulate you in every stage of your business interactions just to give himself/herself an edge in the negotiations, share of the business proceeds, or even claim everything for himself/herself. It is no longer news that the main reasons people lose in business is that the other person cheated them out of the deals. In the same way, a salesman that is nudging you into purchasing something you don't need, using weird persuasive techniques to strip you of your hard-earned money is a dark psychologist. It is not uncommon to see people regret a new purchase shortly after they had splashed the money, they didn't really want to spend on it. "Oh gosh, I shouldn't have bought this thing!" They will beat themselves soon after the dark psychologist salesperson has gone away with their money. Lately, there has been a growing concern

about corporate manipulation, whereby a company turns its employees into senseless, single-minded robots that rehearse the company's mantra every morning meeting and perceive competitors as deadly enemies. Some of these neurotic employees can leave their own families for the company, spending a lot of overtime in the office just to promote the cause of the company while not minding their own personal health and happiness.

4. **Use of dark psychology in social circles:** Everyone has friends, relatives, neighbors, or acquaintances they are very close to. Recent instances revealed that someone is likely to be manipulated 75% more times by people they trust more than those people they have no relationships with. In this case, people you confide in, such as your parents, lovers, siblings, childhood friends, and religious leaders may turn around to hurt you through selfish manipulation of your subconscious. Fake friends, they say, are worse than enemies. Their envy or jealousy of your achievements might drive them crazy to the point that they may be willing to try dark psychology on you. Are you a member of a social group or association? Have you been vilified by the other group members because one member has controlled the thoughts of the other members against you? You see, the applications of dark psychology are more prevalent than one can ever imagine.

5. **Use of dark psychology in education:** Have you ever wondered what in the world could have given birth to a very deadly movement named Islamic State in Iraq and the Levant

(ISIS) that killed many innocent souls and destabilized many erstwhile peaceful communities? That was the power of educational manipulation! Today, in various parts of the world, millions of people (or students) are still being trained to hate others for no obvious reasons. A great proportion of this educational manipulation is enshrined in religion. They coerced people to fight a "holy" religious war against people who have done nothing to incite such a holy battle. The severity of educational manipulation can be felt in every corner where violence, chaos, and societal disturbances are caused by miseducation (or misinformation), from the shores of Europe, America, to Africa.

6. **Use of dark psychology in religion:** Talking about religion is a very sensitive issue, I know. However, religion has now been used by some dastard dark psychologists as a ploy to manipulate, coerce, and rob people of their possessions. Today, church leaders, who are supposed to protect and tenderly look after congregants who look up to them for spiritual upliftment, have turned themselves into their "lords". They milk their followers of their last pound or dollar, flying in private jets while their church members grapple with disheartening levels of poverty. They have sweet-talked or manipulated their congregants into parting with the money they should have spent on themselves and their families.

You see, the outcome of the applications of dark psychology is usually the same—to leave the victim in a poorer state, more dejected, and hurt. This is why you should take every piece of information you see in this book seriously and work on keeping yourself and loved ones safe from the evil people.

## THE DARK SIDE

Everyone has his/her dark side. Some people are natural liars, cheaters, and deceitful. Instead of focusing on how to rebuild or polish their characters and become good people in their respective communities, they may choose to perpetuate their asocial behaviors. What do you expect a liar to do when he/she eventually acquires the knowledge of dark psychology?

It is part of our humanity to utilize our newly acquired knowledge either to do good or evil. A doctor, for instance, knows that he/she has the power to heal or kill a patient. In this scenario, the destiny of the patient is in the doctor's hands, and if the evil part of his/her mind dictates to him/her to end the patient's life, so shall it be!

It is equally scary realizing that the proliferation of affordable dark psychology courses online can equip some fake friends, disloyal relatives, or even envious colleagues with some powers to manipulate you. When a dark psychologist pounces on you, he/she doesn't have any good thoughts or intentions towards you. All he/she wants to accomplish is to bring you down, take your possessions and, in an unfortunate circumstance, take your life. To be sincere, we are in more danger right now than ever before; this is why it is advisable you should acquire all the necessary knowledge about these evil people and protect yourself.

## BE WARY

It is now your responsibility to be wary of people that may want to use dark psychology against you and your loved ones. Protecting your sanity and living a balanced, happy life should be the goal you daily pursue, because those great things you cherish, such as your peace of mind, happiness, and balanced life are what dark psychologists are targeting.

You probably have read or heard people say any of these things:

- Simple manipulation is not dark psychology
- Hypnotism is not dark psychology
- Coercive persuasion is not dark psychology
- Simple mind control is not dark psychology
- Neuro-linguistic programming (NLP) is not dark psychology

Be careful, the first subtle action of a manipulator is to misinform you. Those who are clamoring that simple manipulation, hypnotism, coercive persuasion, mind control, and NLP aren't elements of dark psychology have grossly missed the point. In Science Daily, a reputable publication that provides current information about how pure science affects humanity, has this to say about "dark psychology": *"All dark traits can be traced back to the general tendency of placing one's own goals and interests over those of others even to the extent of taking pleasure in hurting other's -- along with a host of beliefs that serve as justifications and thus prevent feelings of guilt, shame, or the like."*

If someone will use simple manipulation, NLP, or coercive persuasion to make himself/herself better at your expense, that counts as dark psychology because the person does not need your permission to psychologically manipulate you so that he/she can get away with whatever he/she wants, justifying his/her actions with certain beliefs.

As you continue reading this book and unearthing more facts about dark psychologists and their evil tricks, something that should be ringing at the back of your mind should be: "Only I am responsible for protecting myself!". Before you open the doors of your mind to someone, asking these six questions may help you stay safe:

- **Who is this person?** Ask yourself who this person is: What kind of character does he/she have? What is appealing about him/her? Is he the kind of person I can confidently open up to? These preliminary questions will help you discover what kind of person you are about to allow into your space. Character, they say, is like a smoke; there is no way anyone can hide his/her character for a very long time. Like smoke, even when it is covered with a bowl, it will find a way to make itself known. And when you discovered that a person's character doesn't match with yours, and that there is no inkling or chemistry between the two of you, it is a sign that you should literally take cover. Do not be that person who believes he/she can change someone. The only person that will be changed, that will be decimated in an event of manipulation is you, if you are not careful.
- **What does he/she want?** Sometimes people hide their true motives when they approach us for something. A

person who presents himself/herself as prospective business partner may actually be looking for love. You can save yourself from a lot of embarrassment if you could quickly detect what an acquaintance truly wants before letting your guards down on all fronts. You can proactively protect yourself in every area of your life.

- **How much space can I give to him/her?** Not everyone that knocks on the door of your mind should be welcomed in. Some people deserve to have doors slammed shut in their faces, because of the extent of their wickedness. Great and talented entertainers have lost their dear lives because they were not careful who they allowed into their personal spaces. Without mentioning names, beautiful singers who took to taking drugs and energetic sportsmen and sportswomen whose careers got destroyed before their lovers had introduced them to enhancing drugs. Had they been careful about who they allowed into their private spaces; they would still be alive today making good music.

- **How to act when I discover early signs of manipulation:** If you detect early on that the person you are dealing with is a manipulator, count yourself very lucky. The truth is that most victims don't even know they are already in the trap of a dark psychologist until he/she has finished dealing with them. So, after discovering he/she is a manipulator, you have to act swiftly. If you can, sit the dark psychologist down and question his/her motives. However, if you sense he/she could be defensive to the point of being violent, you can easily let him/her go without raising any dust. Just cut off your engagement with him/her.

- **What am I gaining from this?** For anyone who has already gone too deep with a manipulator or dark psychologist, there is still a way to escape. It begins by asking this question: "What am I gaining from this?" Is this situation comfortable for my personal and professional development? Take for instance, if you have married a manipulator or signed a multiyear contract with a manipulating company or business associate, you still need to ask yourself whether you are deriving any tangible thing from the alliance or not. If you are just being used on a daily and you have nothing to show for being in that relationship, it is time to consider the next question.

- **How do I get myself out of this mess?** Very few victims of dark psychology practitioners get to this stage where they can quickly come to their senses and strategize to free themselves from a manipulator's stranglehold. Many of them have already been decimated, abused, used, harassed, and pushed into a complete state of hopelessness before they can recoil from their misery streak. If you are in the situation, you should immediately seek help; it may be difficult for you to take yourself out of the funk you have put yourself. You should consider yourself fortunate to still be alive to rehabilitate yourself. Many have been sent to their graves early; they are no more here to reflect on the mess they have made of their lives by carelessly allowing manipulators to destroy them.

One of the reasons this book was written is to create enough awareness for people so that they don't necessarily fall into all the problems that manipulations, dark psychology, and hypnotism bring about. You can save your friends, families, and colleagues by sharing all that you will discover in this book with them.

Being a victim of a dark psychologist is never pretty: Apart from the financial and social fallouts from the experience, it could lead to a disgraceful mental health issue. For the rest of their lives, the victims of dark psychology often find it difficult to trust anyone; they are always suspicious of people's actions because they cannot afford to be maltreated again. They naturally fortify their defense mechanisms and keep potential manipulators at bay.

Are you wondering why practitioners of dark psychologists don't seem to have any conscience that their actions are hurting others? In the next chapter, you will discover the three main or core dark traits in people who derive some satisfaction in causing discomfort for others.

In their research, Ingo Zettler, Professor of Psychology at the University of Copenhagen, and two German colleagues, Morten Moshagen from Ulm University and Benjamin E. Hilbig from the University of Koblenz-Landau concluded that *"in the same way, the dark aspects of human personality also have a common denominator, which means that -- similar to intelligence -- one can say that they are all an expression of the same dispositional tendency."*

This indicates that whether they are hypnotists or manipulators, their evil goals are the same—to turn people into hopeless beings!

# 5

# THE DARK TRIAD

The dark sides of humanity, or to put it mildly, the dark behaviors of human beings through which they inflict pain and sorrow on others, come in different forms. In this book, attempt is made to distil all those various acts of human wickedness into just three major types. Collectively, they are referred to as "The Dark Triad".

## WHAT IS THE DARK TRIAD?

The Dark Triad is not a phrase you often hear people throw around, but they describe some of the major psychological traits exhibited by people. These traits dictate how people behave, and how they treat the others in their surroundings.

History has it that the term "The Dark Triad" started to gain public recognition in 1990s when a group of psychologists/scientists including McHoskey, Worzei, Szyarto, and Delroy L. Paulhus debated the similarities and differences among the three core components of The Dark Triad, namely, Narcissism, Machiavellianism, and Psychopathy.

Since then, the term has garnered much interest among psychologists/scientists, and studies and/or experiments on how it fully impacts humanity.

## NARCISSISM

Narcissism originates from a Greek mythology that tells the story of a hunter, Narcissus, who got attracted to or fell in love with his own shadow in the pool until he drowned. A narcissistic person has a tendency to exhibit any or most of the following personality traits: Pride, lack of empathy, egotism, arrogance, boastfulness, grandiosity, hypersensitive to criticism, and selfishness.

It is human nature to always desire to be in relationship or have something to do with whoever agrees with us on most occasions. If you are working with or in a romantic relationship with a narcissist, you will feel some degree of discomfort.

There are four distinct dimensions of narcissism observable in various capacities:

- **Leadership/Authority:** Narcissistic leaders demonstrate absolute disregard for their subordinates. Do you know those self-assured company owners or presidents who look down on every other person on their premises? They are only concerned about what they can gain from their employees, pushing them so hard to the point that it may be to their detriment. But then they never cared a hoot about their employees' welfare.

- **Superiority/Arrogance:** Some people who fortunately found themselves in high, covetous social positions or have luckily acquired some wealth may be so arrogant to the point of being cruel. He/she will reveal his sense of superiority to everyone around him/her, making them feel inferior at all times.

- **Self-absorption/Self-admiration:** Dealing with self-absorbed or self-admired persons is the most difficult thing to do. They only see the good in themselves; every other person, to them, is useless, hopeless, and not worth appreciating.

- **Exploitativeness/entitlement:** If you are in a relationship of any sort with an exploitative individual, he/she takes from you to make himself/herself better. In other words, they add value to themselves by reducing you. A husband/wife who often feels entitled will drive you crazy until he/she gets exactly what he/she wants. Come to think of spending thirty or forty years with people like that, you will both be physically and mentally exhausted.

## Why narcissists are very dangerous

Depending on which culture you are coming from, sometimes the societies or cultures confuse narcissism with high self-esteem. They do not necessarily see it as psychological or behavioural disorder. This wrong perception of narcissism gives ample room for narcissists to go out of control. There has been reports of narcissistic abuse lately due to the fact that our cultures—most especially, the winner-takes-all mentality, has given some people an edge to undermine the integrity of the others while claiming they are more important that anyone else.

Another disturbing issue is what psychologists refer to as narcissistic rage, which often occurs when someone who feels too important discovers that people around him/her aren't buying into their assumed self-importance. Many people have ended up being maltreated or suffered what is called narcissistic injury because the narcissists think they have the right to defend themselves, or whatever they believe about themselves.

It must be stated clearly that no one who inhabits the same space with a narcissist will ever like what he/she is experiencing. In certain extreme circumstances, it may cause their victims to suffer mental health issues—just like an abusing wife or husband will cause their spouse to go through some moments of insanity.

Three main approaches often used by a narcissistic individual to remain relevant in his/her own eyes is to manipulate others through:

- **Threats:** They can threaten to do some harsh things to anyone who are not on the same page with them.
- **Guilt:** They make others feel guilty or less important in all conditions.
- **Jealousy/envy:** Presenting themselves as the most

successful person in the room, thereby spurring people into becoming envious or jealous.

## MACHIAVELLIANISM

The word "Machiavellianism" is coined from the name of a 16th-century Italian politician or diplomat, Niccolo Machiavelli. He published a book in 1513 titled "The Prince" which was seen by his readers as a shameful endorsement of the tricky dark arts of manipulating people with deceitfulness and exhibiting unempathetic temperament.

Psychologists have since labelled this trait after him, and a Machiavellian individual employs lies, tricks, and duplication to get whatever he/she wants. He/she does so with apparent lack of emotion. He/she hotly pursues his/her self-interest at the expense of others and lack morality.

If you have ever come across someone in your life who will do anything, including lying and being dubious just to get whatever he/she is aiming at, you have dealt with a Machiavellian person.

It is an undeniable fact that everyone is different. To have a better understanding of how a Machiavellian person thinks, feels, and reasons, we need to consider these attitudes that are usually attributed to Machiavellianism:

- **Poor emotional attachment to others:**
  Machiavellianism is characterized by extremely cold disposition towards others. In other words, they do not, in

principle, express empathy towards anyone; when someone is in pain or enmeshed in some dangerous circumstances, a Machiavellian person just looks the other way instead of showing some sympathy. This explains why they are easily susceptible to harming other people without showing any remorse.

- **Deceitful manipulation:** Even though a Machiavellian individual realizes that he/she doesn't deserve something, he/she will still give it a shot and use lies, tricks, and deceits to take advantage of others. This is common in business, politics, diplomacy, and even among siblings.

- **Duplicity:** Duplicity entails calling things what they are not in order to flatter and deceive people at the same time. A person that shows duplicity in all his/her dealings is likely to use sweet words to cajole people, causing them to do what they didn't intend to do or part with their money or other valuable possessions. This attribute is common to all manipulators whose primary intentions are to make themselves better at the expense of others. They can praise and confuse you with their fake interest in your wellbeing; however, they are not being truthful because down in their hearts, they know that they do not care a hoot about you. Isn't this dangerous?

- **Hardcore selfishness:** By default, it is practically impossible for a Machiavellian to put himself/herself in the position of his/her victim. In other words, they don't seem to feel the same level of pain and agony that their unlucky victims are going through. This leaves them with only one option—to concentrate fully on what they could gain from a relationship. This hardcore selfishness is what motivates a Machiavellian individual to push others to the wall while enjoying himself/herself throughout the entire process. Naturally, friendship between two people is expected to be based on mutual self-respect and considerations. However, when one of them is a shameless and heartless Oliver Twist, asking for more and more until the other is exhausted and dried up, such a friend must be avoided at all cost.

- **Irresistible hunger for power and relevance:**
  Excessive greed and personal gratification are two things that often motivate a Machiavellian in any relationship. They may first pretend as if money, power, and personal aggrandizements are not their primary goals for striking up an acquaintance with you, but their barefaced pretentions won't last long. The eagerness with which they pursue their selfish desires can be harmful as they aren't willing to slow down until they accomplish their evil intentions. This is why you should take flight when you come across such an individual.

## PSYCHOPATHY

Psychopathy is the third of The Dark Triad, and it is considered, in psychiatry, as antisocial personality disorder (ASPD). The word "psychopathy" is usually confused with sociopathy and psychosis. Sociopathy is used to describe a list of asocial behaviors that include manipulation, lack of manners and empathy, aggressiveness, and deceitfulness. On the other hand, psychosis is a condition, usually associated with mental illness, that affects the way a person's brain processes information. A psychotic individual may lose touch with reality, and he/she may be seeing, hearing, believing things that are not real.

## Signs of Psychopathy

A psychopath usually shows some or all of the following signs:

- **Asocial behavior:** A psychopath often reveals some asocial behaviors which indicate a certain degree of irresponsibility on his/her part. He/she may be aggressive to others and show a low moral sense.
- **Absolute disregard for the rights of others:** Psychopaths may find it very difficult to appreciate the fact that others have rights that should be protected and respected.
- **Right versus the wrong:** Owing to their callousness, psychopaths may not be able to differentiate the right from the wrong. When they are hurting people, they do not perceive it as a bad thing. In fact, they derive some weird joy in putting others in trouble. More so, what seems right to them might only be things that tickle their fancy, even though they are publicly considered to be illegal or immoral.
- **Apparent lack of empathy:** Psychopaths are not necessarily empathetic to other people's feelings, whether they are sad or in pain. This accounts for their cruel attitudes towards others.

- **Habitual liars:** On most occasions, psychopaths are liars or have a tendency to lie often. They need to fabricate falsehood from time to time to cover up their selfish behaviors. They never care if their lies could put others in a big problem or not; all they want is to achieve their self-centered goals.

- **Cruelly manipulating and hurting others:** It has become psychopaths' second nature to manipulate and hurt others. They do this both randomly and intentionally. And they do not care what effects their unkind actions would have on others. Can you imagine how annoying it will be when someone who causes you pain does not feel he/she is doing a bad thing.

- **Tendency to break laws:** It is common for psychopaths to have recurring problems with the law. It is in their attitude to disrespect law and order. In addition to undermining other people's rights, they go out of their ways to flout rules and laws enacted for safety in the societies. You are likely going to see a psychopath driving on the wrong side of the road or smoking in non-smoking areas.

- **Common disregard towards responsibility:** Since they have low moral sense, they do not show adequate regard toward any act of responsibility. Psychopaths are much likely not to pay their taxes or participate in community development activities.

- **Reckless behavior:** They act recklessly and show no respect for people in places of authority. They can easily join criminal gangs or groups of domestic terrorists. They can act impetuously in the public, like driving a car through a crowd.

- **Tendency to take risks:** Psychopaths are known for taking risks. Sometimes their risky actions expose others to danger, and they do not really care about the outcomes of their deeds.

## Similarities and differences among the Dark Triads

The main similarity among the Dark Triads is that a Narcissist, a Machiavellian, and a Psychopath lack empathy for others' feelings. They are not concerned about how their hurtful actions will impact the lives of their victims. This lackadaisical demonstration of wickedness is why people generally dislike them. You cannot afford to stay in a long relationship with any of them because it will have some effects on your mental health. All of them are also shameless manipulators; they are naturally fond of deceiving others to achieve their selfish ambitions.

However, while a Narcissist is boastful and full of pride, a Machiavellian lacks moral aptitude and practices duplicity, and a Psychopath demonstrates absolute disregard for the rights of others and under risky and illegal activities that can endanger others' lives.

As you can see, those who habitually exhibit the characteristics of the Dark Triads have no reasons to care about you. They really can't understand whether what they are doing to you is hurtful or not. They do not show empathy; in short, they are not feeling what you feel. And that is why you should protect yourself and your loved ones from them.

# 6

# HARMLESS PERSUASION VERSUS DARK PERSUASION

How do you differentiate a harmless salesperson that knocks on your door to sell you something that you probably need from the one who intentionally comes to your home to carry out dark persuasion on you? Most people will agree that this is a very tricky question. It is an undeniable fact that we are regularly subjected to these two kinds of persuasion: Harmless persuasion and dark persuasion.

In this chapter, you will discover some elements of dark persuasion and red flags you should always be looking for when approached by someone who displays some traits of persuasive manipulation.

## PERSUASION, AT ITS CORE

Persuasion is the process of compulsively passing certain information across to someone whose attitude may be altered or influenced by the information delivered. In itself, persuasion doesn't connote negativism; it is not harmful since the person who is being persuaded has the right to accept or reject the information or persuasion.

In life, persuasion is a common tool used by people for different good purposes. It can be used to engender an effective communication within a team in an organization. Parents normally persuade their children to choose the right paths in life. Teachers often persuade their students to do their best at their examinations.

However, some psychologists believe that persuasive communication, though commonly employed in education and meetings, may turn out to be forceful and threatening. Take for instance, a teacher may choose to punish one of his/her students by talking down to him/her. This kind of punitive approach may elicit negative reactions from the student being targeted. The student may be scared, ashamed, and defensive, having been embarrassed in front of the entire class.

In principle, the nature of a persuasive communication depends on how the receiver of the information interprets it. Take for example, while Student A, shy and unassuming may consider being talked down in front of class as demeaning and improper, Student B, popular and shameless, may capitalize on the teacher's action to become more popular with his classmates.

## WHEN IS IT CONSIDERED HARMLESS?

As briefly hinted above, persuasion may be harmless and good for the receiver. Why? Because not all persuasive communications are meant to harass, demean, and manipulate the receiver, as shown below. We can see examples of this in marketing, literature, legal practice, and even in all professions.

- **Harmless persuasion in marketing:** From the fleeting commercial adverts on your TVs to long, windy infomercials, some companies located somewhere are bombarding you with persuasive information to encourage you to dip your hands in your wallet or purse and buy something from them. Whether they appear at your doorstep physically or reach out to you via email or web chat, salespersons are trying to convince you to intentionally part with some of your money and purchase some things from them. As you can see, it is done harmlessly: No threatening words are used, no one is beating fear into you for the purpose of destabilizing you emotionally. There are reports that some overambitious salespersons do go beyond the sensible marketing stint, pulling some little persuasive tricks on you. However, if you are able to quickly come to your senses, you can tell such an overreaching salesperson to stop it, and he/she will immediately behave properly. He/she may even apologize for pushing too hard. It is clear that such a salesperson, despite being anxious to sell his/her merchandizes, doesn't mean evil for his/her prospective customer. He/she will do everything in his/her power to act nicely and courteously.

- **Harmless use of persuasion in literature:** There are some aspects of literature that require students to persuasively defend their beliefs in reading and writing critique classes. Each student will vehemently speak in support of their personal opinions or perspectives about the book being read or a writing piece under critique. None of them is making an attempt to manipulate anyone; they are just engaging one another in an academic persuasion.

- **Harmless application of persuasion in legal proceedings:** Anyone who has attended a legal proceeding at the court will have seen how lawyers compellingly persuade the judges to consider the case from their perspectives. The lawyers, doing their job, do not mean any evil for the judges; they are merely doing what they needed to do for the goodness of their clients. Persuasion, in such a light, is positive and harmless.

- **Harmless persuasions in other areas:** Everyone will agree that physicians, sometimes and allowed by their profession, do persuade their patients to take some medicines or try a new type of treatment. In the same way, when a police officer persuades a criminal to surrender himself/herself to the law, the officer doesn't mean to harm the criminal at that moment if he/she doesn't make any threatening gestures towards the officer. If you are a fan of football, you will also have seen how coaches yell at their players on the field, persuading to tackle an advancing opponent ruthlessly but skillfully. In all these rife examples, no one is at danger of being dangerously manipulated, undermined, and turned into a victim.

You may be wondering why politicians' speeches are not used as a typical example of positive persuasive communication. While it may be true that not all politicians make conscious efforts to manipulate their followers or party members, however, politicians' tendency to incite crowd against their political rivals makes it unsuitable to consider their speeches harmless or non-insinuating. In politics, it is usually "I" against "He/she" or "Us" against "Them". This can establish a negative atmosphere whereby members of a political party can cause mayhem that could lead to unprecedented destruction and harm for members of the opposing party.

Religious leaders, for example, are good examples of people that adopt persuasive communication to exhort their followers to remain holy and steadfast in their religious callings. They may shout at the top of their lungs at the altars just to make sure that their congregants aren't backsliding, leaving their faith in the Lord to engage in sinful life.

Positive, harmless persuasion is meant to bring the best out of someone else's life. It is a tool for nudging people to take decisive actions in making their lives better.

## Elements of harmless persuasion

For simplicity purpose, these are characteristics of harmless persuasion that you should be looking for. Being vigilant on all occasions can save you and your loved ones from impending calamities. When someone is persuading you for any reasons at all, see if he/she is:

- **Putting your needs forward:** A good salesperson will repeatedly tell you what you can gain from purchasing his/her products or services. Your parents, who disturb you with their countless pieces of advice, sometimes unsolicited, are just rooting for you and your future success. Your teacher who seems to be talking to you harshly in front of other classmates is trying his/her best to guide you. You see, you are at the center of a positive, harmless persuasion, geared towards making you better and stronger.

- **Establishing harmless relationships:** Cruel manipulators don't necessarily care about making you feel welcomed or appreciated in their space. They abruptly come into your life, want to control you, and then leave you dejected and spent after they might have achieved their selfish ambitions. Isn't it crazy for a hopeless guy who slithers his way into a celebrity lady's bedroom only to hold her to ransom, threatening to release all her nude pictures on the internet if she doesn't pay some undisclosed amount of money? Immediately you noticed a sneaky person trying to control you even if you have just met a few days, weeks, months ago, you should consider that as a red flag. It is important to draw a comparison with that; a well-intentioned person will come to your life, tread carefully based on your permission, and continue to hold you in high esteem. Nowadays, the internet has made it possible for people to fall in love without getting to knowing each other better. There have been confirmable reports that some unlucky girls have fallen into the hands of serial killers or pedophiles because they were not quite cautious enough in their approach to seeking friendships from strangers.

- **Listening to your opinions:** if anyone trying to persuade you for whatever reasons fails to listen to your own opinions on the situation, there is every possibility that such a person may be undermining your personal rights. That should give you a sign that the person you are dealing with has a tendency of being a manipulator. Even strict parents tend to give their children the benefit of the doubt to prove themselves nowadays. For every persuasion you received, it is in your hands to accept or reject it. So, if anyone, it doesn't matter who he/she, is compelling or coercing you to do what you dislike, that is purely a manipulative act.

## WHAT MAKES IT DARK?

At this junction you may be wondering what exactly counts as dark persuasions, and what makes them dark? Efforts are made in this book to simplify everything for you. So, sit down and let each fact sink into your mind.

Persuasion becomes dark when these dark persuasion techniques are used by manipulators to steal from you, control you, or compel you to choose a dangerous course of life. Anyone who utilizes any of the following dark persuasion techniques on you is not worth your time and respect:

- **Seduction:** Literally, the word "seduction" means the act of persuading someone of the opposite sex to go to bed with you. While this definition is directly related to the issue of manipulation, whereby men and women use "sex" as a weapon to control one another. However, "seduction" has expanded meanings—it could mean the act of luring someone into believing something so that they take actions without properly thinking it through. The creators of Ponzi schemes apply this interpretation to rob people of their hard-earned wealth. They will tell you to deposit your money in their schemes and earn multiple interests in returns. If your country's harmonized interest rate is around 15%, a Ponzi Scheme may be promising you an interest of 35% on any deposit you made. True to their words, the Ponzi schemers will pay you the promised 35% in the first few months of depositing your hard-earned money in their coffers. However, after some time, having collected a lot of money from different victims, the schemers will turn their backs on everyone and declare bankruptcy, while hiding their loots in foreign bank accounts abroad.

- **Brainwashing:** Brainwashing, which is also known as coercive persuasion, is broadly discussed in Chapter 8 of this book. It is a common dark persuasive technique used by dogmatic religious, political, and cultural leaders. They forcefully put "thoughts" into their followers' heads and rob them the unique opportunity to think for themselves. Hitler did it perfectly and pulled the entire world through a six-year war. Several terrorist organizations are employing the same technique to turn their followers into "human" explosives that wear self-detonating bombs and kill innocent people.

- **Enticement:** A manipulator may decide to first entice his/her prospective victim with something he/she cannot resist or refuse. An unemployed lady may be trapped by a job offer that does not exist. People have been ensnared by fraudsters who presented irresistible financial investments to them, only for them to lose all their money invested in the spurious or fake investments.

- **Coercion:** This is entirely different from the other methods adopted by manipulators in the sense that it is the person controlling them—a spouse, relation, or business partner—forces them to do the exact opposite they intended to do. When held hostage by a kidnapper, the victim is bound to follow all the strict instructions passed down by his/her captor. In this scenario, there is little chance to oppose the kidnapper that could be very dangerous.

- **Isolationism:** In certain cases, a manipulator may stay in the background and direct others under his/her guidance to carry out his/her dark persuasive communication. Those acting under his leadership will then bombard the targeted victim with whatever actions they are directed to undertake. If the victim fails to cower or surrender, they will isolate him/her from their group or association. In this way, they are trying to make the victim suffer from guilt that was projected on him/her by others. In very few circumstances, the targeted victim will be able to free himself/herself from their attacks, which could be prolonged.

In summary, a manipulator is a self-centered, malicious individual whose primary aim is to control, coerce, decimate, and exterminate his/her victim if he/she is left unchallenged.

## DIFFERENTIATING THE TERMS

It is important to identify the similarities and differences between persuasion and manipulation. This will remove any confusion that often arises when people use the two terms. While they do have some similarities, they are quite different from one another.

**Similarities:** Both persuasion and manipulation involve talking or have some discussions with another person. And both persuasion and manipulation are initiated by the individual who is trying to persuade or manipulate the other.

**Major differences:** The differences between persuasion and manipulation can be best understood by considering the three points highlighted below:

- **The intention:** People are usually persuaded to embrace a better way of life or turn away from bad lifestyles that could harm them and destroy their future. A child that keeps failing his/her exams may receive constructive persuasion from his/her concerned teacher. On the contrary, manipulation is intended to turn the receiver into a victim of the manipulator, for the purpose of robbing him/her of some precious things.
- **Truthfulness:** When you receive persuasion from someone who truly cares about your wellbeing or success, he/she will interact with you in all honesty and truthfulness. He/she will frankly address the main issue that may be threatening your career, marriage, or success.

However, a manipulator comes to you with all tools in his/her pocket. If he/she discovers that you are a hard nut to crack, the manipulator will employ falsehood or blatant lies to confuse and mislead you. A Ponzi Scheme owner will tell you all manners of lies just to make sure you part with your hard-earned money and invest it in his/her Scheme.

- **Who benefits from the interaction?** It is obvious that constructive or positive persuasion is meant to encourage you to veer from a wrong path to a much promising career choice or lifestyle. On the other hand, a manipulator comes after you because of what he/she stand to gain from the relationship or interaction. In this scenario, the manipulator will make himself/herself the center or focus of the interaction instead of you.

- **The approach adopted:** Persuasion is mostly soft and benign; there are no overt issuance of threats and acrimonious words or expressions. However, a lot of threats and coercion are employed in manipulation. The goal of a shameless manipulator is to beat fear into the heart of his/her victim before decimating them. Most people lose their mental strength when bullied or threatened; that is exactly the approach manipulators use.

## KNOW WHAT IT IS

You should be aware of these persuasion techniques so that you can immediately detect when people go overboard while using any of them. Manipulators also use them, but they always stretch things too thin just to make sure that they achieve their evil intentions:

- **Anticipation:** When you are being persuaded, what the person who is persuading you wants to achieve is to make you anticipate the good things that may come to your life if you choose to change course and do the right things in your education, business, marriage, and so on. A picture of a better life will be painted for you to fantasize about and work towards attaining.

- **Unity of purpose:** The person persuading you will make you feel that you are on the same page—that there is unity of purpose between the two of you. Take for example, if you want to advance in your business and increase your stream of income, a mentor will let you understand that he/she is there for you so that you can improve your cash flow. At that moment, the person isn't talking about himself/herself, he/she is discussing how you can take your business to the next level.

- **Emotional energy:** Everyone loves it when friends, relatives, and neighbors demonstrate strong interest in their well-being, because they will reveal their feelings towards us through their high-energy emotional expressions. Imagine you have just won the lottery, and a neighbor runs out of his/her flat to greet you on the street with two arms stretched out in from of him//her. That shows the level of excitement in him/her to see you succeed!

- **Commitment and consistency:** Naturally, we tend to

listen to someone who consistently commits himself/herself to directing us in the right ways. We will feel that they have abandoned their own needs to concentrate on making us happier, better, and more prosperous. To be honest, that is one of the best approaches for persuading someone—sticking with it until success comes.

- **"Because..."**: Everyone desires to know the reason why he/she is being persuaded. In that case, an individual who thinks that there are cogent reasons you should change courses and embrace another approach will come to tell you the reasons why. He/she may be your colleague, boss, classmate, or even your spouse. Knowing the reasons for a change might speed up the process of adapting to a newer or more improved system.

- **Reasoning by analogy:** It is common for people to reason by analogy when persuading one another. They can use stories, anecdotes, past testimonies, and popular events to drive home their points. This seems to have much impact on the person being persuaded. They can see clearly that someone was in their position before he/she did something to get out of the hopeless situation. Poor people are persuaded to work harder; telling them the story of people who have got out of poverty through sheer hard work may serve a great motivator.

- **Reciprocity:** Sometimes you are persuaded to take a certain action based on the good thing you have done for someone in the past. The person is merely reciprocating the good gesture by asking you to do the same thing. If you have, by chance, asked a friend to pay a lottery. If your friend surprisingly wins, he/she will surely come around to advise you to try it, too.

- **Authority:** An individual may offer you some pieces of advice based on his/her experience in the same area or field. His/her authority in the matter under discussion is enough to add more weight to his/her persuasion.

- **Urgency:** You can be persuaded by an individual who lets you see the urgency of the issue at hand, and that you have got no time to waste on rejecting his/her advice. In this case, you are encouraged to consider the matter quickly and make a sensible decision on time.

**Warning: As harmless as the techniques outlined above are, be forewarned that manipulators can also utilize them to hurt you. It is up to you to use your discretion in detecting when tricky people are asking for more than you could give. That could be a timely signal that a manipulator has invaded your space. Be wise!**

# 7

# WHAT YOU NEED TO KNOW ON MANIPULATION

People often confuse psychological manipulation with emotional manipulation. Even though the two terms share certain similarities, they are quite different from each other. Psychological manipulation is a kind of social influence on a person or a group of people so as to change their behaviors or perceptions about things through deceptive, indirect, or hidden tactics. However, emotional manipulation occurs when someone, for selfish purposes, tries to control others through exploitative strategies so that he/she can decimate, coerce, and even victimize his/her targets. These kinds of manipulation involve both targeting a victim, but emotional manipulation carries more weight than psychological.

**Watch out: Most of the people that use emotional manipulation on us are those that are very close to us— our lovers, relatives, best friends, and colleagues!**

## THE MANIPULATIVE BEHAVIOR

People are often advised to look out for some manipulative behaviors in people around them. The most important question that normally comes up is: What makes some people be manipulative in their behaviors or attitudes?

There are three unique answers to that question:

1. **Hereditary reason:** A person can come from a lineage or family history that literally has the "genes" for manipulating others. In other words, they naturally exhibit attitudes that redolent with dishonesty and lies. There could be a very strong reason for displaying this kind of behavior. If the family had in the past struggled for power, material resources, love and affection, control, social status and acceptance, it could have shifted their brains towards adapting several deceptive tactics to get by. This struggle might have occurred within the family or with an outsider. As a result of this, to keep whatever they had gained from deceptions, or manipulating others, they will persist in their socially unacceptable ways. Haven't you ever heard of an expression that "deception runs deep in that family!" It means everyone, from their young to old ones are shameless liars. There are many families like that, most especially the political families. They could be rude, deceitful, and manipulative just to keep maintaining their current social status.

2. **Not properly developed during the formative**

**years:** Those who did not grow up properly during their formative years often displayed certain cognitive weaknesses in their behaviors. And to make up for their shortcomings, they can be strangely aggressive, manipulative, and inconsiderate. It is their natural defense mechanisms; sometimes, they cannot personally explain some of their attitudes because they have become part and parcel of their daily routines. Therefore, they may not have room to accommodate feelings for others nor empathize with them. All they want is to prove to everyone that they are culturally, economically, socially, and professionally perfect, even though there is evidence about them that proves otherwise.

3. **Supportive environments for manipulation:** Sometimes, people don't want to be manipulative; however, the environments where they live allow such a thing. So, since it has become a norm or trend within that jurisdiction to be cunning, exploitative, deceptive, inconsiderate, aggressive, and manipulating, it just becomes a status quo for everyone there. In a competitive environment, such as a workplace or an industry, people or business owners tend to compete dangerously with one another. If there are not rules or standards that forbid or discourage unfair practices, there could be chronic manipulations in such an environment. To stay on top of their games, people could be ruthless, malicious, and manipulative.

## ARE YOU BEING MANIPULATED?

Unfortunately, not everyone can consciously detect or know that they are being manipulated. This may be due to the fact that they are living in an environment where acts of manipulation are rife or tolerated; so, they wrongly perceive manipulation as one of the social behaviors in their vicinities. Scientists and psychologists have spent years studying or researching how people can easily detect that a manipulator has entered into their space. Most studies reveal that people could only feel the effects of manipulation; that is when it dawns on them that they have become victims of cruel manipulations.

If you are experiencing any of the feelings outlined below, chances are that you are being manipulated by someone you allowed into your life:

- **Feeling being monitored:** If your instinct tells you that you are being constantly monitored, maybe by a jealous lover, an overbearing parent, or boss, you are inadvertently becoming a victim of manipulation. Those who are monitoring you have only one goal in mind: To dominate or control you! This is quite frustrating because you do not call for this kind of monitoring, and hence you cannot do anything to cause the evil monitoring to cease. You should take action immediately when you discover this: You may challenge those undertaking the monitoring or do something that will frustrate their weird efforts.
- **You are constantly being objectified:** Instead of being respected and treated nicely by people around you, they

pretty much treat you like an object. You are perceived as a "sex object" or any other types of objectification. In romantic relationships, you may be tolerated simply because of what your partner or spouse is deriving from you. In psychology, this condition is referred to "object constancy". Instead of openly showing their hatred, distaste, and anger towards you, they will continue to bear you as long as you continue to tickle their objectification fantasy. Trouble will begin when you no longer fit the bill. Reports show that many couples who were happy immediately after their weddings will start to have some problems in their marriage as soon as the wives began to give birth to children. You know what, since the women could no longer be referred to as "sexy", their unsatiated husbands will start looking for other pretty ladies outside, engaging in extramarital affairs. In essence, people who objectify you don't naturally love you; they are just putting up with you as long as you are satisfying their fantasies. In the same way, an inconsiderate, narcissistic employer may not like you at all; what he/she cares about is the good job you are doing for his/her business.

- **The need to feel superior:** Manipulators do not only target weak or vulnerable people, but they also have the habit of hunting for strong and emotionally stable individuals they can decimate. They realize that destroying a powerful person is a good opportunity to show that they matter. Their Machiavellian spirit will not rest until they have brought a highly placed individual down. If someone is always after you at your place of work or meetings, castigating you openly in the presence of other colleagues, you should mark such a person. He/she is trying to manipulate you and control your thoughts. In politics, the primary goal of an opposition politician is to make you lose focus, diverting your attention from your great policies while spending most of your precious time to respond to their destabilizing tactics.

- **Projection:** After spending some time to study you, manipulators will know what to do to get you angry or to be emotionally disturbed. To make the matter worse, they will turn around and accuse you of doing what they are exactly doing, deceptively covering their actions. For example, a manipulator may wrongly allege that you are planning to criminally implicate him/her at work. Meanwhile, his/her daily actions are to ensnare you at work by fabricating some lies against you. If you are not careful, you may believe their projections and start absorbing wrong energies.

- **Gaslighting:** The word "gaslighting" came from a 1944 movie "Gaslight" where an actor was controlling his wife and made her believe that she was crazy. In the same way, a manipulator nowadays will want to control or overpower you by letting you feel like you are crazy, literally. They will make you feel bad about yourself and position themselves as the solutions you need to be free from your problems. In that case, if you allow them, you have given them a front-seat position in your life; they can control your life the way they like.

- **Perspecticide:** This is a kind of emotional abuse that

occurs in a relationship whereby one partner controls the other to the extent that the victim loses his/her grip on truth and self-consciousness. The victim in this relationship automatically becomes a prisoner in that scenario, having lost his/her senses and cannot stand for what he/she believes. The controlling partner is responsible for everything, including what social, religious, and cultural ideas they must embrace in the relationship.

- **Bonding through trauma:** Manipulators are not always downright harsh and unkind. Sometimes, they act nicely to their victims. This is why some victims in abusive relationships never felt the urge to leave; they enjoy the feeling of being catered for but grossly overlooked the maltreatment they are getting from their manipulating partners.

- **"You are not doing your part":** When in a condition of psychological abuse, the controlling partner will always make the other feel inadequate in everything. He/she will usually cast blame on the other, so they start to doubt their capability.

- **Feeling guilty:** One greatest weapon often utilized by manipulators to absolutely control their victims is to make them feel guilty for nothing. They are constantly put in bad light by their nemesis so that they remain in a dejected or depressed situation. It is quite easy to pull a weak wall down; so also, a mentally weak person can be crushed in no time.

## MANIPULATIVE BODY LANGUAGE

It will save you a lot of trouble if you can quickly identify the common manipulative body language used by manipulators. As far as mischievous manipulation is concerned, the main difference between nonverbal communication and verbal communication is that you can spot the troublemaker in the distance before he/she strikes. Nonverbal communication comprises of signs and body language that you can read and interpret, giving you time to strategize and run for cover. On the other hand, verbal communication doesn't give you much time to run for your dear life because once discussing with a manipulator, there is more than 65 percent tendency that he/she may get you.

Familiarize yourself with the following examples of actual manipulative body language adopted by wicked manipulators:

- **Gestures:** Manipulators are fond of using demeaning gestures to control people. They can manipulate people in the way they move their hands, fingers, heads, legs, and arms. Every culture has its different types of gestures that aim to pass across certain instructions, information, or even threats. The manipulators are well aware of the meaning expressed by each gesture. They will concentrate on using those that are meant to threaten people or berate them so that they can make their victims feel uncomfortable and discomfited.

- **Rubbing hands and necks:** When they are trying to get into your psyche and control you, manipulators tend to rub their hands together. This harmless gesture, as well as neck rubbing, is perceived as an attempt to appear nervous and innocent before you so that they can push you into guilt. On most occasions, victims often cave into such gestures in order not to feel bad or evil, without knowing that the manipulators intentionally set a trap for them.

- **Stroking/scratching arm:** Pay attention to people who stroke or scratch their arms when talking with you. Manipulators do that a lot. They are trying to catch your attention, draw you in emotionally, and then control you. It is sad that as harmless this action is, many unsuspecting victims have fallen prey to hypnotists or manipulators.

- **Chin scratching:** It is believed that manipulators can also act like they are clueless when you are discussing with them. When little kids scratch their chins, they are showing their interlocutors that they are momentarily clueless. In an effort to sway your opinions, a manipulator can pretend to be clueless so that you can easily, out of pity, accept his/her sheepish suggestions.

- **Shifting body:** If a person is in an uncomfortable situation, they shift their body positions continuously. When a manipulator wants to make you feel unsettled, he/she will shift his/her body positions several times when you are chatting with him/her.

- **Foot tapping:** People normally tap their feet when they are scared or angry. When a manipulator does so, he/she is trying to dissuade you from taking a firm position about an issue. He/she wants you to jettison your opposition to the matter under discussion.

- **Eye contact:** Normally in communication, people use eye contacts to convey messages nonverbally. However, a manipulator's frown or grimace is an attempt to throw you off balance and take control or charge of the situation. If you are not careful, he/she may turn the situation against you to benefit himself/herself.

## DIFFERENT TYPES OF MANIPULATORS

You are likely going to come across different types of manipulators in your life. They don't usually possess the same characteristics and employ similar tactics. That is why it is somehow difficult to quickly identify them. Most of us have spent a great part of our lives cozying up with manipulators, thinking they were our friends, colleagues, or neighbors. Unfortunately, as you would have discovered in this book, manipulators are not after your goodness: They always have some ulterior motives, seeking their own selfish gratifications most of the time.

Could you remember dealing with any of these kinds of manipulators?

- **Covert aggressor:** A covert aggressor has also been called a wolf in sheep clothing. He/she doesn't physically or emotionally present himself/herself as an aggressor or a manipulator. In a critical circumstance, a covert aggressor can even be your mentor, business associate, or your spouse. Take for example, when you are listening attentively to all the pieces of advice your mentor is passing across to you, he/she is busy discrediting your ability to have better achievement. This is why covert aggressors are dangerous. Who else will you listen to other than your mentor? In a similar vein, while you are so passionately sharing your goals and ambitions with your spouse, who is a covert aggressor, he/she is secretly discouraging you from attempting them. A covert aggressor makes you feel inadequate and problematic and causes you to lose your self-esteem.

- **Active aggressors:** We can all immediately spot active aggressors when we meet them. By default, they never try to hide who they really are from people around them. Therefore, active aggressors don't really have many friends or associates because their counter-productive attitudes are not bearable to most people.

- **Passive aggressors:** On the other hand, passive aggressors can be described as the green snakes under the green grass. They don't usually come off manipulative or aggressive, but when given the chance or opportunity, once in a while, they can show their true colors. We all have that friend, uncle, stepbrother, boyfriend or girlfriend who can be unpredictable. Everyone knows that when he/she is pushed to the wall, literally, he/she could be very violent and break or throw things!

- **The ruthless competitor:** The primary reason a manipulator comes into your life is to present himself/herself larger than life over you. He/she shows up to compete with you, ruthlessly. If the need arises, the manipulator could be quite destructive just to make himself/herself at your expense.

- **The heartless criticizer:** Have you ever come across a person who has never seen anything good in others? A heartless criticizer will speak unkindly of everyone. Their evil intention is to make you doubt yourself in everything. You will often see yourself as inexperienced, inadequate, and unworthy of living a better life or achieving something great in your career.

- **The shameless threatener:** It is evident that all manipulators threaten their victims. Beating fear into people's minds is one of the strongest tools or weapons. They threaten to expose you to the public or leak your nude pictures online if you don't do what they have demanded. Before you get into such a difficult position, you must be careful to analyse the behaviors of every new person you meet in your journey in life.

- **The silent treatment giver:** Being given a silent treatment among colleagues or friends could be quite emotionally disturbing or draining. A manipulator can utilize this weapon to undermine your integrity and cause you to be mesmerized. Other people at the place may imitate the silent treatment giver if he/she is in a higher position than you and the rest. You should always remember that what a manipulator wants to achieve is to make you feel less than you truly are.

- **Guilt-makers:** This kind of manipulator makes you feel guilty all the time about things. He/she may be a covert aggressor who is hiding his/her real reason from you but busy projecting all poor attitudes on you. For example, he/she may wrongly accuse you for his/her mistakes because something in him/her convinced him/her that the mistake could have been prevented if you had done your part. Bear in mind that it was his/her mistake, not yours!

## RELATIONSHIPS CAN BE MANIPULATIVE

There is somehow a grey area between love and hate in romantic relationships. Many lovers are finding it relatively difficult to differentiate loving relationships from the manipulative ones. However, human senses are designed in a way that we could smell troubles, literally, before they happen. If you are seeing some of the red flags described below, you are probably in or going to be in a manipulative relationship:

- **If you are not really sure if your partner is in love with you or not after dating him/her for several months or years:** Manipulators often do that; they will confuse their partners by keeping them around enough to satisfy their sexual urges or sense of objectification, but not trust them enough to want to marry them.
- **You and your partner always fight instead of sitting down to maturely discuss things.**
- **Your partner often tries to hide many things from you. In other words, he/she is not transparent, and he/she is harboring another agenda.**

- **If your partner is overtly negative:** Knowing that you cannot change anyone, you should be careful starting a relationship with a negative person because they are not going to change their negativity lifestyle overnight.
- **If you often feel that you are being manipulated or controlled by your partner, chances are that you are already in a manipulative relationship.**
- **True love can persevere; however, if your partner often gets angry at the slightest provocation, your relationship is not normal. The same partner would insult you nonstop if you refused to leave the relationship.**
- **When lovers deny each other sex, it is an indication that one of them is manipulative. He/she wants to use "sex" as a weapon to ask for something or make the other person feel unhappy.**
- **No relationship that is marred with resentment can thrive! If your partner is the one that keep malice or remain incommunicado because of a small argument, you are already in a manipulative relationship.**

# 8

# FACING THE FACTS OF HYPNOSIS, BRAINWASHING, AND MIND CONTROL

I n this chapter, you will learn about the three mutually related tools that the dark psychologists often use on their victims or victims-to-be. What you are about to discover will surely shock you! Why? You will soon find out how common dark psychologists utilize these life-wrecking weapons on people.

## THE TRUTH ON HYPNOSIS

Let's begin by separating the truth or facts from myths as far as hypnosis is concerned. Highlighted below are the most common myths about hypnosis that people have passed down from one generation to another:

- **Hypnosis will only work on certain people:** It is surprising that some people have held on to this misconception for too long. No wonder they cannot easily detect it when they are being hypnotized. To say the truth, some people may be more susceptible to hypnosis than others, but the truth remains that every human being can fall under hypnosis.

- **Only weak-minded people can be hypnotized:** This is another fallacy that has been widely promoted by those who are truly ignorant about hypnosis. Your mental strength has nothing to do with falling under the influence of hypnosis or not. It can affect all human beings, irrespective of the fact whether they are emotionally strong or weak.

- **Hypnosis is a state of unconsciousness or sleep:** This statement is not absolutely true: When you are being hypnotized, you may feel like you are in a state of sleep, but you are not practically asleep or unconscious. Many victims of hypnosis can still move some parts of their bodies and clearly remember everything they are doing when under the influence of hypnosis.

- **Hypnosis can't be dangerous:** To a certain degree, being put under the hypnotic effect may not be dangerous in itself, but do you know the ulterior motives of the dark psychologist who is putting you through the process? If he/she wants to harm you during that hypnotic moment, he/she has got an upper hand against you because you were in a totally defenseless situation.

That being said, hypnosis is not a completely bad concept because it has been put to a good use in alternative medicine. Have you ever heard of hypnotherapy? It is an alternative medical treatment that utilizes hypnosis to create an ultra-focus condition during which a person may be guided through a series of positive, life-transforming suggestions and imagery meant to impart a better lifestyle or health choice in them.

Some of the medical benefits of hypnotherapy include but are not limited to:

- **Controlling pain:** If you sustain some pain due to burns, childbirth, cancer, headaches, fibromyalgia, joint problems, or dental procedures, hypnotherapy can help you control the pain.
- **Experiencing behavioural change:** Hypnosis has been employed in successfully treating some health problems such as smoking, bed-wetting, overeating, and insomnia.
- **Dealing with hot flashes:** Hypnotherapy can be used to treat hot flashes that are connected with menopause.
- **Treating cancer side effects:** It is possible to treat cancer chemotherapy or radiation effects with hypnotherapy.
- **Managing mental health conditions:** Hypnotherapy has been used to successfully stabilize people with post-traumatic stress, anxiety, and phobias.

How do you know whether hypnosis is being put to a good or dangerous use? The answer to this question may not be as simple as you expect. The rule of thumb is that it depends on who is administering hypnosis on you, and for what purpose? If you are fully aware of the benefits of submitting yourself to the hypnotic procedure, chances are that you are doing it for your own good. Otherwise, a nemesis might be trying to control you for the purpose of robbing you of something that is quite precious to you!

## UNDER THE HYPNOTIC STATE

Hypnosis is a system that involves some processes. For you to be truly under the hypnotic state, someone has to perform hypnosis on you. This is contrary to the erroneous belief that we naturally get hypnotized by things that seriously catch our attention, such as a very beautiful and gorgeous lady or a fanciful car or mansion.

A hypnotist utilizes some techniques—known as hypnotic induction techniques—to get you hypnotized. Some of these hypnotic procedures are discussed below:

- **Visualization technique:** During guided visualization, a hypnotist deliberately takes your mind away from things or substances around and ask you to focus on some other things that usually give you joy or good feelings. The hypnotist will also encourage you to concentrate on some beautiful situations that you have experienced before and make you fantasize about enjoying the same great conditions now. For example, if you are the type who enjoy visiting exotic places across the world, the hypnotist can ask you to fully imagine you are in your best place right now while enjoying nature and other nice things the environment has got to offer. You will surely lose yourself in such an eerie feeling.

- **Eye fixation technique:** As its name implies, a hypnotist will instruct you to fixate on a particular object. Sometimes the chosen object will have either spiritual or cultural relevance so that you are enthralled focusing your eyes on it. After some time, your eyes are likely going to get tired of staring at the object. At that moment, you will reflexively close your eyes; you may even fall asleep since the muscles around your eyes have been weakened by the concentrating stare.

- **Rapid induction technique:** This technique is a little dramatic in the sense that it involves the hypnotist dragging you from one place to another, maybe by holding your two hands and pulling you around, shouting "sleep, sleep!". Sometimes, an experienced hypnotist may adopt what is referred to as Eriksson's handshake to pull you around. It is reported that most subjects, who are already shocked by this technique, often resist falling under the hypnotic state. They probably have been scared by the amount of pressure exerted on them by the hypnotist.

- **Pace and lead technique:** What is special about this method is that the subject—you—will act out what the hypnotist is doing or saying. Take for instance, if the hypnotist says that you are in a trance now, you will feel yourself collapsing under his/her hypnosis. In essence, you are strictly following whatever the hypnotist is doing or uttering at that very moment.

- **Physical posture technique:** This technique entails putting the subject in a position that is the most comfortable for him/her to relax. For example, you may be asked to lie down or recline in a sitting position. The best position is the one that can quickly get you to sleep. Falling under hypnosis is expected to bring some flush of relaxation that you don't normally have. All your nerves will be calmed, and your muscles will be soothed.

- **Mirroring technique:** A hypnotist can use your natural inclination to unconsciously copy/imitate what someone else is doing without necessarily knowing that. Have you ever been to the cinema and you unconsciously find yourself acting out (or imitating) what the main actor or your most favorite actor is doing in the film? Hypnosis can work that way, too: All the hypnotist needs to do is to bring up some activities that you love and might likely try to unconsciously imitate. Using that tool, it may be possible for you to be pushed into a trance-like situation in no time.

- **Sensory overload technique:** This method is unique in the sense that the hypnotist is trying to overload your senses so that you are totally blanked out. A hypnotist can overwhelm you with a lot of information, sound, or ideas at the same time to the extent that your mind feels overloaded and disconnected. At this junction, you are no longer assimilating anything, just existing with a blank mind. You will have fallen under the hypnosis when that happens.

- **Stealth technique:** A hypnotist will start to soliloquize with interesting expressions that can immediately catch your attention. Once you are carried away by the sweetness of the hypnotist's monologue, daydreaming about what he/she is saying, your mind can become vapid and weak in no time. In that case, you are already being transported into a faraway land where the things the hypnotist is saying are currently happening!

**You may want to ask**: Won't I be able to detect immediately that the person I am dealing with is a hypnotist considering how obvious the techniques elaborated above are? Unfortunately, a professional hypnotist can carry out hypnosis on you without you necessarily discovering what he/she is doing. A typical example of this kind are religious leaders who are fond of using hypnosis. People go to their spiritual leaders for prayers, and in the course of this interaction, their spiritual leaders may conduct hypnosis on them. Instead of being careful about what they are being exposed to, the worshippers will be very happy that their spiritual leaders are holding hands with them or laying hands on their heads!

However, the primary reason you are introduced to different techniques used by hypnotists is to open your eyes to their deeds so that you can protect yourself and your loved ones from their deceptive tactics.

## ARE WE ALL SUSCEPTIBLE TO BRAINWASHING?

As important as this question is, it is impossible to offer a convincing answer without first understanding what brainwashing is. According to Encyclopedia.com, brainwashing is defined as;

*"the technique or process employed in communist-controlled states such as China to attain either or both of two objectives: (1) to compel an innocent person to admit, in all subjective sincerity, that he has committed serious crimes against the "people" and the state; and (2) coercively to reshape an individual's political views so that he abandons his previous beliefs and becomes an advocate of communism. Both objectives, however dissimilar they may initially appear, are attempts to make an individual accept as true what he previously rejected as false and to view as false what he formerly saw as true."*

Europe and Americas also have their fair share of ideological and socio-cultural brainwashing, from promoting Marxism, Leninism to democracy, people have been told to embrace a new set of ideologies they may have found distasteful before.

Over the years, brainwashing has moved from being a political weapon to an educational, cultural, military, or religious tool for the singular purpose of misinforming people to their own detriment. The Soviet Police, the Chinese, and Japanese Armies were all brainwashed at one point in time. The purpose of being brainwashed is to create an atmosphere of homogeneity among a group of people so that they can unanimously pursue the same agenda, no matter how spurious and untrue it is.

The process of brainwashing is very simple: It is a "thought control" approach that aims to change the way a person or a group of people think about something through the application of both internal and external pressure in order to achievement, compliance ,or conformity.

Some of the techniques adopted in brainwashing include but are not limited to:

- **Personal humiliation:** Anyone who refuses to follow the pack and accept whatever ideology the group is embracing is usually subjected to personal humiliation. Other members of the group may taunt him/her simply because he/she is standing his/her ground against falsehood.

- **Total control:** The essence of brainwashing people is to absolutely control them. This is very dangerous because they control their thoughts, imaginations, and even the way they act in public. Anyone who stands out or is different is being picked upon in the society. In this scenario, no one is permitted to express their personal opinions or feelings. Everyone must toe the line of the state or the organization controlling their thoughts, even if it is a falsehood.

- **Creation of uncertainty:** When people are always confused about something or find themselves in a condition of uncertainty, they are likely to be taken in—they can easily be brainwashed. So, the primary responsibility of the organization or government brainwashing the people is to constantly keep all of them in a state of flux. When people are confused, it is practically difficult to separate the truth from lies. And it is not difficult for them to swallow everything they had told without questioning its veracity. Take for instance, President Trump, the former president of the United States, wanted people to believe that all Mexicans are drug peddlers or rapist, which couldn't be true. But he succeeded in creating an atmosphere of fear and distrust among the people.

- **Isolation:** Anyone who doesn't want to play along the group mentality is immediately isolated among the group. The other members are encouraged to shun him/her. They are advised not to have anything to do with the rebel or renegade who refused to jump on the bandwagon. Such a so-called rebel can be isolated for a long period of time until he/she becomes psychologically weak and has no apparent option than to join the group and support their evil agenda.

- **Torture:** In extreme circumstances, a renegade might be recommended for some kinds of torture. This is to beat sense into his/her head and compel him/her to toe the line others are supporting. This technique aims at weakening the target psychologically and mentally. Using force to achieve conformity among ranks and files was rife among the Soviet and Chinese Armies during the WWII. This was done to dissuade any soldier from nurturing their individual thoughts and find a cause to oppose the war they had no reason joining in the first instance.

- **Physical exhausting:** The government or organization brainwashing its people sometimes goes to the extent of subjecting them to a situation of physical exhaustion and debilitation to encourage full loyalty. In brainwashing, it doesn't matter how the people feel, the supreme goal is to make sure people are robbed of their human rights to think for themselves. They are only expected to accept the universality, even though it is never substantiated or explained to them. It is like expecting your pet to do exactly as you desire; in that case, your pet doesn't have an option!

- **Destruction of ego and self-esteem:** To force people to comply with harsh rules, the brainwashing agency will make sure that all its subjects do not have self-esteem or ego. They cannot see themselves as a human being that is capable of thinking creatively and solving many life problems by themselves. The agency turns them into thoughtless beings who have to solely rely on what the agency says to make an opinion.

- **Guilt feeling:** In a situation whereby everyone is brainwashed, anyone who attempts to oppose the general misconceptions will be routinely oppressed and called names until he/she becomes guilty for no reason.

- **Alternating fear and hope:** It is the duty of the brainwashing agency to make sure that its subjects are scared into conforming with the laid-down principles. The agency can accomplish this by alternately beating fear and hope into their minds. For instance, the agency can set up a martial law to punish renegades. However, those who are conforming to the generally accepted ideologies will be praised and rewarded. This will put pressure on anyone who is thinking not to follow the crowd to do evil.

Depending on which environment you find yourself, but it must be stated that anyone can be brainwashed. In fact, most people who are brainwashed do not consider the experience to be awful and destructive; they simply considered it a form of loyalty to their nation or organization that is doing the brainwashing.

However, the following categories of people tend to be more susceptible to brainwashing:

- **Emotionally weak individuals:** Those who are emotionally or mentally weak can easily fall for brainwashing. Their lack of inner strength makes them a really easy target for organizations that brainwash people.

- **Those who lack self-esteem:** Anyone who doesn't believe in himself/herself can become a brainwashing subject. It takes self-confidence and trusting one's guts to stand out in a world that is trying to make everyone act the same way.

- **Those who easily feel guilty:** Since they already have that kind of guilt-ridden nature, their nemesis can capitalize on that to brainwash them. Once such a person is overwhelmed by a feeling of guilt, whatever he/she is told becomes only the truth.

- **Insular people:** Insular people are not flexible; they either accept a thing or not. There is no middle ground when taking a position on matters. So, such a person can easily be won over by someone who brainwashes him/her.

- **Those having an identity issue:** Trying to fit in within a group or a culture can expose you to some ridiculous experiences. Technically, it can make you be susceptible to brainwashing. There are many people in the world who cannot identify with certain cultures—they are willing to absorb the cultures of wherever they find themselves. That's the easiest way to invite culture police who may want to teach you about their culture, thereby brainwashing you. Everyone has his/her intrinsic culture; it is your responsibility to promote your culture and strongly align with it. You can ward off unwanted culture police whose primary duty is to brainwash about how their cultures are more superior to yours.

## HOW MIND CONTROL WORKS

Mind control is the process of controlling the mind of a person or the minds of a group of people. To some degree, mind control and brainwashing can be used interchangeably. Why? Because the procedures employed by a brainwashing organization can also be used by someone who is trying to control another person's mind.

Generally, a dark psychologist can control a person's or victim's mind by carrying out any of the following processes:

- **Creating a new identity for their victim:** A manipulator will brainwash you to jettison your identity so that you can be given a new identity that matches the life he/she wants you to assume. It is like an actor changing his/her role in a film. Let's assume you were a nice guy who is very considerate when dealing with others. However, a manipulator may want you to become harsh and merciless by telling you that "nice people never become a millionaire!".

- **Fatigue:** A mind controller will always push you to exhaustion or fatigue until you do exactly what he/she wants. In this case, to avoid being burnt out by his/her endless trouble, you may be pushed to capitulate to his/her will.

- **Repetition:** One of the greatest tools mind-controlling individual or boss uses is to bore you with repetition. Every day, he/she keeps asking you to do the same thing for him/her. To avoid being driven crazy, you will find yourself doing exactly what he/she requests for.

- **Peer pressure:** To compel you to change your mind about something, you may be subjected to intense social or peer pressure. Not many people can stick to their guns when it comes to facing many people in a community wrongly accusing you for something you have not done.

- **Endless criticism:** When someone is trying to change the way you act or behave, he/she may be attacking you every single day. Everything you do will be criticized by the person trying to control your mind. For example, nagging wives are said to possess the power to change their husbands' attitudes over a certain period.

## CRIMES INVOLVED

Hypnosis, brainwashing, and mind control have been used to commit some crime in our world. A pedophile can hypnotize his/her victim, brainwash him/her and then end up controlling his/her mind. With these three "weapons of human destruction", so to say, a psychopath can get and keep his/her victim for a long time.

In politics, people have been pushed into committing some acts of perjury and treason after being brainwashed by some politicians. In business, some unlucky business owners have lost chunks of their wealth due to hypnotists that have entered into their heads and controlled them like babies.

In relationships, many people are in a kind of "prison of love" because they have been brainwashed by their lovers who are holding them ransom.

In religions, people have been brainwashed to the extent that they cannot separate the truth from mere fabrication. In various corners of the world, every year there are bloody clashes among people of different cultures, faiths, and ethnicities because they have been brainwashed to perceive one another as sworn enemies.

In education, small children have been taught to hate people for no reason. Anarchists are rising up here and there from the different parts of the world because they had been brainwashed to disregard constituted authorities.

Everywhere basic safety of lives and properties has become of a serious concern as authorities battle members of neo-Nazi and other redskin organizations.

Now ask yourself: Who is the cruelest? Is it the person who brainwashes, mind controls, or hypnotizes? Different people will have different answers to this important question. Whatever your answer is, remember that these three categories of people could be very dangerous. You should be careful how you expose yourself to them and their antics. Many of the problems we have in this world can be avoided if people learn how to keep themselves safe. A lot of people who find themselves in one problem or the other should blame themselves for not doing enough to protect themselves.

Dark psychologists are a breed of people who lack moral, human feeling, and moral aptitude. Their evil intentions superimpose their thinking faculty, and they are usually consumed by what they are going to gain from misleading, maltreating, and misusing others.

In as much as that they lack moral compass with which they could know that their deeds are harmful and can exterminate someone's life, we should put up the strongest defense against them so that they would be able to enjoy an inch of space around us.

It is sad realizing that many people have lost their dear lives due to the evil actions of manipulators, mind-controllers, hypnotists, and other types of dark psychologists.

You are lucky today because their secret is being leaked to you!

# 9

# TWO SIDES OF NLP

Neuro-linguistic programming (NLP) is considered to be a pseudoscientific technique employed in communication, psychotherapy, and personal development. It was developed in 1970s in California, United States, by Richard Bandler and John Grinder.

## UNDERSTANDING HOW IT WORKS

This section will explain how NLP works. Fundamentally, Neuro-linguistic programming is actually a technique for altering someone's thoughts and behaviors with the hope of making the person display expected outcomes. In other words, if you want someone to act in a certain way, you can apply NLP on him/her and watch him/her do exactly what you had envisaged.

It must be stated that NLP was initially created to solve some medical problems. It has been used in the treatment of anxiety disorders and phobias; it has also been employed in improving workplace performance and personal development.

The NLP system primarily utilizes behavioural, perceptual, and communication methods to facilitate changing people's thoughts and actions. Incidentally, NLP relies on language processing, but you shouldn't confuse it with Natural Language Processing, which has the same acronym.

Highlighted below are the main assumptions that drive the use or application of NLP in altering people's thoughts and behaviors:

- The core concept of NLP is all about the assumption that people operate by internal "maps" of the world which they have acquired or learnt through their sensory experiences.
- So, NLP is applied on an individual for the purpose of detecting and modifying unconscious limitations or biases existing in a person's map of the world.
- While it is not hypnotherapy, NLP utilizes language programming to consciously bring about positive changes in an individual's thoughts and behavior.
- Everyone is assumed to be demonstrating a bias towards one sensory system described as the Preferred Representational System (PRS).
- What an NLP therapist does is detect your PRS by using some phrases such as "I see your point" (indicating a visual PRS) or "I hear your point" (which signifies an auditory PRS).
- Once your type of PRS has been identified, the next step for

an NLP practitioner is to design his/her therapeutic response around that PRS.

- The entire NLP treatment may involve building rapport with the subjects, gathering appropriate information, and setting practical goals with them

It is important that you understand how NLP works so that you can become aware when you are being secretly put through NLP techniques.

## USING NLP FOR MEDICAL PURPOSE

The NLP technique is being used for medical purposes, as shown below. In addition to its therapeutic usefulness, the healthcare has found many other ways to apply NLP in order to improve health delivery to patients. Primarily, NLP technique has been used to cure anxiety and phobia disorders. On an expanded scale, it has been used in improving people's personal and professional performances.

Therefore, NLP has dramatically revolutionized healthcare in the following ways:

- **Speech recognition:** Before NLP was used for speech recognition, physicians usually had to dictate clinical report notes to transcribers. Today, with speech-recognition technologies, which incorporate NLP techniques, it is possible for physicians to smoothly have their notes transcribed without having to go through the stress of dictating it.

- **Better clinical documentation:** The application of NLP has drastically improved clinical documentation in the sense that manual and complex structures of Electronic health records (EHRs) have been eliminated. This is due, in part, to the revolutionary text-to-speech capability and an advanced clinical data storage system, all made possible by the adoption of NLP techniques.

- **Faster clinical decision:** Nowadays, physicians can make quick decisions based on the data they have at their disposal. It is no longer cumbersome to process patients' medical records; with the click of a mouse, thousands of medical reports can be retrieved, processed, and sorted out for making precise treatment and prescription. Several decades ago, this improved feature was not available; hence, hospitals faced long waiting hours that led to poor hospital administration.

It must be stated that NLP has contributed immensely to the treatment of social illnesses such as anxiety and depression. People who are depressed may be asked to embrace the following mind-altering principles so as to regain their health:

- **Assurance:** The NLP therapist will assure you that you are not your behavior and that behaviors can be changed. This premise is meant to bolster your belief that you are not responsible for your "anxiety" or "depression". That it just happens to you in the course of living your life. Already, the

NLP therapist is helping you not to feel guilty for a condition you have no power to ameliorate yourself.

- **Capability:** Following the first assurance, the NLP therapist will remind you that you are naturally equipped with all the necessary resources you need to overcome your anxiety or depression. He/she will take you through stories of how other people like you have been able to overcome their problems because human beings are endowed with unlimited capabilities.

- **Feedback, not failure:** In order to completely remove fear from your mind, your NLP therapist will let you know that whatever happens in the course of the consultation should never be perceived as failure: His/her advice should be considered as feedback that must be worked on or improved upon.

- **Better communication is the key:** The primary goal of your NLP therapist is to convince that all you need to change to have a better life is your method of communication. People are often instructed that the people in the world mostly respond to what they heard. And to have a better relationship with people around you, you need to improve your communication strategies.

The good news is that NLP has been successfully applied in helping many people achieve a better lifestyle that is reflected in everything else they do. There are instances whereby someone who used to be a socially reclusive person modify his/her communication strategy and end up becoming an orator or famous presenter on TV.

Despite the fact that Neuro-linguistic programming has been solely used for positive purposes, there are indications that some dark psychologists have also added the technique to their arsenals, applying it on their unfortunate victims.

Having deep understanding of NLP procedures should make you to be wary of being put through these same steps. Your knowledge of NLP system will enable you to free yourself and your loved ones from any manipulator who wants to control your life.

## THE OTHER SIDE OF NLP

**This is the scariest part**: Can the NLP system be hijacked by a manipulator and be used to control the mind of his/her victim? Definitely! In this section, you will unearth some sensitive information about dark psychologists adopting the NLP techniques to manipulate and coerce his/her victims.

The Other Side of NLP entails that a manipulator, armed with the knowledge of how NLP techniques work, can control the mind of another person through:

- **Indoctrination:** Passing negative information into his/her victims' subconscious so that he/she could beat fear into them every day. Speaking words that undermine victims' integrity, self-esteem, and hope is meant to hold them back and prevent them from leading normal lives.
- **Disempowering:** Unlike NLP therapist who tries to empower his/her client, a manipulator's primary goal is to

disempower his/her victims. Why? A manipulator knows that when he/she empowers his/her victims, they would become mentally strong and eventually resist whatever manipulation tactics deployed against them.

- **Lack of education:** When victims of manipulations remain in the dark for so long about the causes of their misfortunes, their manipulators are happy because lack of education will continue to keep them in bondage. Therefore, manipulators will do everything within their power to prevent their victims from getting the necessary education that may turn out to be an eye-opener.

Reading this book is a form of education that a manipulator may want to prevent you from doing. If your friend, colleague, or spouse is responsible for your misfortune, you should be wary when training yourself about how manipulators act. In their evil minds, manipulators believe that if your eyes are open, they won't be able to hold onto you for a long time. In reality, you must seriously guard your heart when interacting with a dark psychologist. If you are not conquered in your mind, you still have a chance to hold your head up.

## NLP TECHNIQUES

There are different techniques embedded in the Neuro-linguistic programming system. You and your loved ones will be in a safer place if you could familiarize yourself with the following major NLP features:

1. **Anchoring:** This is the practice of responding differently to a triggering situation. This is somehow similar to classical conditioning. The underlying principle for this technique is that if you keep responding to external stimuli in the same way as you have been doing for years, you are likely going to obtain the same results. For example, if a wife often dismisses her husband's instructions with levity. However, if the same wife turns around and expects her husband to take her words seriously, she may be disappointed because her husband may also choose to treat her shabbily. The only turnaround in their relationship is feasible if the wife changes the way she responds to her husband's words. If she starts showing him some respect and valuing his suggestions, her husband will also change his mind towards her, and they can both enjoy a better romantic relationship. Anchoring, as an NLT technique, provides a unique opportunity to refreshen relationships and helps people to become better at communicating. Imagine a manager that no one loves within an organization because of the way he/she harshly speaks to his/her subordinates. If the same manager decides to be nice and accommodating, he/she will be able to change the unfriendly situations around him/her.

2. **Reframing:** This refers to the practice of identifying adaptive behaviors that can be used in place of some maladaptive behaviors so as to continue to achieve the goals being pursued. In other words, if a student who has been flunking his/her examinations and wants to perform better, he/she can identify the maladaptive behaviors in him/her.

These maladaptive behaviors may include laziness, playing truancy, and not showing interest in his/her studies. The adaptative behaviors to replace the listed maladaptive behaviors include studying harder, attending classes regularly, and learning attentively. When the said student makes the necessary changes in his/her behaviors, better results will be achieved as he/she will be able to pass his/her examinations. NLP is designed to help people improve their rate of performance by consciously taking decisions that could turn things around for good in their lives.

3. **Belief change:** This is one of the primary features of NLP. Everyone is believed to have internalized certain belief system owing to what they are exposed to. Take for instance, we learn from what we see, hear, touch, taste, and smell. Our sensory experiences contribute the largest amount of information that we now internalize as habits. In order to succeed, we must be willing to change our belief systems. A good example to illustrate this issue is that children never harbor any hatred towards anyone; but as they grow up, they start picking hate from what they hear or see from the adults around them. When they grow up, they have already created their own perspective about hatred. To remove this belief system, a new attitude or habit is required. The Behavioural Science claims that it takes people an average of 21 days to create a new habit. To be honest, that isn't a long time. A person with a bad attitude has a lot to lose in life. So, spending time to turn over a new leaf shouldn't be seen as time-wasting.

4. **Future Pacing:** Undergoing an NLP therapy is expected to be a lifelong experience. In other words, an NLP therapist hopes that his/her clients will continue to work on himself/herself so as to achieve success in the long run. Future pacing refers to the practice of continually incorporating good qualities into one's lifestyle for the purpose of remaining mentally and psychologically balanced. It may be hard for someone to keep doing the right things when no one is watching. This is why people attend an NLP therapy with friends and associates so that they can be help one another stay strong and committed.

There is no doubt that NLP was created for a positive and life-enriching purpose. It has become one of the most popular medical features people adopt to change their lives for good. At the same time, some mischievous dark psychologists have been utilizing NLP to constantly harass and mind-control their victims.

How would you know when NLP techniques are being used to destroy you? Well, here are five things you should always look for when undergoing an NLP procedure:

- **Positive energy:** The positive energy that emanates from confidence-boosting words of the NLP therapist are meant to strengthen you psychologically and mentally. Most people with broken spirits cannot easily see or appreciate the good things about themselves. So, soothing and powerful utterances of an NLP practitioner is meant to uplift their souls. If you, by accident, find yourself in an NLP session where negative, morale-destructing expressions are used, be rest assured that you are in the wrong place.

- **It is all about your well-being:** The main reason people go through the NLP processes is to make themselves better, to be more productive, and have more clarity about life. When you see an NLP therapist focusing on himself/herself during an NLP routine, that should be a red flag that you are dealing with the wrong person. Manipulators will always put their own interests ahead of others. In this way, they will violate all NLP rules and leave you worse than you have been before coming to the NLP session.

- **No coercion:** None of the standard NLP techniques require the application of external force or pressure. In other words, there is no coercion when you are undergoing an NLP procedure. If someone who claims to be an NLP therapist is compelling you to do what you think is inappropriate, it is advisable that you should stop such an NLP practice and run for your life. People can only truly change when they are convinced that what they are doing is worth it. Forcing an individual to memorize, internalize, or undertake some processes forcefully will run counter to the underlying principles of NLP.

- **Trust is important:** Those who have successfully gone through the NLP process claim that trust is an integral aspect of the entire procedure. An NLP therapist will first of all try to win your trust by being so nice and understanding with you. You will then, in return, entrust him/her with your time and full participation in the process. Flee from any NLP therapist who is trying to gain your trust through threat, force, or being disrespectful. Normally, you cannot follow the directions or advice given by an NLP therapist whom you do not trust. In short, trust is the building block required to connect wholeheartedly with a therapist and make a success of the entire process.

- **It is your life!** Remember it is your life! If you sense any danger in an NLP therapist, you have the right to bring the whole thing to an abrupt end. We are living in a world where evil people are everywhere masquerading as good people. You can find manipulators everywhere; and they are never ashamed to strike any time. So, use all you have learned from this chapter to protect yourself and your loved ones. It is your life, and it doesn't have a duplicate.

Take it upon yourself to share your discoveries in this book with your friends, colleagues, and relatives who might benefit from them. This is a rare book that exposes all the secret machinations of the dark psychologists so that you can be always seek protection from their evil deeds.

# III

PROTECTING YOURSELF

# 10

# ARE YOU A VICTIM?

Now that you are well aware of the dangers dark psychologists can pose to your dear life, it is time for some self-reckoning. Are you a victim of manipulation? To perfectly answer this question, you have to be absolutely honest with yourself. Have you been living in self-denial that you are not a victim of manipulation, hypnotism, or evil Neurolinguistic Programming (NLP)? Or is it possible that you have been a victim of malicious dark psychology without necessarily recognizing it?

The Psychology Today reportedly stated that nearly 2.5 percent of women and 1.3 percent of men in United States who are in manipulative relationships face severe health, mental, and psychological issues. These statistics paint a serious social problem that is begging for immediate solutions.

- Does someone make you feel like you are worthless?
- Do you give more room to someone in your head that you can't get space to accommodate other more important things in your life?
- Are you living in dread of being socially isolated and always craving for attention?
- In fact, has your life been made miserable because someone you trusted took advantage of you and you are so upset about this situation?

If your answers to the questions above are in the affirmative (Yes! Yes!! Yes!!!), then you have been a victim of evil manipulation for some time without realizing it. This is not the time for self-pity; it is time to take some proactive actions in protecting yourself and your loved ones, preventing the same cycle of misery from repeating itself in your life.

## PREVENT YOURSELF FROM BECOMING A VICTIM

It is in your power to prevent yourself from becoming a victim of manipulation in the first place. It is assumed that this book has taught you a lot about how manipulators, hypnotists, and other dark psychologists operate. Empowering yourself with this amount of useful knowledge will surely save your life.

How do I stave off a mischievous manipulator? You may want to know. The answers to this important question is not far-fetched.

- **First, learn to say "No!"** Unfortunately, most victims of severe manipulations are kind-hearted and considerate individuals who always say "Yes!" to things or people. We are talking of people who will never do anything to hurt others or put them in harmful circumstances. If you are too kind, manipulators perceive your benign attitude as a weakness. So, they will lunge at you swinging all their destructive shots, because they have realized that you will never say "No" to any of their evil machinations. No one is pushing you to say "No" to everything; you should apply your discretion in selecting what to say "Yes or No" to. The rule of thumb is that you should always say "No" to anything that won't benefit you now or in the future. Take for instance, if a demanding or manipulative lover asks you to follow him/her to Las Vegas to play poker or gamble. And you know down in your mind that you don't know how to gamble. It is totally wrong to sheepishly accept such an invitation and tag along with him/her to Las Vegas. You may end not only losing your hard-earned money, but also losing your precious life.

- **Second, put yourself in a safe position.** More often than not, we are the one opening our doors to manipulators or taking some actions that could draw them to us. Ten years ago, one of my best friends and I won big in the lottery. We shared the money equally because we contributed an equal amount of money to buy the winning tickets. While I deposited my money in the bank thinking seriously about what investments to make or which business to start, my careless friend went on a spending spree. It didn't take long for people around him to know that he had suddenly found some fortune. My friend bought a Rolls Royce, moved into one of the expensive flats in London, which was tastefully furnished. He spent most of his night partying and womanizing. Less than a year later, he started to complain about not having enough money to pay his bills. The rumor had it that one of his many pretty girlfriends used some kind of charm on him and stole a huge chunk of his wealth. On the other hand, I wisely invested mine, and I am still benefiting from the clever decisions I made till today. Never put yourself in a situation that will make you vulnerable to a manipulator's gimmicks.

- **Third, stop being an attention-seeker.** To be honest, manipulators are always searching for attention-seekers. Why? Because it is easy to manipulate them emotionally! When someone's emotions have been used against him/her, such a person is already in a weaker

position or state; he/she will just obediently follow the manipulator's orders. In life, some things are stranger than fiction. We have seen a very strong and confident man turning into a weakling in the hands of a manipulative lady. In the same vein, a woman that is constantly abused finds it very difficult to get herself out of such an abusive relationship. These two unique examples reveal how one's emotion can be used as a trap that is difficult to escape from. It is a common saying that anyone who loves money too much can be magnetized by it. Do you know how many people across the globe have been lured into committing crimes or engaging in prostitution in the name of money?

- **Fourth, validate yourself.** If you are the type who constantly looks outward for validation or acceptance, you are simply putting yourself up for manipulation. Your manipulator already knows that you will surely come for his/her approval before you set out to do anything. That realization, in itself, is scary, because your manipulator can make your life miserable by simply refusing to validate or approve any of your plans. It is not uncommon for friends to seek opinions from one another about which merchandize to purchase, which boyfriend/girlfriend to marry, or which car or house to buy. While it is not a bad thing to do so; your final decision about some important things in your life should come from you. Did you know if your bosom friend was not being truthful about the pieces of advice he/she was giving you? Maybe he/she was speaking out of jealousy or envy. We have seen instances whereby someone's best man or best lady turns around and snatches his/her best friend's husband/wife.

- **Fifth, know what it is in it for you.** Armed with all the essential knowledge about how to easily identify who a manipulator or hypnotist is, you can quickly elude being trapped by their manipulative tricks. If you are dealing with an arrogant, self-centered person, whether a colleague, business associate, or even a relative, that red flag should warn you to immediately flee for your dear life. Here are some examples of manipulators you should avoid at all cost: A business partner who is always speaking for his/her own gains does not think you stand to gain anything from the business transaction; a spouse who often accuses you wrongly and fails to appreciate your sundry contributions to the relationship. In those people's eyes you do not amount to anything. They can choose to objectify you and treat you with all manners of disrespect. So, you should always ask yourself when in such circumstances: What is in this for me? If you can't find any cogent reasons for staying in a relationship or having a business relationship with a partner, get yourself out of it.

- **Sixth, never blame yourself.** One of the evil intentions of a manipulator is to project bad attitudes on you so that you can feel sorry for yourself. Take for instance, a manipulative boss may choose to always blame you for every mistake that occurs at your workplace, even when the said mistake was committed by another employee. If you let evil people's projections get to you, you will end up blaming yourself for an offence you have not committed. So, never blame yourself. Stand your ground and defend your cause. By doing this, you are inadvertently strengthening your mind and putting the manipulator's camp in disarray.

- **Seventh, just disconnect.** Finally, the most sensible thing you can do to protect yourself against a manipulator or hypnotist is to just disconnect. It is not practically reasonable to assume that you can outmaneuver a manipulator. Some victims of manipulation who could have saved themselves the embarrassment from the experience and run for their lives chose to stupidly stay in the deceit and harassment. You would have heard some abused women saying: "I will stay in the relationship. I hope I can change him, or he will change". To be honest, no one can change someone who doesn't see anything bad in what he/she is doing. The most honorable step to take when abused, manipulated, or hypnotized is to disconnect yourself from such a horrible experience.

## MOST COMMON TRAITS OF A VICTIM

You are halfway to protecting yourself and your loved ones if you have taken some or all of the steps highlighted above. However, the best thing to do is never to invite a manipulator into your life at all. How can you achieve this? In this section, you will discover some common traits that manipulators and users of dark psychology often go for.

Check out below the list and descriptions of common traits that can attract a manipulator to you:

- **Being overtly emotional:** Emotional people are the weakest category of victims manipulators are constantly searching for. All a manipulator needs to do is to tap into their emotion and use it against them. When I was young, there was a kind lady, a Christian down the street who was always willing to help people. Sometimes, she went as far as sharing her meals with those who had nothing to eat, even when it was apparent that the food was not enough for her. Can you believe that she became the main target of many manipulators? Some came to her, begged her to lend them some money only to disappear and never repay their debts. The worst scenario occurred when a man she made friends with reportedly borrowed her car for an occasion. The rumor had it that the manipulator drove the fairly new car across the border into France and never came back.

- **Being Emphatic:** If you are someone who likes to be emphatic about issues, not letting go when you should have, chances are that you may be an easy target for manipulators. When something isn't working in your favor, or when you don't see any reason to stick to it, the best thing to do is to disconnect yourself. Unfortunately, emphatic people are not like that; they want to stay in the game until the end. Many of them, surprisingly, get manipulated in the course of the events. Some people have boyfriends/girlfriends who cannot cook, clean, or even help them when they are in trouble. But because the sex is good, they choose to stay in such a relationship for the long haul until their manipulative lover uses "sex" as a weapon against them.

- **Hypersensitivity:** The primary reason manipulators like hypersensitive people is that they will never let go or disconnect for the fear of hurting others' feelings. An abused wife would like to remain in her marriage because it shameful, in some cultures, to be a single mother. A businessperson who has been defrauded by one of his/her employees may decide not to fire the employee because other workers might be affected by their decision. Therefore, being hypersensitive puts you at the mercy of your manipulator, despite the fact that you have an option to flee or end such an ungratifying relationship.

- **Being lonely/afraid to be alone:** Lonely men and women are mostly susceptible to manipulators' tricks. A manipulator can come into a lonely person's life by first offering some fake companionship. Once you allow him/her to get his/her foot in, the rest will be history. So, even though you are lonely, don't show to the world that you are obviously afraid to be alone. That might cause a manipulator to take an advantage of you.

- **Emotionally/personality dependent**: People who are emotionally/personality dependent on others find themselves easily manipulated by dark psychologists. One of the reasons politicians are popular is that their followers see them as a personality that is larger than life and are attracted to them. Therefore, this makes them worship their political idols like a small god and get manipulated.

- **Afraid to disappoint others**: Not everyone has a stony heart; some people are so kind, sensitive, and considerate that they can inconvenience themselves in order to make others happy. Such a person easily becomes a target for manipulators who knew quite well that the targeted victim is a "Yes, Sir", "Yes, Ma" person. It is a good thing to show consideration for others; however, it is equally harmful to let the whole world think that you are a weakling when it comes to controlling your exuberant emotion.

## SIGNS

Manipulators are so crafty to the extent that their victims may not even realize that they are being manipulated. In extreme circumstances, the victims could even pick a quarrel with you for saying harsh about their manipulators whom they have considered to be their benefactors. Recently, a 23-year-old lady shocked the local TV viewers when she said her kidnapper has been good to her and accused the police of interfering with her private life. The report revealed that she was bamboozled by the marathon sex she was getting from the man.

If you are not sure whether you have been subjected to some forms of manipulations or not, the following **seven signs** would help you determine that:

- **Picking holes in all your arguments:** At home, in the office, or among friends, a manipulator will often let you state your opinions first before picking holes or mistakes in them. You see, these kind of manipulators do not appear to be domineering or controlling at first, however, they want you to always feel inferior or incapable in every setting. We all have people like that in our life: It could be an arrogant boss who often likes to belittle his/her employees. It could also be a grandparent or neighbor who never sees anything good in what you do.

- **Manipulation of facts:** A manipulator commonly tampers with facts so as to put you in a disadvantaged position. They hotly debate everything with you and makes you feel uncomfortable whenever you are around him/her. I used to have a teacher like that when I was in secondary. His eyes were always on me in the class, and all answers I gave to his questions were never properly stated. His impudent actions often made me shirk his classes.

- **Those who make you display negative emotions:** In a gathering or at work, a manipulator will always paint you in a bad light. He/she will utter things or take actions that will get on your nerves. The manipulator's primary goal is to push you into a frenzy and cause you to lose your cool. In most cases, the manipulator wants to see you curse, throw punches, and destabilize a meeting. When you demonstrate all those negative attributes, the manipulator has pretty much accomplished his/her mission.

- **Giving you no time to decide:** This sign is common among family members where either of the parents is dictatorial in his/her approach to their children. This can also be found in a workplace where the boss is aggressive and absolutely inconsiderate. Cruel manipulators are really a bother; they do not care whether you have an opinion or not. All they want is that you do exactly what they say.

- **Incessant silent treatment:** Pay attention to this very important sign manipulators use—the incessant silent treatment. No matter what you do to get in touch with a manipulator, he/she will not respond at all to your calls, emails, letters, or otherwise. The singular reason behind this action is to discomfort you or put you in a state of perpetual flustering. Can you imagine someone who claims to be your best friend suddenly going incommunicado with you? Such an experience can lead to emotional depression or anxiety. That is exactly what a manipulator wants to achieve by becoming eerily silent on you.

- **Reverse victimization:** Instead of acknowledging that he/she has made you his/her victim, a shrewd manipulator would act as if he/she is your victim. We could all relate to that! We used to have a neighbor who was rude and self-centered. He would play loud music all day; his dogs would bark from morning to the evening. However, instead of accepting the fact that he was the nuisance, he often accused my family of being too loud and inconsiderate. Why? Because we often welcomed visitors on the weekends, and he alleged that our visitors' cars and deep-throated laughter greatly unsettled him. He had forgot that he was the one making us uncomfortable with the noises emanating from his quarters seven days a week.

- **Transferring the guilt to you:** A few years ago, one man told me a story that made my eyes well with tears. He said one of his employees, who happened to be his sales manager, absconded with a huge sum of stolen money. He had trusted the employee to the point that he allowed him to go to the bank on his behalf to withdraw any amount of money. On this fateful day, the employee cashed out £50,000, but instead of bringing it to the office and handing it over to his boss, he went away with it. When the case was brought to the court, his defense lawyer pleaded with the judge that his client (the shameless thief) was a kleptomaniac right from his childhood. And any huge amount of money could make him misbehave. The guilt was transferred to the boss for not identifying this quality in his employee. Therefore, based on his mental health claim, the employee was ordered to return the remaining amount in his pocket, which was just £10,000. He was eventually set free!

Keep those seven signs in your mind. Any time you detected any of them in someone, immediately take flight. You can also use the same knowledge to save someone else, may be your loved ones.

## ACCEPTANCE

Acceptance is an important step that victims of manipulations should take. When you accept yourself the way you are, you would not need any external validation to live a happy life. Many people who look up to others to approve of every plan they make for themselves are inadvertently making them susceptible to manipulation. Dark psychologists often seek out such people.

Even though self-acceptance is hard to achieve, it is something everyone can do. It may take you some time to do it right, but it is definitely worth it. Here are ten practical ways you can increase your self-acceptance:

- Celebrate your uniqueness because you don't need anyone to make you feel awesome about who you really are.
- Let go of things you cannot control. Don't give yourself sleepless nights on what are not essential for your day-to-day survival.
- Identify your strengths and use them to your advantage every time.
- Set some achievable goals and go all out to get them. You will feel more accomplished once you have achieved them.
- Throw a celebration for any accomplishments made, whether small or big.
- Cultivate the habit of planning everything ahead to avoid unexpected disappointments.
- Think positively of yourself and everything that concerns you. It is your business worrying over whatever opinions others have about you.
- Constantly practice self-appreciation by being kind to yourself. Don't be your own worst critic.
- Be actively living. Passiveness will cast a shadow of doubt on your personal capability.
- Seek help from the most reliable people and always remember not to completely let down your guard until you have realized that the person who is mentoring you is not a manipulator.

## NEVER BLAME YOURSELF

Whatever situation you find yourself, or whichever uncomfortable experiences the manipulator pushes you through, Never Ever Blame Yourself. Self-blaming is a potent weapon the dark psychologists usually use to rob their victims of their resilient spirits.

Self-blaming will do more danger than you could ever think of. It will make you powerless and weak to confront the manipulators and hypnotists. You will constantly be at their mercies; in that situation, they can get away with whatever they do!

Blaming yourself can, as a matter of fact, increase your anxiety level. You are going to be huffing and puffing about something that was not your mistake in the first instance. Please save yourself of all those negative emotions and live your life happily.

Write it clearly on paper and hang it where you can always see and read it: "I WILL NEVER BLAME MYSELF FOR ANYTHING IN LIFE!" Internalize it, live it, practice it, and preach it. Let it become an integral part of your daily living. Doing this will consequently increase your morale and your mental health will be solid and unyielding to manipulative pressures.

## TREATMENT AND THERAPY

Overt or uncontrolled exposure to manipulations could result in a shift in the victim's mental health. After a while, they become violent, erratic, and depressed.

Physicians and therapists do not have a single treatment for people who have been manipulated for a very long time, who are obviously displaying the symptoms of excessive exposure to manipulation. However, they offer treatment for each symptom that is detected in the victim. The essence of the treatment is to help boost the victims' mental health so that they could be mentally strong again.

The list below shows a regimen of medical treatments and therapies used to treat victims of dark psychologists:

∼

### Symptom displayed by the victim of manipulation

*Depression*

### Possible treatment

*Medications and therapies for depression*

∼

### Symptom displayed by the victim of manipulation

*Severe anxiety*

### Possible treatment

*Medications and therapies for severe anxiety*

∼

## Symptom displayed by the victim of manipulation

*Negative habits copied from the manipulators*

**Possible treatment**

*Behavioural therapies*

∿

## Symptom displayed by the victim of manipulation

*Being too negative*

**Possible treatment**

*Exposure to positivism and some behavioural therapies*

# 11

# SEE IT FOR WHAT IT REALLY IS

*"I think it's always important to be vigilant of what you're doing and aware of your surroundings."*

— LEONA LEWIS

## LISTEN AND OBSERVE

**M**ost of the battles we fight in this life are done individually. In other words, we are solely responsible for own our safety and successes based on the series of actions we take. No one is going to be out there helping you to check out who is trying to manipulate you or not; it is your duty to listen and observe everything in your vicinity. You have to consciously analyse the behaviors of people around you in order to detect any verbal and non-verbal cues that may point out a manipulator or hypnotist.

## A DEEPER UNDERSTANDING OF INFLUENCE

You need to have a deeper understanding of how manipulators influence their victims. If you are armed with this knowledge, chances are that you will not easily fall victim to a manipulator's guiles.

One of the definitions of the word "influence" that I really like to use in this book can be found in Merriam-Webster Dictionary. It states that "influence" is "**the act or power of producing an effect without apparent exertion of force or direct exercise of command.**" As harmless as their physical actions may seem, the primary aim of a manipulator is to make their victims' lives miserable.

How do they necessarily accomplish this? The influence dark psychologists exert on their victims come in different forms, some of which are described below:

- **Neutral influence:** As cunning as many dark psychologists are, they will pretend that they are not directly connected with your misery, meanwhile they are mainly responsible for the untold hardships you are going through. A manipulator can delegate another person, maybe your close associate or even your spouse, to directly influence every decision you make. If you are not quite suspicious, you may be fighting the wrong person while your main nemesis is hiding in the shadow. In certain cases, you may even end up going to your manipulator to seek advice about what you should do about your situation, not knowing he/she is the one calling the shots.

- **Positive influence:** As its name implies, everyone desires to be positively influenced, in as much as we believe it is for our good in the long run. But you should be careful about this; manipulators don't necessarily first appear in front of us as manipulators—they can begin as your mentor, leader, boss, or even your lover. To a certain degree, they will try to influence us positively by offering pieces of advice meant to grow us personally and professionally. They will show us love and cares; they will handle our case with all dedication and selflessness. Who doesn't like to be affectionately spoiled? However, by the time they have entered into our heads and won our trust, they would strike, showing their real nature.

- **Negative influence:** Those who are following the wrong crowd may receive some negative influence from their group or gang leaders and members. A saying goes thus: "You are who you associate with". Ten years ago, one of my friends, Fred, had had a sudden transformation that obviously shocked his parents and friends alike. Fred was such a quiet bloke, always shy and self-effacing. During his work experience at a local bank, he met a guy who introduced him to drinking and womanizing. Fred captured his colleague's habits in no time and became so bold that he could walk up to any lady and woo her. And when he drank beer, he wouldn't stop until dozens of beer bottles littered his bedroom. That was how far negative influence could ruin a person's career and life!

- **Life-changing influence**: Some influence on people could be life-changing, for better or for worse. If anyone is coming to you demonstrating some attitude of selfishness, please wake up; he/she could be a manipulator. Whatever you do in association with others, in as much as it is not for your own good, think twice before you continue going down that path. We are endowed with a natural instinct with which we could sense some dangers far before they occur. I don't remember who said it, but there is an important lesson in this quote: *"An insincere and evil friend is more to be feared than a wild beast; a wild beast may wound your body, but an evil friend will wound your mind."* Let us always remember that we have the right to reject any unwanted act of influence over our life. If we fail to do so, we may find ourselves being subjected to continuous manipulation that may leave us more damaged than we could ever imagine.

## INFLUENCED BY ANOTHER PERSON'S BODY LANGUAGE

Body language (also known as kinesics) is one of the commonly used non-verbal tools in communication. Over the years, people have passed information across from one person to another using different types of body language. At the schools for people with impaired hearing, body language has been utilized in educating a generation of people that might have otherwise been uneducable. As we celebrate the good applications of body language, it is sad to realize that dark psychologists also employ this communication to influence and take advantage of another person.

Highlighted below are the most common types of body language used by manipulators:

## TYPES OF BODY LANGUAGE

You have read about some types of manipulative body language in Chapter 7. In this section, you will read about additional kinds of body language that dark psychologists are also using.

- **Squinting or looking slyly:** Squinting is perceived as a seductive gesture if it is done by a man to a woman, or vice versa. As harmless it appears, it can make someone restless and confused if it is done by a total stranger. Most especially, a lady may be thrown off balance if a man she has never met before continues to look at her slyly for hours. This feeling of discomfort may make the target or lady lose focus on whatever she was doing at that time. Manipulators have used this body language successfully to confuse and command their victims' feelings for minutes, hours, or days, depending on how often they can lay their eyes on their victims.
- **Clicking fingers:** A manipulator can click his/her fingers, whether noisily or noiselessly, to draw your attention to himself/herself. It is a ploy or tactic they usually use when they want to unsettle you and make you doubt yourself. Take

for instance, you may be in a meeting where you are offering your opinions on the issue under discussion. Immediately your senior manager, who is chairing the meeting, begins to click his/her fingers, you are likely going to be checking yourself whether what you are saying is reasonable or not. If you have not been aware of the fact that such a gesture could be used to manipulate you, there is every possibility that you may be forced to abruptly conclude whatever you are saying.

- **Nose-Picking:** Even though it is an asocial behavior, some people pick their noses to express some displeasure at whatever they are seeing or hearing. If you don't have enough confident, you may be responding to such a gesture from time to time.

- **Deep-breathing:** When you are interrupted by someone who deep-breathes "Hmm!" several times when you are talking, he/she is trying to give others a negative impression about whatever you are saying. He/she may want other people to doubt the truthfulness of your words.

- **Incessant yawning:** When a person yawns often when you are saying something, he/she is either showing that you are talking too much, or that your words do not make any sense to him/her. Yawning is a sign that he/she is bored with whatever you are saying.

- **Tongue-clicking:** When someone clicks his/her tongue when you are contributing to a discussion, he/she is trying to alert other people that you are lying. Continuously clicking their tongues is a crafty way manipulators undermine the significance of what their victims are saying.

- **Fake coughing:** A manipulator can cough several times to dissuade his/her victim from expressing his/her confidence on an issue. The coughing is fake, and almost everyone understands what it means—it simply indicates that the cougher disregards what the victim is saying or alleging.

As innocuous as the above-mentioned forms of body language are, they have been used repeatedly by manipulators to render their victims weak and powerless in meetings, among other colleagues, and in family get-togethers.

## REMAINING NEUTRAL

You may have heard about the different coping strategies people adopt when it comes to dealing with manipulators; one of the most effective strategies is to maintain a neutral baseline behavior without any bias. What this entails is that you should never express extreme emotions about your circumstances.

It is almost impossible for a manipulator to completely take over your senses if you always operate in neutrality. In other words, if a seducer-cum-manipulator comes to you using all his/her tricks to seduce you, if you are the type who responds modestly to seduction, a seductive manipulator will have little or no influence on you. In the same way, if you are not consumed by greed and illogical love of money, it is almost impossible for fraudulent manipulators to get you.

In principle, a neutral behavior is comparable to being neither cold nor hot about any issue. This frame of mind is required to checkmate every move a manipulator makes towards you. **This is how it works**: If you come to me and spend hours telling me how profitable a deal is going to be, how much millions of pounds I am going to make from the business, and how easy it is to execute it. If I do not appear a sceptic to you as well as not expressing excitement about the deal, you are likely going to misjudge my reactions: You may think I don't like doing the business with you. In that scenario, you, the manipulator, will not be interested in wasting your time convincing a doubter.

More often than not, people bring manipulators into their lives by the way they express their emotions when baited. Usually, dark psychologists will throw their prospective victims some baits and watch carefully how they will react to them. If you don't exude overexcitement about their baits, manipulators are likely going to be confused about how to handle you.

Neutral behavior is replicable; in other words, you can develop it if you undertake the following procedures:

- **Live without any bias:** Don't be too quick to assume that something is good or bad for you. Give it time and see if it will eventually be good for you or not. For the fact that one of your relatives introduced a business idea to you doesn't mean he/she couldn't cheat you in the business. If I were you, I would welcome any suggestions from my spouse with a neutral mindset. In that way, when things go wrong, I would not live the rest of my life biting my fingers. Doesn't that action make you a natural sceptic? Not at all! When dealing with a potential manipulator, you should do everything in your power to protect your heart. If a person is not already conquered in his/her mind, such a person still has some hope that he/she would overcome every deceit of the dark psychologists.

- **Never accept anything at face value:** When you cultivate the habit of not accepting things as they are presented, you will see that everything has another side. Most dark psychologists won't let you see their other sides when finding a way to get into you. So, if you have been careful from the outset, you will have made it very difficult for them to pitch their tents with you.

- **Use your mental analyzer:** Quickly analyse with your head if this person seeking your attention and time worth getting it. We all have instincts that will let us know we are playing with trouble by opening our heart or door to a manipulator. If at that instant you feel some uneasiness creeping over you, quickly excuse yourself and cut off the communication. A manipulator won't be so violent at the beginning or else he/she won't have a chance to craftily get into you.

- **Momentarily embrace a second thought:** Most of the victims of manipulation often blamed themselves later for not having a second thought about their manipulators when red flags were all flying everywhere when they first came into contact with them. When unclear about what to do about a sudden proposition from acquittances, relatives, and strangers, please have a second thought about it.

## INCREASING YOUR AWARENESS

You are reading this book now because you want to increase your awareness about how to prevent dark psychologists from messing up your dear life. The truth is that the actual process of protecting yourself during the acts of dark psychology can be hard to achieve, and the main method you can adopt is to increase your awareness to prevent it from happening in the first place.

What steps can you take in achieving this? In Chapter 10 you have read about the seven signs that reveal the devious acts of the dark psychologists. Here, you will learn how to counter dark psychologists' tactics without actually causing a stir:

- **Stand your ground:** Whether you are in a meeting or a family get-together and a manipulator is trying to pick holes in your arguments or words, stand your ground! If you confidently support your position or argument with convincing evidence, you are likely going to force the manipulator to keep his/her mouth shut.

- **Call for evidence:** If you find yourself in a dire situation where your detractor, a manipulator, is trying to manipulate facts against you, ask him/her to show his/her evidence. In the absence of any sensible evidence, your tormentor will lose face for making an evil attempt to destroy you.

- **Practice neutral behaviorism:** The most potent way to prevent anyone from rousing negative emotions in you is to practice neutral behaviorism. Don't be unnecessarily attached to anything. Just let things fly and never be afraid to have a second thought about them. You know what? What makes you angry in one second can become a ridiculous issue that will crack you up in loud laughter the next second.

- **Ask for the rules of engagement:** Don't let anyone put you in a box that you don't belong in. When having a meeting or relationship with someone who turns out to be a manipulator, always ask for the rules of engagement. Why are we doing this, and what are the rules we are playing by? It would be difficult for just one person or a group of people to isolate you, keep you incommunicado, accuse you wrongly, or make you feel guilty when the rules of interaction have already been laid down and each party is expected to play his/her part accordingly.

## GOING WITH YOUR INTUITION

There is no hard-and-fast rule when it comes to dealing with dark psychologists, who often come in different forms and categories.

This is why it is imperative you go with your intuition in whatever approach you adopt. You should weigh the pros and cons of going with one's intuition, and in the end, if your gut feeling tells you that something is inappropriate or wrong, it is better to be safe than sorry.

We are built differently, and each of us has his/her unique way of detecting danger that hasn't happened yet. It is a kind of in-built intuitive system developed over one's lifetime. Don't regret later for not paying attention to what your body, so to say, is telling you.

You will never go wrong to do things that will protect you from unkind actions of shameless dark psychologists. More so, pay attention to every revelation made about them in this book and share them with your loved ones so that they too could be fully aware of the danger looming in the dark outside.

# 12

# RAISING YOUR WALLS

---

*"The most common way people give up their power is by thinking they don't have any,"*

— ALICE WALKER

---

## YOU HAVE RIGHTS

L et this ring loud and clear in your mind all the time: You Have Rights! Irrespective of where you live or what culture you come from, there are local and national laws enacted to protect your human rights.

Human rights, as defined by Oxford Learners' Dictionary, is *"one of the basic rights that everyone has to be treated fairly and not in a cruel way, especially by their government."* A dark psychologist that subjects you to a series of damning actions has violated your fundamental human rights. Hence, he/she is liable to be punished under your local and national laws.

A manipulator has treated you unfairly and cruelly, and he/she should be handed over to the appropriate law enforcement agencies for prosecution. However, when you are dealing with a very clever manipulator, he/she may not leave any traces for you to discover he/she is behind your ordeal. In that scenario, you probably have nothing to use against him/her as evidence.

When dealing with cunning dark psychologists, always make sure you document everything. If the manipulator poses himself/herself as a business partner, you can record every meeting or ask him/her to append his/her signature to every business deal you both agreed on. You will be able to use those pieces of evidence to seek some legal redress.

However, don't get carried away, what most dark psychologists are seeking, is your mind so that they can easily manipulate your emotions. In that case, it is almost impossible to quantify the extent of the damage they have done to you.

The Article 5 of the United Nations Universal Declaration of Human Rights states that *"No one shall be subjected to torture or to cruel, inhuman or degrading treatment or punishment."* In so far that your country is a member of the United Nations, you are protected by this charter. It aims to protect you from mental or emotional assaults meted out by dark psychologists.

When you know your human rights, you will have the confidence to prevent anyone from undermining them.

## MANAGING YOUR EMOTIONS

---

*"The sign of an intelligent person is their ability to control their emotions by the application of reason."*

— MARYA MANNES

---

Controlling one's emotions may not be as simple as it appears, but the good news is that everyone can successfully manage their emotions if they try. It is imperative that you learn how to manage your emotions so that you can properly protect yourself.

Highlighted below are some practical approaches anyone can adopt in controlling his/her emotions:

- **Just pause for a little while:** When you discover that your emotions are running wildly, and they are in the process of getting the best of you, please pause for a short time. If you are in a condition whereby negative emotions overwhelm you and you don't necessarily know how to keep your thoughts under control, please stop! One great technique often used to stop a flood of negative thoughts is deep breathing. Refrain from saying anything, just breathe deeply for some minutes. It is helpful if you could decide to change your environment for a short time or leave the presence of the cruel dark psychologist rousing negative thoughts in you. If you could do those suggested actions, you would feel a lot lighter as the negative thoughts begin to disappear from your mind.

- **Positive affirmations or rehearsals:** Psychologists believe people can replace the negative thoughts flocking to their minds with positive affirmations. Take for instance, if you are overwhelmed about the thought of losing your wealth, you may replace that annoying thought with a positive affirmation such as: "**My wealth is everlasting! I will live till old age in great wealth!!**" Repeating this positive affirmation from time to time helps you sound the negative voice that has been keeping you unsettled for some time. Positive affirmations are also referred to as "positive rehearsals". You constantly tell your subconscious or mind great and wonderful things about you, about your current and future circumstances. By doing this like a routine, you are likely able to recreate a positive and powerful mindset that you need to achieve tangible successes in life.

- **Hear but don't speak:** We could call this a biblical mind-conditioning technique. It is written in James 1:19 (King James Version), that "*Wherefore, my beloved brethren, let every man be swift to hear, slow to speak, slow to wrath.*" It doesn't matter whatever your manipulator is saying to irk you, this technique advises you to listen, but refrain from saying anything at all. Hence, if you do just that, you will be able to control your angry reaction and keep the situation under control. Remember that the primary goal of a manipulator is to see you troubled, angry, and unsettled. It is your power to prove them wrong and confuse them in their strategy.

There are other ways people use to control their emotions. However, we are only recommending the positive techniques described above. It is equally important to differentiate the helpful methods from some harmful ways people have been utilizing in managing their emotions.

Let it be clear that the following are not recommended for controlling your emotions: If you adopt any of the harmful approaches described below, you are inadvertently doing more harm to yourself than any good:

- **Use of mind-altering substances or drugs:** You may be able to temporarily control your mind by abusing drugs or other substances, but in the long run, you are doing a serious harm to your body and life.
- **Binge-drinking:** There are some people who often boast of keep "calm" by consuming a lot of beer and alcohol. To be honest, anyone who does so is only putting himself/herself up for some damage in his/her body. Stay away from binge-drinking.
- **Denial:** It is funny for people to control their feelings by living in denial. Unfortunately, reality will soon strike while they are trying to hide their true feelings from what is exactly happening to them.

- **Attachment:** It is common for people to attach themselves to lovers, friends, nice colleagues, and neighbors as they try to overcome some uncomfortable experiences in their lives. Be careful: No one can be trusted, and they make yourself vulnerable through unreasonable attachment to people. If care is not taken, you may be running from Peter only to get pummeled by Paul.

## BUILD YOUR SELF-ESTEEM

Your self-esteem is exactly how you feel about yourself. People with low self-esteem often look down on themselves; they usually belittle their own achievements and seem to be suffering from inferiority complex. When your self-esteem is pretty high, it will take a stranger some tough time before he/she can enter into you.

Understand that having a high self-esteem is not the same as being unreasonably arrogant. It means that you know your worth and won't do any senseless thing to put yourself in a risky situation where anyone will take advantage of you. Dark psychologists are always looking for those with low self-esteem so that they can make their lives unbearable for them.

With this information, it is imperative that you build or improve your self-esteem. By doing this, you will avoid turning yourself into a victim.

You can boost your self-esteem by doing some or all of the processes highlighted as follows:

- **Channel your inner superstar:** We all have a superstar in us that is begging to be revealed to the world. Realizing that you are born with some inherent skills, talent, and uniqueness will always equip you with the right amount of confidence that you need to face any situation in this life. Those who look down on themselves and their abilities are possibly in doubt whether they are born with any talent or not. If you can just let your inner superstar speak for itself once in a while, people around you will respect you and hold you in high esteem. One of my university friends was the shyest person I have ever seen in my life; he was so timid to the point that he simply could not look anyone in the eye. One day, we were in an important event and everyone there agreed that he should be the Master of Ceremony. After his initial resistance, he surrendered and mounted the podium. Everyone was already simpering because we knew doing public speaking wasn't his thing. It was like throwing fish into a pot of hot water. After mumbling for a few minutes, he summoned up courage and obviously shocked all of us there with his hidden oratorical gift none of us had ever detected in him. The bottom line: Bring out the hero in you and show it to everyone.

- **Be mindful of everything:** It is dangerous to live thoughtlessly around a dark psychologist. It is like living in a vacuum where one doesn't have a grip on the events happening around him/her. Only hopeless or downtrodden people live thoughtlessly. You should be that person who actively participates in everything occurring around you.

Show the world that you have a strong personality, and that you are not a push-over for any manipulator. When we were in secondary school, it was not the prettiest girl or the most handsome guy that was too difficult to get; it was those loud and difficult ones that often gave guys/girls tough time before agreeing to becoming their friends. Do you know that there is nothing like an old or young politician when it comes to finding supports to pass a new law? Even an MP that had served for decades of years must seek out those newly elected MPs, no matter how young they are, to get their support to move his/her legal agenda forward. This indicates that when you present yourself as a formidable personality, people will have to ask for your permission before getting themselves into your space. In the same way, a manipulator will think twice before approaching someone who is very confident and well aware of the things going on around him/her.

- **Live in the present:** Your past is none of your business, and you should never allow it to shape or define your current lifestyle. One of the evil things people do to themselves is to stick to their inglorious past and let it rob them of living an amazing life. If you were a failure before but your situation has changed for the better, please embrace your present "you" with pride and boldly speak with authority. As long as you are holding onto your uneventful past, you are making yourself unqualified or unfit for a wonderful, new experience. Dark psychologists understand that they can easily use your past to hold you ransom.

- **Don't compare yourself with anyone:** The best way to avoid throwing yourself constantly into a despair is to stop comparing yourself with others. Everyone is unique; we do things differently and our results are not the same. What you are capable of achieving, it may be difficult for others to record similar level of success. Even twins that were born on the same day never grow up acting in the same way—they are genetically and behaviorally different. Albert Einstein once cautioned those comparing themselves with others in one of his popular quotes: *"everybody is genius. But if you judge a fish by its ability to climb a tree, it will live its whole life believing that it is stupid."* Nothing kills a person's esteem faster than comparing himself/herself with others.

- **Take good care of yourself:** Pay attention to your health and stay alert. Exercise and eat good food. Take care of your physical appearance, always present yourself neat and well-dressed. Remember that first impressions matter a lot. More so, you need to have enough sleep and rejuvenate your brain so that it can function properly. When you neglect your self-care, you may end up suffering from stress or other illnesses that may hinder you from presenting a glorious image of you to the world. If a manipulator is thinking of getting into you, but he/she sees that you have a good physique and mental sharpness, he/she will re-think his/her plans. Sometimes, people unintentionally invite dark psychologists to attack them by the way they weakly present their personas. It is just common sense to think that a weak person will become an easy victim. And that is exactly how dark psychologists think!

## SAYING "NO"

You can't believe how high a wall of protection you can raise by simply saying "No!" Kind-hearted and considerate people often think that they are making the world a better place by generously saying "Yes!" to everyone. To some degree, they may be right; the world needs kind and caring people who are always willing to offer a helping hand to those in need.

Unfortunately, dark psychologists don't reason the same way. They perceive kind-hearted people as weaklings that they can easily take advantage of. Good people are hurt the most in this wicked world, and that is why you must learn how to say "No".

Train yourself to identify what works for you and what doesn't. Remember that saying "No!" doesn't mean that you are rude or inconsiderate; it just signifies that you are no longer going to put yourself in a situation where you are vulnerable to dark psychologists' assaults and manipulations.

More so, you should never feel guilty for saying "No", even if the other person keeps on insisting on getting a "Yes". You should emphatically say "No" in the following situations:

- When the matter under discussion adds no measurable value to you or your business. You don't want to give room for interactions that will waste your precious time and allow a total stranger to get a foothold in your life.

- If the purpose of the connection violates the human rights of others. It is criminal to undermine the fundamental human rights of others. You may be liable to criminal charges for doing so.

- If it contradicts your personal principles or ideologies. Take for instance, if you are the type of person who dislikes falsehood and underhand business dealings, you should immediately say "No!" when someone is suggesting such things to you.

- When you suspect that you are interacting with a manipular or a dark psychologist.

- If you are not made the center of the conversion, and your interlocutor appears manipulative in words and body language.

- When your gut tells you that you should say "No".
  Sometimes you may not feel convinced about something. At that moment, your body wants you to say "No" to whatever the other person is suggesting.

There are no fixed rules about what you should say "No" to. At this junction, you should use your discretions and follow your instincts. Not everything that glitters is gold; sometimes what you think is tangible and worth exploring may turn out to be a waste of time for you. In an extreme circumstance, they could be traps that will lure you into the dragnet of a dark psychologist.

## BE SKEPTICAL

Never take any information or suggestion at face value or as it is presented; it doesn't matter if it is coming from your spouse, friends, or business partners. You should cultivate the habit of always scrutinizing facts to be sure you are assimilating nothing but the truth. Be so skeptical that everyone around you knows that you are not gullible.

There are times when people get deceived by believing information that cannot be quantified. Some people have complained of being duped and manipulated by palm readers, shamans, or spiritualists who helped reveal some vague information about their future. In essence, this practice is referred to as the 'Barnum Effect'.

Some people have the habits of listening attentively to palm readers or spiritualists who claim to have had the supernatural powers to see far into the future. It is not uncommon to see people visit those kinds of spiritualists every week to hear more prophecies about different aspects of their lives. In turn, the shamans or spiritualists hold a lot of influence on them and, when necessary, manipulate their victims' thoughts and actions.

The spiritualists have, in certain situations, capitalized on the absolute trust their victims reside in them to defraud them, getting money and other properties from them. It is almost impossible how many millions of people worldwide have lost huge chunks of their personal wealth consulting fortune-tellers.

## PREVENTING AND BREAKING FREE FROM HYPNOSIS, BRAINWASHING, AND MIND CONTROL

Most of the information presented in this book is about how to prevent yourself from becoming a victim of a dark psychologist and breaking free from Hypnosis, Brainwashing, and Mind Control. There are two main ways you can accomplish this:

- **Understanding who you are:** Do you have a high self-esteem? Are you capable of frustrating every tactic a dark psychologist deploys to catch you? Do you know that, paraphrasing Mahatma Ghandi, *"No one can hurt you without your permission?"* After doing some self-analysis and discovered you are still found wanting in some areas of your life, it is very important that you strengthen those areas before putting yourself in the public. Dark psychologists are always on the lookout for weak-minded people to prey upon.

- **Strategize your defensive mechanisms:** You have learned a lot of defensive mechanisms in this book that can help you avoid the possibility of becoming a victim of hypnotism, brainwash, and mind control. Now, it is time you designed a defensive strategy that will work best for you. This may entail combining a few of what you have already read about in this book. Take for example, you may need to improve your self-esteem, learn how to say "No!" emphatically, master your body language to drive away potential manipulators, and refrain from being publicly emotional.

## DEVELOPING YOUR POKER FACE AND OTHER BODY LANGUAGE

The best weapons to use against an enemy, as they say, are the same ones he/she uses to attack you. This aphorism is true on most occasions. When you are dealing with a manipulator, it is sensible to learn some of the body language and signs he/she is using to oppress you. You will then use them back on him/her.

One of the potent weapons you can develop is a poker face and other related body language. When you wear a poker face, you are intentionally confusing your enemies, because they cannot accurately read your emotions. They cannot confirm whether you are happy, sad, or having mixed emotions. More so, you can also employ some body language which you believe will protect you from a dark psychologist, most especially from people who use body language as a means of manipulation.

Other body language techniques that you can focus on include:

- **Cold reading**: This refers to a practice of obtaining a great deal of information about someone by analyzing his/her behaviors, age, fashion, gender, hairstyle, body language, manner of speech, education, sexual orientation, religion, and so on.
- **Mind reading**: This is about reading a person's mind

without necessarily asking him/her any questions. This practice requires some preternatural power or telepathy, and two individuals can communicate with each other without using their five senses.

- **Lip reading**: When dealing with a manipulator who speaks other languages than the one you understand, you can use lip reading to predict the person's behavior through the way he/she pronounces words.

# 13

# IN A RELATIONSHIP WITH DIFFICULT PEOPLE

I f you are in a relationship with a difficult person, there is every possibility that a certain form of manipulation exists in that relationship. In reality, people don't get attracted to anyone they don't have natural affection for. However, staying in a relationship with someone you hate indicates that you are either being manipulated unknowingly, or the other person has stayed in the relationship because he/she has already objectified you and deriving maximum pleasure from that.

## MANIPULATIVE AND TOXIC RELATIONSHIPS

We have probably seen examples of manipulative and toxic relationships all around us. By default, a toxic relationship is the one in which those engaged in it are unhappy about such an alliance. Unfortunately, most of those involved in manipulative and toxic relationships sometimes find it very difficult to call it quits because of something that binds them together.

Some common examples of toxic relationships include:

- **Controlling relationships:** One of the people in a relationship can be so controlling that he/she chooses to treat the other with absolute disrespect. A controlling partner will tell you everything you have to do in the relationship, to the extent of choosing the kinds of clothes or shoes that you should wear every day or what types of food or drinks you are allowed to consume. This kind of attitude will make the other involved in the relationship feel like a powerless person who is being bossed around. When you see someone who is henpecked, he/she is always unhappy with his/her partner. At every slightest misunderstanding, they could end up punching each other in the face. This level of toxicity could result in health issues or even mental health problems.

- **Jealous people:** Everyone has a certain degree of jealousy in them but being in a relationship with a very jealous person could become a serious nightmare. Your phone will be secretly checked; all your private messages will be gone through to detect if you are cheating, even when there are no reasons to embrace such a suspicion. People in a jealous, toxic relationship are often affected by anxiety, because they could never imagine what their jealous partners are up to. Pathological jealousy, which is otherwise known as Othello Syndrome is considered to be very dangerous because the jealous partner could be absolutely delusional and obsessive. In one of the rare studies conducted on delusional jealousy in the United States in 1998, where 20 participants were randomly chosen and 13 of them were men. The research revealed that out the 13 men, 9 actually attacked their spouses. A weapon was used by three of them and 12 had harmed their spouses. This reveals the extent of inconvenience associated with a toxic relationship.

- **A negative thinker:** There is no way a negative thinker can make a beautiful relationship with anyone. Every single thought in his/her heart is evil. Even if you are doing your best to impress him/her, your good gesture will still be misinterpreted. You know, sometimes, people who have had a traumatic experience in the past will always be suspicious of the actions of others, irrespective of how great they are. This is why it is imperative that you spend time to study people very well before falling in love or starting a relationship with them. You may be fortunate to have discovered earlier on that such a person may not be the best fit for you.

- **The nagging one:** This doesn't need a lot of explanation: A nagging wife/husband is a complete pain in the butt. In this kind of relationship, you get talked down to like a baby. All your actions are questioned, and your decisions are weighed thoroughly for the purpose of finding some faults to spend days whining about. It is only in a family that a nagger can make life unbearable for others. If you happen to work with a nagging colleague or boss, you will find the most of your working hours devising ways to handle such an occupational disturbance. Only a few workers can survive in an atmosphere where they are constantly accused of one wrong or the other. Such an action will kill their motivation, and they may be constantly unproductive in that environment.

- **Cheaters:** Whenever cheating enters a relationship, it is like a fire has been thrown into a bush—it will burn everything in its path. The partners will begin to doubt everything they do, accusing each other angrily. Most of the domestic abuse cases in the United Kingdom is attributed to infidelity. This is why it is not surprising that the most commonly cited reason for divorce in the UK is infidelity. According to the Global Investigations statistics, the percentage of married women who admitted to being unfaithful rose 40 percent from 10.5 percent in 1990 to 14.7 percent in 2010. In the same fashion, up to 57 percent of males revealed they had cheated at least once in their relationship. Those who are trapped in a cheating relationship where the partners are accusing each other of infidelity knows that it is not always an easy place to be.

- **The liar:** No good relationship can be established on falsehoods. If you are in a relationship with a liar, you are already putting yourself up for regular abuse and manipulation. It may be difficult for you to identify who a liar is when meeting them for the first time. However, if you can be patient and study them, chances are that you may be able to see them as they are, and not as they portray themselves. One thing about staying in a relationship held together by habitual lying is that you will never get to know the truth about the other person. We have seen it in films how conmen borrowed expensive cars to deceive gullible ladies that they are rich. Once they have swept such ladies off their feet, they will do everything in their power to keep their identities hidden by escalating their lies.

- **Abusive relationship:** In the United Kingdom, the statistics of abusive relationships paint a gloomy picture. It is estimated that 1 out 4 women, and 1 out of 6 men are subjected to some forms of abuse in relationships. The sad reality is that this abuse leads to an average of two women being murdered every week and about 30 men losing their dear lives to abuse every year. Domestic abuse accounts for 16 percent of all violent crime in England and Wales and has more repeat victims than any other crime. One of the headaches associated with abusive relationships is that those involved often pass the blame to the other person. There is a lot of psychological projection going on, with each partner projecting blame on each other. In this case, it will be practically difficult for them to sit down and solve the problem amicably as none of them is accepting the blame for causing the abuse.

- **An insecure partner:** Those who have been in a relationship with an insecure partner often complain that it is totally toxic and manipulative. Instead of embracing the fact that he/she is somehow insecure and do something about it, the person may be acting erratically to present himself/herself as someone he/she isn't. It takes two to tango; unfortunately, if one of them lacks the confidence to tag along, such a relationship may be problematic.

- **A demanding person:** A demanding person is manipulative in nature. He/she doesn't have any considerations for others. All he/she wants is that his/her orders be carried out immediately, and without any questions. Why many relationships turn sour is that when you demand too much from your partner, they are likely going to feel that they are being used. In a relationship where one partner objectifies the other, such an alliance cannot last for a long time. As soon as the objectified person realizes he/she has been used to satisfy the fantasy of the other person, he/she will abruptly put an end to that objectification. Take for instance, if a married woman only likes her husband because of the expensive gifts he is buying for her, their relationship will soon hit the rock once the man finds out that he is only being valued as "Mr. Spender". Everyone wants to be unconditionally loved or appreciated in a relationship. Similarly, you cannot keep a woman for long if she realizes that she is only being valued for sexual pleasure.

- **Narcissistic partner:** As you are fully aware, a narcissistic person is completely self-centered, arrogant, and inconsiderate. A relationship works if the people involved in it value each other and mutually and show respect to one another. A narcissistic lover is only concerned about what he/she can get from the relationship.

He/she doesn't care if the other person is maltreated, under-appreciated, and manipulated. This accounts for why narcissistic individuals are not good at maintaining relationships.

- **Undue competitor:** When you are in a relationship whereby the other parties involved are unduly engaging in cutthroat competition with you, there are going to be some serious issues. A competitor wants to be better than you at all cost; so, instead of amicably dealing with things within the relationship, the other person will be forcing his/her ideas or opinions on you. That could set a dangerous pattern that may jeopardize the relationship, because no one admires being manipulated or ordered around.

- **A perfectionist:** No one is perfect; we all have our flaws as human beings. If you are in a relationship with a perfectionist, there is a tendency that such a relationship will soon collapse. Why? You cannot always have an unreasonable expectation of your partner—you must understand that people make mistakes. And that they should never be held hostage because of those mistakes. A lot of relationships could have been saved if the parties involved had exercised some patience with their partners.

You can see why there are so many relationship problems in the world. We are entering into relationships with people with different personalities and psychological makeups. This is why universal relationship advice never works on all situations because people are psychologically different. You will save yourself some trouble if you can be patient enough to study your partner before heading into a relationship with him/her.

## AMONGST YOUR FAMILY AND FRIENDS

There are also some forms of toxic and manipulative relationships among your family and friends.

Addressing his disciples in Matthew 10:36, Jesus Christ dropped a bombshell: *"a man's enemies will be the members of his own household."* This assertion has remained forever relevant even in our present age.

Do you know why? Your families and friends know a lot about you; they know your strengths and weaknesses. This gives them an edge over external manipulators if they choose to attack you with dark psychology. And if they do, you will feel the most pain from their attacks.

What could make your family and friends subject someone to dark psychology? You may want to know. There are a few reasons why your brother/sister or a close friend/acquaintance may want to harm or hurt you:

- **Envy:** If you happen to be more successful than some of your relatives or friends, they may be tempted to use dark psychology on you. Some of their attempts may be to lure you into giving them money or some pricey possessions they won't have had access to if they didn't use hypnotism or manipulative tactics on you. Sometimes, they may not want to see you die or be incapacitated, but their initial expectations could be that you become as hopeless as they are.

- **Competition:** There is usually a rivalry among siblings; your brother or sister will aspire to be better than you. In case they cannot achieve that naturally or by working hard, they may be tempted to give dark psychology a try.

- **Family discords:** There are many reasons why members of a family can become sworn enemies. Take for instance, when they are dividing their family properties after the demise of their parents, who did not leave a Will, they may do so disproportionately and cause one or more person to feel cheated in the process. The affected person (s) may resort to seeking justice through the use of dark psychology on any of his/her siblings.

The case is slightly different when it comes to friends and acquaintances. Your friends can only have as much information about you as you let them. And never forget that today's friend could be tomorrow's enemy. Warren G Harding once said, *"treat your friend as if he will one day be your enemy, and your enemy as if he will one day be your friend."*

In essence, the impacts a friend or an acquaintance can have on you depend how much you expose yourself to their influence. If you are a moderate person who doesn't make himself/herself vulnerable to friend-initiated dark psychology, you may be able to protect yourself from their evil intentions if they happen to think of hurting you.

Human beings are so unpredictable; so, do all you can to put yourself and your loved ones in a safe situation where unexpected dark psychological attacks will have no serious effects on you and your loved ones.

This doesn't mean that you should always suspect one or more of your friends as a potential manipulator; if you use your discretion very well, over time you can detect who is to be trusted and who to be sent packing from your life.

## IN YOUR WORK

You can choose your friends and acquaintances, but you cannot, on most occasions, choose your co-workers. And there is nothing as difficult as working with manipulators. At first, they may disguise as a caring manager training you how to do some of the tasks assigned to you at the workplace. Over time, you will see that they are becoming more demanding and manipulative in nature.

Unfortunately, a large number of female employees have been harassed by their superiors who wanted more than just working with them. And if a female employee refuses sexual advances from a male superior, he may make life difficult for her.

You surely have some well-defined options when it comes to dealing with a manipulator at work. Here are some time-tested approaches you can adopt to proactively deal with a manipulator at your workplace:

- **Compose yourself:** Understand the fact that no company

or office welcomes heartless manipulators; you are, to some degree, protected by your company's rules, irrespective of the position of the manipulator. So, compose yourself. Ask sensible questions to clarify whatever the manipulator might be querying you for. Of course, a male manager that wants to sleep with his subordinate, who is a female worker, will never say it directly. Instead, he will be accusing her from time to time for not doing her job very well. So, ask relevant questions to clarify the issue under discussion. If necessary, involve another high-ranking manager in the discussion.

- **Stay away from the manipulator:** If you can, always stay away from the manipulator. You can request to have your seat rearranged so that you are not always sitting next to him/her. When in meetings, do not attempt to interrupt the manipulator so that you don't give them the chance to lambast or attack you in meetings.

- **Don't say "Yes" to everything:** Honestly, you don't have to say "yes" to every task given to you by the manipulator who keeps looking for an opportunity to attack you. You can claim that you are busy on a task so that they look around for another person to take it up. Remember that your colleagues are not your friends nor family members; interact with them with caution. If a sex-obsessed senior executive is asking you out to drink with him, you have the right to say "No!".

- **Know Your Rights:** Don't forget that you have rights at your workplace. So, if you are sure someone is pressing you too hard to compromise your integrity, you can complain to the establishment using their normal procedures for registering grievances. It is dangerous to keep enduring harassment and manipulation at work, thinking that the perpetrator will change. That's an erroneous thinking, because most manipulators are excited seeing their victims in pain.

## CAN THEY STILL CHANGE?

It is common among victims of manipulation to assume that their manipulators can still change. Will they? Well, there are some instances why they may. We are talking about salvaging relationships that shouldn't have, in the first place, turned sour. A husband and a wife can choose to reconcile after discovering that they were both at fault. An employee can forgive an erring employer and reconcile with him/her. Some relations and friends may have learned that their actions were wrong and have duly apologized for their misdemeanors.

However, be careful! Not everyone who apologizes really means it; some old friends or associates may reconcile with you because they realise they cannot enjoy similar benefits they have been having without you. So, use your discretion in each circumstance.

Can all manipulators still change? The answer is an emphatic "NO!" Some evil-minded people who approach you for the singular purpose of hurting you, defrauding you of your prized possessions, or even taking your precious life will never see any reasons to leave you alone. Those are the categories of manipulative people that you should never give a second chance, because they will hurt you more.

## DEFENDING YOURSELF AGAINST MANIPULATORS

The best way to defend yourself against evil manipulators is to not give them unfettered access to you. Keep them far away from you. Don't be that kind-hearted person who is always willing to give people a second chance without finding out, beforehand, if they are going to add value to your life or business.

Always remember that you have nothing to gain from manipulating and toxic relationships. So, take the steps to protect yourself from toxic relationships:

- Get out of any relationships that do not serve your purpose.
- Do not let your colleagues or acquaintances know your weaknesses; they could use them to manipulate you.
- Identify the purposes of a relationship before starting it; if your interest is not clearly expressed in the agreement, get out of the relationship.
- Never allow a manipulator to get a chance into entering your life without knowing if he/she has something good to add to your life.
- Use your discretions and natural instincts to spot out manipulators far before they attack you. Chances are that you will always have a natural way to identify a mischievous troublemaker before he/she makes his/her tent in your life.
- Stop making yourself vulnerable to dark psychologists' attacks. The easiest way people expose themselves to danger is to present themselves as emotional and weak.

# 14

# AGAINST ONLINE ATTACKS

Dark psychologists have gone a new platform for launching their debilitating attacks—the internet. In recent years, lives of some innocent people have been turned upside down due to the nefarious activities of online manipulators. This malicious practice is called cyberbullying, whereby a handful of evil-intentioned people hide behind the anonymity of the internet to bully or attempt to manipulate the behaviors of others.

The 2020 statistics on cyberbullying is pathetic: About 36.5 percent of people reported being bullied online in their lifetime, while 17. 4 percent confessed that it has occurred to them in the last 30 days. And 87 percent of young people complained to have been bullied mainly on online platforms.

The impacts of these evil online practices are as well significant: About 64 percent of those who are bullied say that they do not feel safe at schools. And they exhibit some social and mental health issues if the bullying persists longer than expected. To manage their situations, many cyberbullied people often take to excessive drinking or abuse substances. In serious circumstances, they could commit suicide or harm others in their vicinities.

## FACTS AND LIES

Internet is still pretty much an open platform that is poorly regulated. This entails that much of the information online is not moderated. This gives the opportunity for those with evil intentions to easily spread lies about others. Most of them get away with the falsehoods they are broadcasting, except in rare cases when the attention of the moderator of the platform is drawn to the content, which they will later make an effort to delete.

The idea of fake news further exacerbates the reliability of the online platforms. Sometimes even governmental agencies spread rumors to deceive unsuspicious citizens. Before he was voted out of office, Donald Trump and his administrative officers held sway over ordinary Americans that it was even difficult for them to differentiate truths from lies. In the same way, other organizations have released untrue information online that are publicly quoted by people all over the world who do not have the resources to confirm if the information was true or not.

You may be confused about what you should believe on the internet then. Well, some decorum is finding its way to the internet and social media companies are increasingly working round the clock to strike out fake news, destructive information, and unconfirmed rumors from their platforms.

Before you believe anything online, use these yardsticks to help you separate truths from half-truths or lies:

- **Authority sources:** Make sure the information you are spreading is coming from the authority sources. Take for instance, you could see a blue tick (v) beside the name of the person or organization releasing that information. This means that those sources have been confirmed to be real/true by the social media companies.
- **Believable experiences/stories:** You can also help yourself only to the truth online by accepting believable stories. These are factual stories that are almost always true. Take for instance, if someone says the Sun rises in the East and sets in the West, you probably don't need to fact-check that because it is the truth.
- **Confirmed information:** Sometimes you may not know the sources of some information. But if they have been confirmed by other authority sources, that piece of information could be true. For example, you may not know who said something many years ago, but if a reliable person quoted the same statement that was made many years ago, the truthfulness of the statement can be attributed to the reliable personality that authenticates it.
- **Well-known facts:** You may not need to fact-check well-known facts. We all understand that some religious data or

information are incontestable. In that scenario, you can save yourself some time to clarify them.

That being said, internet is still a very dangerous place that one must carefully navigate, most especially for little children.

## BE AWARE OF DARK PATTERNS

When you search online for any service, you must be careful who is responding to your call for help. The anonymity of the internet has made it possible for dark psychologists to hide behind a computer screen and secretly find their ways into people lives.

According to FBI, the internet crime rate has increased proportionately in the past years. In 2019 alone, there were 467, 361 internet crime complaints made, which translated into 1,300 complaints per day. In total, there was an estimated $3.5 billion losses to businesses and individuals.

The nature of the crime committed online is getting darker each day, from a pedophile lurking in the dark looking for kids to prey on to dark psychologists making continuous attempts to manipulate people with the click of a mouse. From dating sites, many unconscious lovers have thrown themselves into the arms of manipulators who make their lives truly unbearable. Many manipulative and toxic relationships are being formed every day, and people do not necessarily seem to have learned any lessons.

So, what should you in the face of mounting takeover of the internet by the dark psychologists? Well, there is no one-size-fits-all answer in this regard. But, as you will soon discover, there are steps you can take to protect yourself and your loved ones online.

Keeping yourself safe is a daily battle you must wage. The internet is a large ocean full of malicious sharks. And what they are looking for is you, your property, your heart, or somehow your life. It is your responsibility to make sure they don't get whatever they think they are looking for.

For you to know how dark the internet is becoming, young people are facing an unprecedented level of threats online. In an interview conducted to find out about how some teens were bullied online, the following observations were made: And the most common kinds of cyberbullying teens experience include:

- Offensive name-calling (42%)
- Spreading of false rumors (32%)
- Receiving explicit images, they didn't ask for (25%)
- Constant asking of who they are, what they're doing, and who they're with by someone other than a parent (21%)
- Physical threats (16%)
- Having explicit images shared without their consent (7%)

## MANIPULATIVE INFORMATION

Most of the fake news or information online are directed at certain groups of people, and their covert purpose is to manipulate them. Take for instance, there are certain categories of people called the Leftist and Rightist. These groups constantly produce online content that will solidify their socio-political beliefs, convictions, and ideologies. It doesn't matter if the messages they are sending out are true or false; what is important to them is to continue to control the thoughts of their followings, telling them exactly whatever they are waiting to hear and totally brainwash them.

Recently, people are subscribing to websites that offer daily horoscopes. The most shocking aspect of this is that they absolutely believe everything they read about their stars, whether they are Aries, Scorpio, or Capricorn. Through this holistic adhere to horoscope and reading of tarot cards, some people have carelessly made themselves vulnerable to dark psychologists' attacks.

More so, dark patterns are noticeable in some online marketing and advertising. People are being manipulated to reluctantly spend their hard-earned money on things they don't need in the first place. A blogger lists some of the tactics employed by dark marketers to manipulate buyers, and they include:

1. **Trick questions:** Buyers are asked some tricky questions they may not have answers for. In the course of that, they may be lured into paying for goods they don't really want.
2. **Sneak into basket:** This is a deceptive and manipulative practice whereby online shoppers are tricked into buying something because the algorithm has suggested them to be useful alongside a good product they are purchasing.
3. **Roach motel:** This is a kind of cockroach bait used to catch the insect. In this case, a roach motel could mean disguising a

product as very attractive only to compel shoppers to click on buying it.

4. **Privacy Zuckering:** This is a typical dark pattern that has received much attention lately. E-commerce or online stores sometimes add a hidden line to their "terms and conditions" which allows them to secretly sell customers' or shoppers' private information to a third-party.

5. **Price comparison prevention:** Sometimes shoppers are deceived into believing that they are getting the best price on a product. Why? Because shopping marketplaces or the search engines have hidden comparison of prices from them. So, they are not aware that there are other online stores offering the same products at a cheaper price.

6. **Misdirection:** More often than not, shoppers are misdirected while navigating an online store. They could receive suggestions about useless products that they don't need.

7. **Hidden costs:** What makes online manipulation worse, as far as online shopping is concerned, are the hidden costs storeowners sometime include in the price lists. If you are not careful, you may end up paying more for a product that it actually worth.

8. **Bait and switch:** This is an advertising dark pattern that has been in practice for ages. In this case, a store advertises a product at a bargain price. And when buyers purchased them, they are sent counterfeit products with poor value. Sometimes, shoppers may not be able to differentiate the

original from their counterfeit products because they look exactly alike.

9. **Confirmshaming:** Some online stores shame shoppers from confirming their final list of purchased products in their shopping cart. They do this to intentionally defraud them, adding hidden costs to the final price paid for the shopping.

10. **Disguised ads:** These ads are disguised as content from another source, meanwhile they are placed on a store by the storeowner. So, when a potential shopper sees it, he/she may be excited to shop elsewhere, without knowing that the same store owns the ads.

11. **Forced continuity:** Nowadays, storeowners can use algorithms that can urge shoppers to continue shopping. This dark pattern is referred to as forced continuity, because if the shopper wants to exit shopping, he/she will be directed to another listing page on the store.

12. **Friend spam:** Have you ever been a store and you suddenly see a pop-up that says, "Your friend has bought this!"? This dark practice is called friend spam—because stores will spam you based on the products your friends have purchased previously.

It is apparent from the examples provided in this section that internet remains a dangerous medium that is full of countless manipulative tactics. From dating, horoscopes, to online shopping. In this dispensation, you can also learn about Neuro-linguistic programming (NLP) online or join an association of witches/wizards or Satanism right on the internet. The dangers posed by all these online interactions are enormous.

## MAKE CHECKING FACTS A HABIT

The truth is that you don't want to become a victim of all these online manipulations. The first place to start in protecting yourself is not to believe everything you see on the internet. Fact-check every piece of information to make sure it is originating from a very reliable source. Do not follow the crowd to embrace a new technology without confirming that it has something good to offer you.

Today, there are millions of online thought leaders and influencers. You don't have to follow any of them if they don't preach the causes you are passionate about. Some of the online motivators are, in fact, manipulators in disguise because they will force you to practice their mantras from time to time. Some of them will even take the conversation with you out of the internet and start calling you to get a better grip on your life.

You can avoid plunging yourself into misfortune by questioning the veracity of the things you see online. Lately, prostitutes don't advertise their services openly; they will put a deceptive advertisement on the internet, like "Get in touch with us for your body health services!" Body health services? Yes, that is how crafty and dodgy manipulators are. And when you fall into their hands, they will control you like a baby!

You are one of the luckiest beings on earth for reading this. According to the great physicist, Galileo Galilei, *"all truths are easy to under-*

*stand once they are discovered, the point is to discover them."*
You should make it your duty to always seek the truth because, as the
Bible says, only the truth can set you free.

Use the following four essential steps to confirm the veracity of
anything you see on the internet:

- **Step 1: Identify spurious or fake content:** Always be
  alert. When you see a piece of information that seems to be
  too good to be true, let your fact-checking instinct come
  alive.
- **Step 2: Verify the source of the information:** You
  may need to look at the link that carries the message,
  investigate the author of the information, the date it was
  published, contact information of the author, and see
  whether the author is an authority on the subject-matter.
  This technique can help you screen out fluffy content.
- **Step 3: Check out if the content is relevant:** You may
  want to confirm if the content is accurate, recent, and
  applicable to the purpose you want to use it for. Is it some
  practical report, a satire, or an imitation?
- **Step 4: Weigh the veracity of the evidence:** Is the
  evidence portrayed in the information correct? Are there
  similar citations that could prove that the information
  released on the internet is true and not fake?

If you patiently followed the four steps highlighted above, you will be
able to reduce the number of falsehoods you consume on the internet.

This will help you to concentrate on nothing but the truths and protect yourself from dark psychologists' attacks.

## PROTECTING YOURSELF ONLINE

To some extent, you can protect yourself online. Apart from bookmarking most of the useful online content that you would like to access from time to time, there are further actions to safeguard yourself while on the internet.

Outlined below are ten practical approaches you could use to protect yourself online:

- Never open emails or messages from strangers. Many people who got themselves into trouble with manipulators started by communicating with them online, without first knowing or meeting them.
- You should make sure that your devices have up-to-date security protections. That will help you keep malware, spyware, and hackers at bay.
- Make sure you are using strong passwords that cannot be easily compromised.
- You should use two-factor authentication on all of your online sign-ins. This will prevent any impostors getting into your systems and stealing your vital data.
- Refrain from clicking on all links that appear strange; they could be a virus or a hacker looking for a way to get into your system.
- It is not advisable that you should use public WIFI that is

mostly unprotected. Malware or spyware can get into your system through that.

- Make it a habit to back up your data regularly. When your system is down and requires a reboot, you may have back-up data to use.

- Be careful not to expose your financial information online. Internet criminals can get valuable information from your computing system and use it against you.

- You should educate every member of your family how to play safe on the internet.

- Never share your personal information with anyone. Some careless people who freely provide their private information to strangers have ended up becoming victims of online manipulations.

Above all, use your discretion and stay safe. Most of the precautions described in this book are doable only if you try them.

# 15

# IMPROVING YOUR EMOTIONAL INTELLIGENCE

The most important thing you should concentrate on improving is **Yourself!** Why? No amount of evil intentions the dark psychologists plan towards you will work if you have high emotional intelligence.

The Oxford Learners' Dictionary defines "Emotional Intelligence" as *"the ability to understand your emotions and those of other people and to behave appropriately in different situations."* With good emotional intelligence, you will know the right thing to do at the right time to save your life. Unfortunately, not everyone has great emotional intelligence. Some people still need to work on themselves to improve their emotional intelligence.

## WHY IMPROVE?

It is imperative that you improve your emotional intelligence so that you will be able to withstand whatever tricks the dark psychologists are playing on you. Why Improve?" No one can help you if you don't help yourself first. And the main way to help yourself is to do everything in your power to better protect yourself against dark psychology. And you can accomplish this by tuning up your emotional capability.

People need high emotional intelligence because:

- They need to handle all things that come their way in life, and they should be able to perform sensibly when under stress.
- They need to ward off potential manipulators who may be looking around for emotionally weak individuals to manipulate their thoughts and actions.
- They can apply their instincts to issues and resolve problems quickly without losing much or nothing at all in the process.
- High emotional intelligent people are fully in charge of their senses when in any circumstances. In other words, their actions are not influenced by external forces.
- They can identify problems in the distance and do whatever it takes to avoid it.

## TAKE AN EMOTIONAL INTELLIGENCE (EI) TEST

How do you know your emotional intelligence (EI) level? You should take an emotional intelligence test or a combination of emotional intelligence tests. The outcome(s) of these tests will show how emotionally resilient you are to handle all difficult issues life will bring your way.

An individual can measure his/her emotional intelligence through three unique techniques:

- **By using a self-report or self-assessment**
- **By using other reports conducted by a third-party**
- **By utilizing ability measurement tools**

A number of tools have been developed by different organizations to accomplish the task of measuring a person's emotional intelligence. They include questionnaires, quizzes, and scales. There are four main classes of intelligence that are measured by different tests; they include:

- **Abilities-based tests**
- **Trait (or character)-based tests**
- **Competency-based tests**
- **Behavior-based tests**

**Emotional intelligence (EI) scales:** There are different scales developed for the purpose of measuring people's emotional intelligence. The most commonly applied EI scale is a 33-item scale purportedly designed from studies carried out by Schuette and colleagues in 1998, which was an adaptation from the 64-item scale previously published in 1990 by Salovey and Mayer.

Here is the 33-item emotional intelligence scale upon which people's emotional resiliency is measured:

1. I know when to speak about my personal problems to others.
2. When I am faced with obstacles, I remember times I faced similar obstacles and overcame them.
3. I expect that I will do well on most things I try.
4. Other people find it easy to confide in me.
5. I find it hard to understand the non-verbal messages of other people.
6. Some of the major events of my life have led me to re-evaluate what is important and not important.
7. When my mood changes, I see new possibilities.
8. Emotions are one of the things that make my life worth living.
9. I am aware of my emotions as I experience them.
10. I expect good things to happen.
11. I like to share my emotions with others.
12. When I experience a positive emotion, I know how to make it last.
13. I arrange events others enjoy.
14. I seek out activities that make me happy.
15. I am aware of the non-verbal messages I send to others.

16. I present myself in a way that makes a good impression on others.

17. When I am in a positive mood, solving problems is easy for me.

18. By looking at their facial expressions, I recognize the emotions people are experiencing.

19. I know why my emotions change.

20. When I am in a positive mood, I am able to come up with new ideas.

21. I have control over my emotions.

22. I easily recognize my emotions as I experience them.

23. I motivate myself by imagining a good outcome to tasks I take on.

24. I compliment others when they have done something well.

25. I am aware of the non-verbal messages other people send.

26. When another person tells me about an important event in his or her life, I almost feel as though I have experienced this event myself.

27. When I feel a change in emotions, I tend to come up with new ideas.

28. When I am faced with a challenge, I give up because I believe I will fail.

29. I know what other people are feeling just by looking at them.

30. I help other people feel better when they are down.

31. I use good moods to help myself keep trying in the face of obstacles.

32. I can tell how people are feeling by listening to the tone of their voice.

33. It is difficult for me to understand why people feel the way they do.

**Emotional Intelligence (EI) Questionnaires:** These are questionnaires specifically designed to measure people's EI. One of such a questionnaire, designed by Mind Tools (2019) is provided below for your use:

**Note:** Responders are encouraged to offer true answers to the statements below as they are currently, and not as they hope they could be:

1. I can recognize my emotions as I experience them.
2. I lose my temper when I feel frustrated.
3. People have told me that I'm a good listener.
4. I know how to calm myself down when I feel anxious or upset.
5. I enjoy organizing groups.
6. I find it hard to focus on something over the long term.
7. I find it difficult to move on when I feel frustrated or unhappy.
8. I know my strengths and weaknesses.
9. I avoid conflict and negotiations.
10. I feel that I don't enjoy my work.
11. I ask people for feedback on what I do well, and how I can improve.
12. I set long-term goals and review my progress regularly.
13. I find it difficult to read other people's emotions.
14. I struggle to build rapport with others.
15. I use active listening skills when people speak to me.

For each of these statements, the responders would rate themselves from not at all, rarely, sometimes, often and very often (Mind Tools, 2019).

**Emotional Intelligence (EI) Quiz:** Quizzes are also popularly used to measure people's intelligence. The sample quiz below is developed by Institute for Health and Human Potential.

**Statement:** I do not become defensive when criticized.

**Possible answers:** Strongly agree, Agree, Neither agree nor disagree, Disagree, and Strongly disagree.

**Note:** Your choice of answer can say a lot about you and your temperament. And these are the interpretations for each selected answer:

**Strong Agree:** I utilize criticism and other feedback for growth.

**Agree:** I am positive.

**Neither agree nor disagree**: I maintain a sense of humor.

**Disagree:** I try to see things from another's perspective.

**Strongly disagree:** I recognize how my behavior affects others.

**Emotional Intelligence Quadrants:** This comprises of four distinct quadrants that measure each aspect of human intelligence, namely self-awareness, social awareness, relationship management, and self-management.

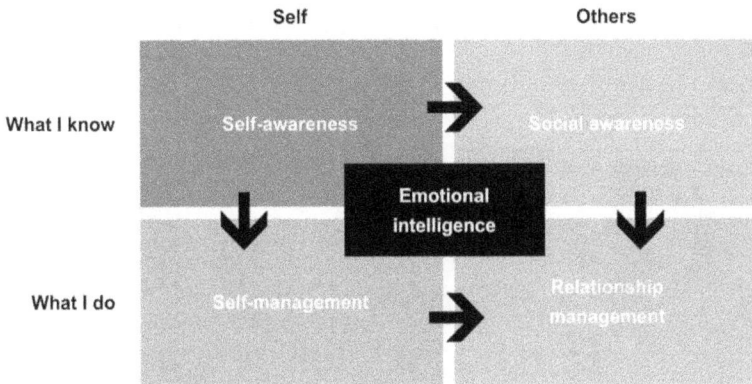

**Emotional Intelligence Score**: Each emotional intelligence test has its own scoring system. You can either have a high or a low score. When your score is low; all you need to do is to check the areas where your scores are low and do something about strengthening or improving upon those areas. When you work on improving yourself for some time, you can come back to take the test (s) after several weeks of self-development to see how you will do again in the tests.

**The primary purpose of taking an Emotional Intelligence test is to let you know which aspects of your life is weak and may be taken advantage of by dark psychologists.**

## 5 SIGNS OF HIGH EMOTIONAL INTELLIGENCE

When your emotional intelligence is pretty high, you will be able to do the following very well:

- **Good decision-making:** Your decisions about every area of your life will be spot on and powerful.
- **Better stress management:** You will demonstrate high resiliency that is useful in proactively managing stress.
- **Improved interpersonal skills:** Your interpersonal skills will improve dramatically.
- **Self-perception:** You will always see yourself in a better light and hold yourself at high esteem.
- **Self-expression:** You will be able to express yourself confidently and purposefully.

## HOW TO IMPROVE?

Having seen how important high emotional intelligence is, it is imperative that you should do everything in your power to improve your emotional intelligence. You can take some of the steps described below to achieve that:

professional success. Below are 10 ways to increase your EQ:

### 1. Communicate boldly.

Let your communication with people be assertive and sensible. If you are too passive, people around you may misunderstand your good intentions.

### 2. Respond, don't react to stressor.

When you find yourself in a situation where your emotional resolve is being tested with conflicts and stress, do not react but respond accordingly. Let people see you as reasonable and calm in any situations.

### 3. Better listening skills.

It is usually said that intelligent people listen when discuss with people so that they can obtain clear messages and respond sensibly. If you are talkative and never listen to what the others are saying, your answers might be inappropriate for issues under discussion and people might consider you to be of low emotional intelligence.

## 4. Always be motivated.

Self-motivation is the key; don't wait until people come around to motivate you. You are your own savior when it comes to adopting coping strategies to deal with life's uncertainties.

## 5. Always maintain a positive attitude.

Let it be part and parcel of your attitude to constantly maintain a positive attitude about things. Because being overtly negative can affect your mental health and destabilize everything about you.

## 6. Practice regular self-awareness.

If you know who you are, no one can underestimate your worth. Most of the people who become victims of manipulations are those who are self-effaced and don't particularly know their self-worth.

## 7. Calmly accept criticism.

The easiest way to test anyone's emotional intelligence is to see how they react when criticized. If you are a boisterous arguer who won't let people get a word in edgeways, you may be excluded from many intelligent discussions because people can't handle your vituperation when angered.

## 8. Be empathetic.

One of the best qualities of emotionally intelligent people is that they show empathy to people around them. They share in their weaknesses and feel like they are in the same unfortunate position as the people they are sympathizing with.

## 9. Use your leadership skills.

It is important that you use your leadership skills wherever you find yourself. You won't always be a subordinate; so, when a duty of honor comes up, act as honorable as possible. Take for instance, if you are a senior executive in a company, it is your responsibility to calmly attend to the needs of those working under you, including showing them a great example of leadership.

## 10. Be approachable and sociable.

If you are cantankerous and always pick quarrels with people, you may not be perceived as someone with high emotional intelligence.

## IT TAKES TIME AND PRACTICE

Can you learn how to improve your emotional intelligence? Definitely. The good news is that people are not born with high emotional intelligence; they most learn them, as you would study any subject at school. However, it takes time and practice to get good at it. It requires consistent practice for it to be truly developed.

You can use the following techniques to develop your emotional intelligence:

- **Understanding your emotions.** Analyse each of your emotions and understand how to use them well. So many things in your life will go wrong if you misapply your emotions. Keep quiet where you are supposed to hold your peace. Never be overanxious about things that do not matter and protect yourself from manipulators who are always looking for those who are too emotional.

- **Matching your emotions to the right scenarios:** After analyzing your emotions, you will fully understand which emotion to use in a certain circumstance. In this case, match your emotions with the applicable tasks and scenarios. This will help you to do the right thing at the right time.

- **Map your emotions:** Sometimes you may need to map your emotions and put them under control when necessary. This entails that you interact with individuals based on their relevance at a particular point in time. You cannot transfer emotion to those who do not merit it. For example, you cannot use the emotion for a business partner with your child. Such inappropriate use of emotion will point you out as immature. In reality, people have a measure of expectation from everyone; it is in your power to decide who gets what. It is practically unreasonable to be angry with a person who has not offended you in anyway. If that happens, people will have every reason to doubt your emotional intelligence.

# CONCLUSION

After reading this book with detailed information about how to deal with the threats all of us face every day, you should be really happy for the deep knowledge you have garnered from it. It is almost impossible to find a book out there that exhaustively treats the subject-matter of dark psychology as much as this book does.

No one should ever be subjected to the dehumanizing experiences of manipulation, hypnotism, and destructive Neuro-Linguistic Programming. Instead of keeping quiet and letting people be treated in a way that undermine their human rights and humanity, I took upon myself to write this book. Take this as a warning for you and your loved ones, because if you could judiciously follow the comprehensively researched content in this book, you will be better off after digesting it.

When someone is ill, they can go to see the doctor for a cure. Unfortunately, most of the people who have been or are currently being manipulated don't realize they are victims. They think it is a natural experience that they must go through. Good thing, this book will serve as an eye-opener for many victims who still don't know that their lives could have been more glorified than they are now if they had learned about manipulators years before.

This is not a book that should be read one time and dumped on a shelf; you should constantly consult it so that you could continuously gain insights into the machinations of dark psychologists and remain ahead of them in the curve of personal development. You have got to do what it takes to remain in a safe position, while helping friends and relatives to discover the same safe haven offered in this book.

The topics covered in this book are evergreen, always applicable to our day-to-day survival in this wild world. Keep digesting all the important information about how you can master your emotions, improve your emotional intelligence, identify manipulators, hypnotists, and NLP practitioners. Prevention is the best method for safety. As long as you. are armed with the cogent information highlighted in this book, you will be able to ward off dark psychologists by doing things that will frustrate their moves towards you and your loved ones.

You have a lot to lose by allowing a dark psychologist to enter into you. It may already be late to redress the situation. An average dark psychologist has an evil intention they want to actualize on their victims. Many people have lost valuable properties, wealth and, in some serious circumstance, their precious lives. You only live once; it is your perpetual responsibility to keep yourself and your loved ones safe.

You can as well see this book as pages of life coaching about the dangers of dark psychologists and how to avoid them. This will help you to actively visualize the information in the pages. They must be engrained in your mind from time to time so that they can be useful for you.

I think you should congratulate yourself; The first step in defeating evil is to know, in detail, how they operate. Then you will use your knowledge about them to disarm and frustrate them.

Do not hesitate to share the invaluable knowledge in this book with your friends, loved ones, and acquaintances. Doing so, you might be able to save someone's life. Dark psychology is pretty much in use on a large scale in our world. It is through this level of education about their influence that we could all work together to put an end of their menace.

Apart from that, people will continue to fall victims to dark psychologists, who run into millions all over the world.

# RESOURCES

Beheshti, N. (2020, May 15). Toxic influence: An average of 80% Americans have experienced emotional abuse. (https://www.forbes.com/sites/nazbeheshti/2020/05/15/an-average-of-80-of-americans-have-experienced-emotional-abuse/?sh=565b44067b49

Birkett, A. (2020, September 5). Online manipulation: All the ways you're currently being deceived. Online Manipulation: All The Ways You're Currently Being Deceived (cxl.com)

Britannica    (2021).    Hypnosis.    https://www.britannica.com/science/hypnosis

Broadband Search (2021). 51 critical cyberbullying statistics in 2020. 51 Critical Cyberbullying Statistics in 2020 - BroadbandSearch

Clark, J. (2021). What are emotions, and why do we have them? https://science.howstuffworks.com/life/what-are-emotions.htm

Cohut, M. (2017, September 1). Hypnosis: What is it, and how does it work? https://www.medicalnewstoday.com/articles/319251

Cook, S. (2021, February 7). Cyberbullying facts and statistics for 2018-2021. Cyberbullying Statistics and Facts for 2021 | Comparitech

Cowen, A. (2018, May 9). How many different kinds of emotions are there? http://kids.frontiersin.org/article/10.3389/frym.2018.00015

Daskal, L. (2016, March 31). How to make yourself mentally strong this year: These 15 habits will you keep you at your sharpest, whatever comes your way. https://www.inc.com/lolly-daskal/how-to-make-yourself-mentally-strong-this-year.html

Federal Bureau of Investigation (2020, February 11). 2019 internet crime report released. 2019 Internet Crime Report Released — FBI

Global Investigation (2021). Infidelity statistics in the UK (Infographic).Infidelity Statistics in the UK [Infographic] – Global Investigations

GoodTherapy (2019, March 26). Manipulation. https://www.goodtherapy.org/blog/psychpedia/manipulation

GoodTherapy (2018, December 2). Neuro-Linguistic Programming (NLP). https://www.goodtherapy.org/learn-about-therapy/types/neuro-linguistic-programming

Goulston, M. (2013, December 19). Never be manipulated again. https://www.psychologytoday.com/us/blog/just-listen/201312/never-be-manipulated-again

Jones, J. (2021). Dark psychology & manipulation: Are you unknowingly using them? https://drjasonjones.com/dark_psychology/

Kaufman, S.B. (2019, March 19). The light triad vs. dark triad of personality: New research contrasts two different profiles of human nature. https://blogs.scientificamerican.com/beautiful-minds/the-light-triad-vs-dark-triad-of-personality/

Lidow, D. (2019, August 11). We must curtail online manipulation before it's too late: Here are four things we can do. https://www.forbes.com/sites/dereklidow/2019/08/11/we-must-curtail-online-manipulation-before-its-too-late-here-are-four-things-we-can-do/?sh=44b80aa7e000

Living Without Abuse (2021). Statistics. Domestic Abuse Statistics | lwa.org.uk : LWA

Louv, J. (2021). 10 ways to protect yourself from NLP mind control. https://ultraculture.org/blog/2014/01/16/nlp-10-ways-protect-mind-control/

Mental health.gov (2020, May 28). What is mental health? https://www.mentalhealth.gov/basics/what-is-mental-health

Mind Tools (2021). Understanding the dark triad: Managing "dark" personality traits. https://www.mindtools.com/pages/article/understanding-dark-triad.htm

Morgan, N. (2017, April 20). Why learn about body language? Here's one reason. https://publicwords.com/2017/04/20/learn-body-language-heres-one-reason/

Naim, R. (2016, April 25). 10 types of people you don't really need in your life. https://thoughtcatalog.com/rania-naim/2016/04/10-types-of-people-you-really-dont-need-in-your-life/

Ni, P. (2014, June 1). How to spot and stop manipulators. https://www.psychologytoday.com/us/blog/communication-success/201406/how-spot-and-stop-manipulators

NLP-TECHNIQUES. ORG (2021). What is NLP? NLP Techniques. NLP training. NLP coaching. https://www.nlp-techniques.org/

Office Dynamics International (2013, September 8). Persuasion skill—the good, the bad, and the ugly. https://officedynamics.com/persuasion-skills-the-good-the-bad-and-the-ugly/

Overby, S. (2019, June 6). Can emotional intelligence be learned? 4 techniques to practice. https://enterprisersproject.com/article/2019/6/can-emotional-intelligence-be-learned-4-techniques

Parvez, H. (2015, April 16). What is the importance of learning body language? https://www.psychmechanics.com/importance-of-learning-body-language/

Psychologia (2021). Infographic: Psychological manipulation. https://psychologia.co/emotional-manipulation/

Psychology Today (2021). Emotional Intelligence Test. https://www.psychologytoday.com/us/tests/personality/emotional-intelligence-test

Quora (2021). What's dark psychology? https://www.quora.com/Whats-dark-psychology

Quora (2021). When is persuasion a form od bad manipulation? https://www.quora.com/When-is-persuasion-a-form-of-bad-manipulation

University of Minnesota (2021). How do thoughts and emotions affect health? https://www.takingcharge.csh.umn.edu/how-do-thoughts-and-emotions-affect-health

Villines, Z. (2019, September 17). Red flags: Are you being emotionally manipulated? https://www.goodtherapy.org/blog/red-flags-are-you-being-emotionally-manipulated-0917197

Wildenberg, L. (2017, May 5). 10 types of people you don't need in your life. https://www.crosswalk.com/slideshows/10-types-of-people-you-don-t-need-in-your-life.html